D1486152

The Tennis Set

The Tennis Set

REX BELLAMY

With a foreword by Mark Cox

CASSELL·LONDON

CASSELL & COMPANY LTD
35 Red Lion Square, London WC1R 4SG
Sydney, Auckland, Toronto, Johannesburg

First published 1972

ISBN 0 304 29011 4

Printed in Great Britain by
The Anchor Press Ltd, Tiptree, Essex
and bound by Leighton Straker Bookbinding Co. Ltd, London
F. 772

Foreword

Rex Bellamy is an unusual man and has, typically, written an unusual book. It was born from a conviction that tennis enthusiasts had been saturated with facts and figures, but had hungered for more character and peripheral detail. With *The Tennis Set*, they have been given good cause for satisfaction. As every Bellamy fan will know, he has an extraordinary facility with the pen but seldom resorts to using it as a weapon. Thus his book is sheer entertainment.

He stimulates the appetite of the reader by his unbridled enthusiasm. He clearly relishes the opportunity of sharing his experiences. He blends together his ingredients of thoughts held and impressions received, seasons them with wit, then invites us to savour the memory. His writing is always refreshing because it is never tarnished with prejudice or cynicism.

As tennis journalist for *The Times*, Rex has established an international reputation second to none. In his articles there is a subtle mixture of humour and romance that would appeal to the most prosaic reader. In his criticism there is a courtesy that makes it digestible for the most sensitive player.

Because he has always taken more than merely a professional interest in the game and its performers, Rex is well qualified to colour in the public's black and white picture of tennis. He was an outstanding athlete as a schoolboy, so has always had an instinctive understanding of the problems facing professional sportsmen. He has effectively bridged that fractious gap that often exists in relationships between the players and the press. Thus he is in an enviable and singular position—a journalist trusted, liked, and respected by the exponents of the game, the players themselves.

If his book echoes with a spectacular ring of truth, it is because he has personally endured the agony and enjoyed the ecstasy of those he writes about. They happen to be friends. By the time you have read *The Tennis Set*, you will find that you know them too.

MARK COX

Contents

Illustrations

Acknowledgements

One of the pleasant aspects of writing this book was the ready assistance received from everyone I approached. Indeed, so much material was assembled that much of it will demand the accommodation of another volume. To those who helped, I am grateful. Most of all, to *The Times*, because nearly all the subject matter was gathered while I was reporting for the paper. I appreciate the freedom to use amended versions of many reports published in its columns. My special thanks also go to Mark and Alison Cox for contributing a Foreword that has put me on my mettle.

My professional colleagues—reporters, photographers and players—have also been a great help. If I listed all their names, the book would be no more than a postscript. The photographs have been supplied by Marilyn and Ed Fernberger of Philadelphia (at a time when they were already busy enough, promoting the world's best attended indoor tournament); by the dapper Arthur Cole of the magazine *Tennis World*; by Richard Evans, a freelance who turns up in the most likely places between trips to some of the most unlikely; and by Russ Adams of Reading, Massachusetts, who can always be depended on to have cheese and crackers somewhere among his mountains of photographic gear.

The books I found myself consulting most often were the *BP Year Book of Tennis*, edited by John Barrett; *The Education of a Tennis Player*, by Rod Laver and Bud Collins; the *United States LTA Year Book*; and *A Game to Love*, by Ann Jones. To John Barrett, Rod

Laver and Mrs Jones, my thanks for their permission to dip as I pleased. Other works used for reference, for extracts, or both, include the newspaper *Herald Tribune* and the magazines *Lawn Tennis, Tennis USA, Tennis World, World Sports, World Tennis* and Philippe Chatrier's estimable *Tennis de France*. In terms of background information, I also owe beers to Jimmy Jones, editor of *Lawn Tennis*, for his diverse writings on the game, and to Will Grimsley, author of *Tennis: Its History, People, and Events*. A word of thanks, also, to my friends at Harp Lager, whose gift of the abridged edition of *Roget's Thesaurus* provided a good companion for a travelling writer.

Most of all, I owe an immense debt to my wife. She patiently shouldered the role of author's widow while I was married to the typewriter, sometimes until the small hours. She checked most of the manuscript and chuckled often enough to make me feel I was working well. And after I had once worked through the night under the lubricating influence of Dewar's and water, she quietly carried out blankets and pillows when (early that morning) she found me lying on the floor of the hall—paralytically and immovably plastered. Clearly a terminal case of writer's cramp.

Introduction

This book is an attempt to capture the character of the international tennis circuit and of the men and women who play on it. If any other purpose is served, it is to recall some of the drama and some of the laughter of four years of open tournaments from 1968 to 1971. That period may come to be remembered as the golden age of the modern game, though the International Lawn Tennis Federation (ILTF) and World Championship Tennis (WCT) may devise some means of granting it an extension. It will also be remembered for a coincidence concerning two players: Ken Rosewall and Virginia Wade. They won the singles at the first and last open tournaments, at Bournemouth in April 1968, and at Melbourne in January 1972.

To a great extent I write as the fancy takes me. Because a reporter cannot see everything, and in any case the memory can be selective in an arbitrary way. Unless directly attributed to someone else, the opinions expressed are all mine: *The Times* should not be lumbered with the responsibility for any of them.

There are seven major ILTF tournaments. The omission of separate chapters on the South African and Australian championships is no reflection on their status. But it would be pretentious to comment at length on tournaments I have never attended (that is only narrowly true—the day after handing this manuscript to the publishers, I fly to Johannesburg). In any case, the casts of both championships are with us in these pages. The scene changes, but the play and the players are the same.

The promotional skill of Owen Williams has made the South African championships one of Johannesburg's leading sporting and social occasions, and has lifted the tournament to fourth or fifth place in the hierarchy of the ILTF circuit—behind Wimbledon, France, the United States, and possibly Italy. But as the stature of the South African event has risen, that of the Australian has fallen. One reason is that fourteen Australian men, including the best, are with WCT and therefore play most of their tennis in the United States. They are also barred from the Davis Cup competition, which Australia have not won since the formation of WCT in 1967. The Davis Cup was important to Australia. The challenge round was an exciting attraction, its profits were essential to the health of the Australian game, and it ensured that famous overseas players would be available for at least part of the season. All that is over. Australian tennis has temporarily receded to the place geography designed for it—remote from the mainstream of the world game. But there are hopeful factors: the Australian game now has at its helm Wayne Reid, one of the youngest and most progressive administrators in tennis; there is a chance that tournament entries may be improved by the development of a Far Eastern circuit; and the Australian championships remain the only way to begin the quest for that mythical but coveted prize, a Grand Slam.

If I concentrate on ILTF tournaments, it is merely because they were the heart of open competition. Their traditional pre-eminence is being shaken by the energetic challenge of the slick WCT circuit, inaugurated in 1971, and by the fact that the United States, rather than Europe, threatens to dominate the professional game.

That first WCT circuit spanned four continents and nine countries and carried a million dollars in prize money. The final, played in Dallas, was a brilliant, thrilling and emotional occasion. The supporting cast to Rod Laver and Ken Rosewall included Neil Armstrong and Charlton Heston. Jack Jones, singing at the hotel, insisted twice nightly that everything was beautiful. But WCT in general and Rosewall in particular (he collected a cheque for 50,000 dollars, the biggest prize in the history of the game) did not need convincing. The touching thing for all of us was not so much the event itself as its significance: the great actors of the independent professional game had come in from the wilderness to a stage worthy of their talents. The WCT circuit marked their graduation from a wasteland of one-night stands to the lush pastures of a secure place in big-time sport.

Armstrong was a reminder that tennis had reached the space age. There was another when I reached the ticket counter at Kennedy Airport with John Barrett, perhaps the most imaginative and dynamic influence in British tennis.

'Only about a hundred and seventy passengers,' said the clerk. 'Plenty of room. So you can sit where you like.'

Dallas was memorable, too, for a congenial team of journalists— from the United States, Paris (Judith Elian), Rome (Rino Tommasi), London (John Barrett) and Knotty Green (me)—who took pleasure in each other's company and in that of those other professionals playing or working under the banner of WCT. One evening, in the Venetian Room of the Fairmont Hotel, Jack Jones introduced all the tennis celebrities—including that loyal supporter of the professional game, Charlton Heston—and each in turn stood up and took a bow in the spotlight. This pleasant duty done (pleasant because he is a tennis player himself), Jones began to talk about his next song. Whereupon a lady called from the back of the room:

'Could we have a request please?'

'What's the request, madam?'

'Would you ask Mr Heston to stand up again?'

Dallas was quite a week: fun and (underneath the glamour) important.

It is neither my wish nor my intention to discuss in detail the least interesting, least dignified, most infuriating aspect of the game —the administrative squabbles featuring the ILTF, their national associations, and the independent WCT organization. Politicians ask us to share their headaches; players ask us to share their pleasures; the players are better company. But much of this book concerns men who were outlawed by the ILTF as from 1 January 1972. So we must briefly examine the situation as it stands now (in March 1972) and what happened to bring it about.

There are two professional circuits. The ILTF, representing the national associations, has nominal jurisdiction over all players except those under contract to WCT (the exceptions include seven of the top ten men in the game). To extend this picture, there are within the ILTF (specifically, the United States LTA) two powerful promotional figures—Bill Riordan, who created the expanding American indoor circuit, and Gladys Heldman, editor and publisher of *World Tennis*. Out of a discontent based on restrictions in prize money and competitive opportunities, she conceived a women's professional tour that has the allegiance of most of the best players. It is because of the combined influence of WCT (head-quarters, Dallas), Riordan (Salisbury, Maryland) and Mrs Heldman (Houston) that the United States is becoming the hub of pro-fessional tennis.

Another formidable force, darting about from one side to the other, is Donald Dell. He was ranked in America's top ten from 1960 to 1962, captained the Davis Cup teams of 1968 and 1969, dabbled in tournament promotion, but is fundamentally a Wash-ington lawyer who looks after the business affairs of many leading WCT and ILTF professionals—including Arthur Ashe, Zeljko Franulovic, Tom Gorman, Jan Kodes, Bob Lutz, Tom Okker, Charles Pasarell, Marty Riessen and Stan Smith. He therefore has a foot in both camps. If there were three camps, he would grow another foot.

Dell is a success. If you want to hire the kind of star tennis players who wear jock-straps, you get in touch with WCT, which is easy, or with Dell, which is not. He spends all his time arriving or leaving. If he is not on an aircraft or the telephone, he is in a corner talking to somebody, somewhere. When he is neither talking nor listening, it seems that the wheels of tennis history have stopped turning. If the telephone had not been invented, Dell would have invented it. He is always in touch with everybody simultaneously. If he was marooned on a desert island, Dell would work on the birds until they could negotiate in rational American. Then he would do some kind of deal with them—and they would get the worst of it. I doubt if he ever needs tickets. He turns up everywhere so often that they think he is on the staff, or is maybe a sort of tennis Kurt Waldheim. When Dell is interred, they should put a telephone in one hand and an air ticket in the other. He would like that: dying with his boots on.

That is the American scene, or part of it. The ILTF does not exist: except as a hesitant collective voice (with a heavy European accent) for the national associations. It has no full-time staff, no home or will of its own. The ILTF is like a Government without a Cabinet. Its only solid and continuous presence is that of Basil Reay, secretary of Britain's LTA. He has spent a quarter of a century doing ILTF work in the LTA's time and his own.

The officers of the national associations are mostly part-timers who work hard and do an admirable job for the game in their respective countries. But when they start discussing international—as opposed to national—tennis, it can be like switching on the radio and hearing a programme that has been off the air for ten years. Through no fault of their own, they do not get around enough.

Although the national associations are concerned essentially with the amateur, pay-for-play game, they also have a wealthy, international grand prix circuit (Jack Kramer's brainchild) that is vital to them as a shop window, a source of income, and an inducement to keep leading players out of the ranks of WCT. The ILTF were forced to take up WCT's challenge in the promotion of professional tennis. But they cannot continue to do it on a part-time basis. Amateurs cannot adequately govern a professional sport.

'It would be a very good thing if, working on committees, we had more people who were close to the circuit,' says Robert Abdesselam of France, one of the most distinguished and enterprising of tennis administrators. 'I don't see why people who have a direct financial interest should not be asked to help. The guy who is professionally round the courts knows a great deal more than a lawyer or businessman who can only look after the affairs of the game once a month.'

A small group of independent professionals—independent, that is, of the ILTF—had existed for a long time, notably under Kramer's promotion. But in 1967 they were a tribe without a chief. Two men decided to take over. One was George MacCall, who captained the United States Davis Cup team from 1965 to 1967. He was already a popular man within the game, and the best-known professionals signed for him. But the second candidate for the job, an imaginative New Orleans sports promoter called Dave Dixon, was not nonplussed for long. He chose to create a separate group by rounding up the spare professionals and raiding the 'shamateur' ranks. That decision changed the course of tennis history.

Either MacCall or Dixon in isolation would not have hurt the ILTF. But their combined activities drained off not merely the cream, but some of the milk as well. Britain's advocacy of open competition now gathered force, inspired by Herman David, chairman of the All England Club (Wimbledon). Britain's LTA made their famous decision to 'go it alone' if they had to. They sent two trouble-shooters, Derek Hardwick and Derek Penman, on a world tour to lobby support. They got it. In 1968, open tournaments were sanctioned, thanks largely to the astute diplomacy of Britain's John Eaton Griffith within the councils of the ILTF. 'Amateurism,' he says, 'is not an act of God. Every country has its own interpretation'.

Dixon, the original catalyst, did not stay in tennis long. The first WCT tour was a failure. But the pieces were picked up and put together by Dixon's backer, Lamar Hunt, a Texan oil millionaire with diverse sporting interests; by Dixon's colleague Bob Briner, one of those exceptional men who achieve power yet remain liked, respected and trusted; and by a former British Davis Cup player, Mike Davies, who knew the professional game inside out. Al Hill, Hunt's nephew, acquired a 15 per cent interest compared with his uncle's 85 per cent. A New Zealander, John McDonald, was installed in a London office to act as overseas link man. Another key figure was a gifted public relations director, Ron Bookman, whose personality alone was of immense value to WCT (Briner left in 1969, Bookman in 1971, but otherwise the team is the same).

The show was on the road. The staff alone was as big as the original stable of eight players. The MacCall group had been absorbed, thirty-two fine players were under contract, and WCT were ready to take command of their own destiny. In 1971 they promoted their own circuit of twenty-one tournaments carrying a million dollars in prize money. The exclusively professional game had a strength, coherence and sense of purpose it had previously lacked. Competition and incentive had been intensified. Joining WCT became a privilege and a commitment: a privilege because it marked a graduation in terms of proficiency, and a commitment to a consistently high playing standard, to a way of life, and to a new personal and corporate responsibility. A dream that Ken Rosewall put into words—'a successful pro circuit as part of an open game'—had come true. But the open game was not to last, though its demise was deferred by the mediation of Teddy Tinling, a couturier with a shrewd brain and an extensive knowledge of international tennis.

The ILTF were frightened that they might lose control of professional tennis, even within their own sphere of influence—and as we have seen, they could not afford that. They still had many advantages—their traditional circuit, the support of the national associations, and control of the most famous stadia. They could have closed their ranks, refused WCT any income (other than prize money) from ILTF tournaments, and at the same time kept faith with the principle of open competition. In short, they could have said: 'Look, play in our tournaments if you wish. We'd love to have you. But like everyone else you'll have to play just for prize money. Nothing on the side.' This would have meant WCT's withdrawal from all ILTF events except a few that would be useful to their prestige. But that was going to happen anyway.

There were talks at Wimbledon in 1971. There was a dispute about terms for WCT participation in ILTF events, notably the Kramer-Hardwick dream of a united world circuit (the policies and priorities of the two sides were so essentially different that, even had the circuits been married, there would ultimately have been a bitter divorce).

The ILTF then took one of the most indefensibly fatuous decisions in the history of tennis or any other sport. They outlawed WCT from every area of ILTF activities. They deliberately slammed the doors of the game's most famous tournaments in the faces of nearly all its most famous players.

The best players on both sides enjoyed having an occasional crack at each other in open competition. The public enjoyed it, too. And the experience of the past four years had proved that open competition had an enormous contribution to make to the development of the game. But the ILTF slammed the doors anyway. This was hardly calculated to arouse public sympathy. Nor was the fact that the ILTF had betrayed the cause they had espoused at Britain's insistence in 1968.

The golden age was over, but there was a gratifying legacy. Shamateurism had been abolished. Increased commercial sponsorship, attracted by open competition, had surged into almost every area of the game. The fixture list had expanded. The earning capacity of the players had soared.

The lusty advance of WCT had a revitalizing effect on the rival ILTF game. The ILTF had to pull up their socks to meet the challenge, or the trickle of players to WCT would become a flood and the ILTF professional game might wither. In addition to all they achieved for the exclusively professional game, WCT took tennis as a whole to fresh venues, made the old and new publics more tennis-conscious, set higher standards in promoting and presenting the game, and pushed players' rewards to a level the ILTF had to match.

Cliff Richey, a professional then teetering between the ILTF and WCT, said nothing that had not been said before when he told us at the Albert Hall in January 1972: 'Lamar has done more for tennis than any other one man in the history of the game.'

The legacy of those four years includes the successful inauguration of two separate big-money circuits (the WCT series and the ILTF grand prix). Players earn points according to their singles performances at each tournament, and the leading scorers qualify for rich and spectacular showpiece finales which have become exciting new fixtures in the calendar.

A disquieting feature of the revolution was the tendency for men's and women's tournaments to be separated. There are mixed feelings, too, about the introduction of the tie-break (an opus composed by Jimmy van Alen—a wealthy eccentric from Newport, Rhode Island—and arranged by Rod Laver and others). But the tie-break is useful as long as it is not allowed to assume too much importance. Wimbledon probably got it right: a best-of-twelve-points system that approximates to traditional scoring, is enforced only after a set has reached 8-all, and is not applied at all in the fifth set of a men's match or the third of a women's. Van Alen has a lot more ideas. One worth thinking about, for the benefit of an expanding public, is that 'fifteen', 'thirty' and 'forty' should be replaced by 'one', 'two' and 'three'.

The changes in the game have also affected the traditional team competitions. These events provide the fixture list with the punctuation of variety. Intense patriotism is not a flower that flourishes in the closely knit cosmopolitan world of tennis. But it is a special and healthy challenge to play for a team, a country, instead of for oneself—a formidable test of nerve to hear the umpire calling 'Advantage Britain' instead of 'Advantage Taylor'. A player's responsibilities suddenly widen.

Nowhere is this emotional strain more evident than in the best of the team events, the women's world championship for the Federation Cup (inaugurated in 1963, and perhaps the finest testimony to the ILTF's occasional capacity for enterprising innovation). Yet the best known women's event remains the Wightman Cup match between Britain and the United States. 'Certainly for me, the Wightman Cup has much more atmosphere and team spirit,' says Winnie Shaw. 'It still seems almost the more important, though it shouldn't be. You seem to build up for it more. The tension is between two countries, instead of all together. And each Federation Cup match is over so quickly, whereas the Wightman Cup match lasts three days in the States and two here.'

But the depth of American talent has made the Wightman Cup series one-sided. A more exciting event on the drawing board is a new competition between the United States and Australia.

The most famous men's team competitions are the Davis Cup, the world championship, and the King's Cup, a European equivalent played indoors. The Davis Cup has been sadly devalued by the exclusion of WCT and has become a second-rate event. But the abolition of the challenge round (the holders now have to play through the competition like anyone else) is a welcome if overdue piece of legislation.

The Davis Cup's restriction to ILTF players again springs from a fear that WCT may seek to control the competition or demand too high a price for playing in it. But it would be easy for the Davis Cup nations to say: 'We shall continue to run the Davis Cup as we think fit. But we believe in open competition. So anyone is eligible to play in it.' It is unlikely that many, if any, WCT players would take part in the circumstances that exist now. But the door would be open—and it is the job of sports administrators to open doors rather than close them.

What the competition really needs is a revised, compact format so that the professionals (whether WCT or ILTF men) could compete without spending too much time away from their regular sources of income. Because there is a tendency to regard men as professionals when they are playing tournaments, but as *ad hoc* amateurs—gaining little or no financial return—when they are playing in the Davis Cup. In the days when Arthur Ashe was still an ILTF professional, he opposed Rod Laver at Wimbledon in a match that could not happen in the Davis Cup because Laver was a WCT player. Such is the erratic logic of the game's administrators.

Ashe's exclusion from the South African championships had much to do with the fact that South Africa were chucked out of the Davis Cup competition for two years. But there was a lot of fuss before that, because several East European countries scratched when they were due to play South Africa. Had the existing rules been properly applied, those countries would have been suspended or punished in some other way. Instead, only South Africa and Rhodesia suffered. There are, of course, much wider issues here. But the subject of politics and sport has become rather a bore, certainly to sportsmen, and in any case is not within the scope of this kind of book. The only point I want to make is that any country entering for a competition should honour their commitment by playing through it until they are beaten. No country should be allowed to scratch from a competition with impunity merely because they dislike the political, racial or religious complexion of the team due to oppose them. Any nation not prepared to play South Africa should state bluntly that they will not enter the competition as long as South Africa are allowed to do so.

The King's Cup was a good idea to fill a competitive gap in the European calendar during November and December. But the indoor fixture list has expanded so much that the gap no longer exists. The leading players usually have better things to do than playing in the King's Cup, and in its present form the competition seems doomed to mediocrity. Like the Davis Cup, it could perhaps be restored to health by a drastic change of format.

Indoor tennis has been one of the most exciting features of the game's expansion. We could have some fun together going round Britain's Dewar Cup circuit. Or attending two London tournaments that, in the winter of 1971-2, were visited for the first time by that witty American freelance, Barry Lorge—who observed that he was 'underwhelmed' by Wembley but that the Albert Hall brought 'tiers' to his eyes. Shame on the man. We could even pop over to Philadelphia for that massively efficient tournament promoted by Marilyn and Ed Fernberger. Or take the fifteen-seat 'white knuckle fight' over Chesapeake Bay to the United States indoor championships at Salisbury. One day, perhaps, we can do all that together. But for the moment we must not be greedy. A glittering outdoor circuit lies ahead of us.

Drews End,   R.B.
Knotty Green.
March 1972

Postscript. Much has happened since this introduction was written. Brenda Kirk and Pat Pretorius achieved for South Africa a Federation Cup triumph that was like something out of school-girls' fiction. The first 'multinational' South African championships kept faith with all the praise previously lavished upon the tournament—though in this and other major events there was a decline in quality because WCT were excluded. But Allan Heyman's legal brain seems to have instilled some sense into the ILTF, and open competition with WCT may be restored in 1973. There is still much to be done: not least a better deal for the women's and doubles events in the allocation of prize money, and a co-ordination of the two most important grass court circuits (let there be three weeks of British tournaments as preparation for Wimbledon, immediately succeeded by three weeks of American tournaments as preparation for Forest Hills). The facetious, of course, will continue to insist that the game can be improved only by slower courts and faster women.

R.B.

June 1972

I

The Writing Game

Every day of our lives begins as a blank page in a history book. It is the reporter's job to fill that page, to answer the question 'What's happening?' (which tells those of us in tennis that a bizarre shirt has turned up, with Arthur Ashe inside it). On the face of it, a reporter is merely a trained gossip. But I am going to convince you that there is more to it than that—just as the rock-climber, with his ropes and his boots and his respectable comportment, will rationalize that his motives are far finer than those of the boy who scrambled up cliffs and trees in search of birds' eggs and apples (and was later admonished because he tore his pants on the way).

The reporter has to enjoy writing. He has to care about people, about the society which he reflects and to some small extent may influence. He has to be curious, to show a detective's initiative and pertinacity in collecting, sifting and assessing facts. He has to know the difference between his personal preferences and his professional judgement. If that judgement tells him to take an unconventional and unpopular line, he must have the moral courage to do so.

The reporter has to get his facts right, or no one will trust him. In practice, he does sometimes err—because he is human, because he can tire at the end of a hard day, and because he has to work fast, even if he feels unwell or unhappy. But although errors of fact can be explained, they cannot be excused. The reporter's interpretation of the facts must continually be re-examined and possibly revised. In his opinions, as distinct from his facts, he can afford to be wrong as long as he does not make a habit of it. At worst, he has to stimulate his readers and help them towards a wider and deeper appreciation of the issues he is discussing.

By its nature, news is concerned with the exception rather than the rule. If a qualifier beats the top seed, that is news. If the top seed beats a qualifier, that is not news. But although the reporter must have a quick eye for the exception, for the flaw in the pattern, he must also reflect the texture of the whole. If he is a specialist (and in these days most of us are), he has to remember that he is working on one small stretch of a vast horizon, and that the part must be related to the whole.

Above all, he has always to be aware that the best story in the history of journalism would be so much garbage unless it reached the office on time. The one tyrant he can never escape is his deadline.

If he works for a newspaper, rather than a specialist magazine, the reporter has also to remember that he preaches not merely to the converted. So he attracts and holds the interest of wandering flocks on peripheral pastures. His piece contains such basic facts and tactical and technical comments as will enlighten the initiated. But it is also brightly and smartly dressed so that it will interest and inform the uninitiated. Thus can the reporter kindle fires where none existed and, at the same time, join his public in some harmless fun. The reporter must communicate his enthusiasm, as well as his knowledge. As he ploughs his field, he must sniff the flowers on the way. His secret, if there is one, is to write an informal, chatty, yet professional report—as if to some relative or friend who knows a little about the game, would dearly like to be there with him, and, failing that, wants to catch the flavour of the occasion through the reporter's eyes.

That relative or friend is also aware that sporting celebrities are people, not machines. So he or she has a natural curiosity about them which the reporter should satisfy, as long as he does not overdo it and turn his articles into shameless gossip. The reader, for example, knows the players a little better if he is aware that Tom Okker and Marty Riessen tend to be absorbed in backgammon when they have time to kill, that Ion Tiriac is hot stuff on a pair of ice skates and eats glass as a party trick, that Roy Emerson is a joker capable of telephoning his opponent at two in the morning to ask what time they are playing, and that Helen Gourlay is dextrous with chopsticks and has a fondness for chocolate sauce and chutney (though not to the point of consuming them simultaneously).

This sort of information catches the fancy of a public apt to regard famous sportsmen or sportswomen as a race apart. In a sense—the exploitation of a special skill—they are. But that applies to many who stand, as it were, in the wings of fame rather than in the spotlight at the centre of the stage. Tennis players are not pampered freaks. They are capable of the same kindness and the same frailty as the rest of us. They, too, have problems. They cannot spend as much time with their families and friends as they would like to. They rush about from airport to airport, from tournament to tournament, packing and unpacking in one hotel room after another, and washing their smalls at the end of the day. They worry about tickets and passports and currency and excess luggage. They sometimes feel happy and sometimes feel sad—and have to play anyway. The machinery of their game runs smoothly one day and, for no good reason, is creaking and erratic the next. It may be that you would like to swop your problems for theirs. But in the last two minutes you have at least been reminded that they are not just tennis players: that they are also men and women. So if they sometimes play badly or behave badly, remember that they may be nursing some slight injury or may be anxious about a sick relative or some business affair that is going badly.

In exceptional cases there may be less weighty reasons for strange goings-on that puzzle the innocent spectator, but cause unreserved and apparently heartless hilarity among a cluster of attentive players and camp followers who are in the know. If a player is observed practising with demoniac dedication—and wearing a track suit and multitudinous sweaters in heat fit to fry an egg—you may reasonably speculate that, the night before, he drank until he was as full as a boot, and is now paying the bill. If you are watching a match and wonder why some player keeps missing the ball, or why the spring has gone from his stride, do not condemn the laughter of his friends. They may be aware that he has a hangover, or spent the night with some lady indulging, perhaps to excess, a mutual passion for the most primitive of horizontal exercises. Even King David's iron virtue was known to melt a little when the furnace of temptation was hot enough.

The reporter, while aware that he is writing about people, has to comment dispassionately and objectively on what they are trying to do and how well they are doing it. If someone plays badly he must say so: with no excuses, save in the most remarkable instances. His heart may feel compassion because he knows, for example, that a player has had bad news from home. But his head, and his training as a professional critic, tells him that once a player steps on court, that player has a responsibility to himself, to the game, and to the public. The clown may be crying inside. But when he bounces into the circus ring, he still has to make the children laugh.

At the same time the superficially hard reporter (who is really a softie at heart, or he could not write with feeling) should in his own small way extend the reader's understanding of the players as human beings. He remains sensitive to character, mood, and environment. He observes the principle that the good reporter has his eyes, his ears, and his heart open to anything that catches his fancy—and then uses such professional talents as he has, in order to make it catch the fancy of his readers. Like an imaginative cook, he uses such tricks of the trade as putting wine in the gravy.

But he has to remember that gravy is a sauce, not a meat. The reporter needs a basis of expert knowledge. So he does his homework, listens to the experts, and watches constructively. He has probably been doing it for years: and unless he is as thick as a Roman wall, he has learned a lot on the way and become, to a degree, an expert himself, except in such fields as the refinements of technique. It would be a great help if the reporter was himself an expert player. But it is given to few to have the talent and time to excel in two professions at once. The reporter's knowledge of the game is only one facet of his job.

Reporters learn a lot, and never stop learning: by watching players and by nattering with them. Consciously or not, a host of professionals have expanded and still expand my understanding of a game to which we bring a common enthusiasm, though our involvement takes different forms. In 1970, for example, Lew Hoad had an exciting run in the Italian championship and then expressed himself on the subject of clay court tennis: 'I would have thought that somebody like Orantes or Metreveli would have handled me easily,' he observed, thoughtfully savouring the quality of a glass of the right stuff. 'But nobody ever takes a risk. They just stand back and hit the ball. If I hit the ball five times, I have to do something. With all the balls that come short, everyone who has a chance to go to the net should do it.' Because as a match progressed, he added (taking a deep draught of the liquor that waters great truths and makes them blossom), it became harder to hit passing shots—for the simple reason that the incoming volleyer was becoming ever more facile in learning which flank needed to be covered.

Nothing sophisticated about that. But here was a professional talking sense. They do it all the time, if you catch them in the right mood. There must be a few diamonds in Roy Emerson's mine of experience. But it is not easy to dig them out of a man who seems to regard every day as Christmas Day and every minute as a bonus of laughter. But on one subject—the player who makes excuses for defeat—he is forthright and adamant. If a player is unfit, says Emerson, he does not go on court. If he goes on court, he is fit. If he loses, there can be no excuses. That is Roy Emerson's lesson for today and every day: and he practises what he preaches.

One way and another, the specialist reporter continually widens and deepens his reservoir of knowledge and wisdom. But his growing confidence has its hazards. His open-minded detachment may be submerged beneath the weight of acquired prejudice and the set views born of years of experience. He may become more of a tennis specialist and less of a journalist. This is bad. The convincing advocate of his own opinion is a good writer. But he must beware the closed mind, which is a warped mind.

Although the reporter may know the game and care deeply about it, he has to remember that gravity can be dull company unless (as I once discovered while climbing on rotten rock) he happens to be falling off a cliff. The man who takes himself seriously is seldom taken seriously. We may respect his responsible attitude, but it does not follow that we find his company an irresistible stimulant. It is often tactically wise to be apparently frivolous in order to make a point: to influence through such charm as the reporter can contrive and such laughter as he can provoke.

Though they could not strictly be classified as sports reporters, Oscar Wilde, C. E. Montague, and to a degree the gentler Jane Austen, all had this ability to hit us between the eyes while we were giggling. They used words as if conjuring with brightly coloured balls: and through the dazzling wit we saw, and still see, the images they wanted us to picture and the points they wanted us to grasp. One of these genteel jesters always travels in my hand baggage on long journeys through air and time and trays of crowded food. They keep me amused. Moreover, they are an insurance when I suspect the onset of staleness.

One of the built-in snags of the writing game is that, after the freshness of the first ten years or so has begun to fade, the chore of collecting and assembling facts and meeting deadlines could become a stereotype, and harden the sensibilities. Luckily, the good reporter has the antidote: he is a romantic by nature and the romantic within him is always struggling to get out. In his haste to hustle along well trodden paths, he retains the capacity to be moved—to recognize and cherish the great moments that caress the palate of the mind. But in the manipulation of words and phrases, every day of his working life, the reporter (like the man or woman hitting tennis balls) may sometimes lose his imaginative, inventive zest. At such times a Wilde, a Montague or an Austen can help him recapture the sheer joy of using a wondrously versatile language—just as the sight of Rod Laver, Ken Rosewall or Ilie Nastase in full flow, flashing and dancing like mountain streams, can remind the jaded tennis player what an exciting game he is playing.

The tonic is good for us, as long as its heady juices do not make the reporter try too hard to be clever: or the tennis player strive to play exactly like Laver, Rosewall or Nastase.

Because he is a romantic, the newspaper reporter listens to the larks singing and remembers that he has to interest not merely the initiated, but everyone. It is relatively easy to sell food to the hungry and clothes to the cold. It is far more difficult and exciting to sell to those who have no interest in, nor need for, the product you are marketing. And that is one of the reporter's jobs.

Good sports writing is spiced by variety and contrast. It is relatively easy for the reporter to be crafty, in two senses, when he has time. But most of his work is hurried, because it consists of daily reports written or extemporized to a set length to meet a specific deadline. A few are born with a flair for extemporization, but most have to acquire it. The important thing is to have a good note. This is particularly necessary at Wimbledon. Every day the first edition story for *The Times*, consisting of about a thousand words ex-

The Writing Game

temporized (that is, with nothing written out in sentence form) has to be flowing across the wires from the centre court to Printing House Square between 6.30 and 7 p.m., while play is still in progress. Why not, you may ask, take time off for writing? But have you tried assembling material on a succession of matches taking place on fifteen courts, and taking time off for writing?

Later in the day, between 8 and 10 p.m., it is possible to settle down with a typewriter and a pipe, a lager and some good companions, and pound out a thousand better organized words for the later editions. It is because reporters are thus heavily engaged that doubles matches, usually played late in the day, often receive less publicity than they deserve.

Time is always short for the reporter at the end of the day—when the setting sun is casting long shadows across the courts, the birds are singing lullabies fit to wake the dead, and the players are washing off the sweat, sinking a few beers, and planning dinner. The year Ann Jones won Wimbledon, an innocent in the Wimbledon trade passed on the stimulating news that, in addition to a thousand words for the sports page, *The Times* wanted a long 'profile' for the centre pages and a third piece for the front page. The subsequent snatch of conversation went something like this:

'How' (rather anxiously) 'are you going to tackle it?'

'I'm going to order two beers, light a pipe, attach the seat of my pants to that chair, and keep typing until I've finished. If you want to help, get the beer. Otherwise, get lost.'

(Willing lad that he was, he left me in peace and returned later to help with the dictation.)

You will gather that there are times, in the heat of battle, when the cushioned niceties and proprieties of small talk are thrust aside; when the soft and gentle nature of sports reporters is temporarily overridden by the hard-boiled urgency of the professional. When a Wimbledon reporter is under pressure, with his nose pushed up against a deadline, you pester him at your peril. Might as well ask a Bob Hewitt or a Cliff Richey (or for that matter, anyone else) for his autograph when he is match point down and has just had a bad line decision.

As our friends across the sea would put it, Wimbledon is something else again. It is the tennis reporter's most difficult task of the year because of the sheer weight and complexity of work: assembling accurate material on perhaps sixty matches a day and banging it swiftly into shape. Twice. You may see a reporter engaged in apparently casual badinage with a colleague, or some player or official. 'What a life,' you may mutter. But they are not just passing the time of day. The reporter is checking facts, or gathering information and comment on something he has not seen. After all, he cannot be in umpteen different places at once, though he may give you that impression when you read the paper next morning. He is lucky in that everyone is willing to give him the help he needs. Because the tennis set is a closely-knit team and every section of it appreciates the problems of the rest and is aware of the demons that drive them.

The scene in the press room from about 6 p.m. onwards has to be seen and heard not to be believed: the ceaseless pounding and tinkling of typewriters, the rattle of exchanged information, the to-ing and fro-ing between desks and telephones, the shouted dictation in a dozen different languages, the tobacco smoke, the continual inflow of beer and outflow of empties. These are gloriously crowded hours. There is nothing quite so exciting as being under pressure when you know (or you think you know) that you can handle it. At such moments the heart sings—as with Alpine guides, so morose at sea level, when they climb above the tree line and happily get to grips with the sharpest challenges of their calling. On those evenings at Wimbledon, the reporter needs all his buttons on and raises thanks if there is none missing.

In the early 1950s I knew a sports writer (let his name be withheld, to spare his blushes) who was a genuine craftsman, a good professional who never missed a trick. For years our paths never crossed again. Until one day he turned up at Wimbledon, his first visit, to help a colleague gather the ingredients for daily dishes served to readers of one of the national newspapers. He was enthusiastic, bright-eyed and impressively dapper. And he did help—struggling urgently from court to court along packed promenades, collecting choice morsels of information for his chum, like a squirrel hunting nuts with winter coming on. Towards the end of the day, briefly looking up from the typewriter in search of the elusive right word, I observed that respected journalist cross the threshold of his new world. It was the usual Bedlam. His smart suit was rumpled, his hair awry, his face streaked with drying rivulets of sweat. He looked as if he had awoken from some terrible nightmare only to find the house on fire.

'Jesus Christ!' the man gasped. 'I didn't know people still worked this hard. You can stuff Wimbledon.'

Rod Laver recently pondered whether tennis writers ever 'tighten up at the typewriter during Wimbledon'. Did we 'choke on a big match, and stress the wrong aspects' or 'try too hard and come up with botched prose'?

It is sometimes true that, after a particularly good match, the reporter approaches his typewriter as nervously as a virgin bride on her way upstairs. The reporter is aware, because he is a humble lad at heart, that it may be difficult for him to do the match justice. But he is also aware, because he is a professional, that he has to do his best—and that it should be better than anyone else's. He is also curious: because he is not sure what is going to happen when his well worn fingertips start flitting dextrously across the keys. He may have to do a consciously laborious job, thinking hard all the time and wishing it were easier. Or he may find that some muse takes over (the muse compounded of flair, experience and confidence) and guides his fingertips for him. At such times the reporter sometimes kids himself, especially when the imagination has been lubricated by a glass or two of his favourite tipple, that he is a vehicle, a messenger, a middleman: that some disembodied creative force is merely using him. But he is kidding himself, because the truth is simply that he feels good and the match has moved him. He is doing it all on his own, and none of the gods, with the possible exception of Bacchus, can take any credit.

Nervousness is good, for reporter and player alike. Both need to feel the nerve ends twanging a little—but not too much—if they are to strike their best form. If the vibration of those nerve ends is not exactly right, then the task is going to be awkward and there is nothing but hard work ahead. The reporter's song of praise may be in the wrong key.

Most people can produce a fleeting enchantment with the spoken or written word when inspired by a combination of circumstances that summons the poet who lurks within us all (and is waiting for a chance to do his stuff). But the reporter, like the player, must reluctantly accept the fact that his best form is not his true form. In both fields, the professional is distinguished from the amateur by his ability to work well when he is not in the mood for it.

We have discussed some of the urgent difficulties of the trade and we have peeped into its Wimbledon workshop. The Roman counterpart used to be equally stimulating, but for different reasons. The press room at the Foro Italico is large and marbled. Only in recent years has it been partly cushioned by noise-resistant partitions. Italians tend to talk more (and more loudly) than most of us. It sometimes seems that they never use one word if ten will do. So your imaginative ear will pick up the echoes of the evening chorus of reporters talking and typing. The sound waves, the din of decibels, rebounded from wall to wall and ceiling to floor like a shower of ping-pong balls caught in a whirlwind. In the midst of just such a cacophony, on my first visit to the Foro Italico, I heard a strained Italian voice ascending from the vicinity of my size sevens. Could it be that the crazy reverberations had ventriloquial qualities; that some freak of architecture was tossing echoes into areas apparently uninhabited by the human larynx? But on leaning back from the typewriter and adjusting my angle of vision, I discerned that delightful eccentric, Gianni Clerici, of *Il Giorno* (Milan). He was sitting on the floor under the table, with a telephone in his lap—the receiver at one ear and a finger stuck in the other. For a moment we looked at each other, mute puzzlement on one side and mute desperation on the other. He had the sad-eyed, haunted look of a child caught raiding the drinks cabinet, or a spaniel apprehended while munching the joint.

'It is the noise, Rex,' he said softly. 'Under here, it is not so bad.'

No more was said. He carried on with his subjacent dictation. I resumed the assault on my portable. A good moment had taken root in the memory. An original, is Gianni. I am told that he once turned up at a formal reception wearing a one-piece bathing suit.

High in an office building, somewhere in London, are those cherished though often unmet colleagues, the copy-takers. Equipped with typewriters and earphones, they sit patiently through a barrage of dictation from reporters all over Europe—every reporter apparently convinced (and sometimes tetchy with it) that his story is the most urgent and important of the day. If only those copy-takers knew what a comfort it is to hear a familiar voice when a reporter has had trouble getting through—maybe from the beach at Monte Carlo, some hotel in Sofia, the high perimeter of a twilit stadium in

Sarajevo, the crusted ruins of Athens, or, more prosaically, after grubbing about for a telephone box in the night-darkened back streets of Stalybridge (and perhaps dictating by the fitful light of a dwindling supply of matches).

It will not have escaped your speculations that, like a rumour passed along from mouth to mouth, a report may become strangely transmuted as it is tossed from reporter to copy-taker, sub-editor and printer. Between them, they often stumble over the inherent hazards of the craft. Through human or mechanical failings, opinions can be distorted and errors of fact, grammar or spelling can creep into articles. The breakfasting reporter is pleasantly surprised when a piece appears exactly as he wrote it. The stories of printed howlers are legion. My favourite concerns a famous provincial paper which, on opposite sports pages, carried double-column photographs of two tennis players and two jockeys. Some gremlin switched lines in the captions so that the photograph of the tennis players was explained thus: 'Miss Fiona and Miss Jennifer Morris, sisters from Salisbury, Rhodesia, who contest the final of the women's singles at the Heaton lawn tennis tournament, who both have fancied mounts at Thirsk tonight.'

From all directions—mostly from outside but sometimes from inside the office—the reporter is repeatedly pressed to give an airing to the bees in someone else's bonnet, to take a line that is not his own, to publicize some personal or sectional interest. He considers all he hears and reads in the way of special pleading. Then, impartially, he makes up his own mind. Newspaper reporters are not propaganda agents, nor public relations men. They do not represent players, nor administrators, nor indeed any group interest. It is not their job to promote tournaments, to sell tickets, to advance the cause of a sport—nor to minister to the morale of the men and women who play it.

The freedom of the press is no empty cliché. Those who would restrict that freedom, if they could, might achieve a temporary gain for some private interest. But they would achieve it at the expense of society as a whole. The reporter has to be both well informed and candid. If his reports are inhibited by the fear of giving offence, then he is in the wrong job: he is probably a kind man, but as a journalist he must be ineffectual.

A reporter's integrity—by which I mean his insistence on always writing only what he honestly believes—is not for sale. Most of the reporters I know are so bloody-mindedly independent in their opinions that they always do an honest job, because they have never learned how to do anything else.

Britain's corps of tennis writers is the largest and best informed in the world (the best informed not because they are clever, but because they have the advantage of covering the sport almost full-time). They are an oddly assorted bunch. All, like the players they write about, recognize the importance of measuring their own strengths and weaknesses: and working accordingly. Inevitably, there is plenty of character in the crew.

To avoid burdening you with a trade directory, I will introduce, as representatives of many good companions, those few who are most often my sparring partners on foreign assignments.

First, the evening paper reporters. Barry Newcombe (*Evening Standard*) is a bouncy little chap, bluff but kind, who brings enormous gusto to work and play alike. His conversation tends to be fast and clipped, as if he were in a hurry to finish because he would rather listen. Devoid of prejudice, he has a ready supply of common sense and enviably combines the twin talents of news-gatherer and writer. John Oakley (*Evening News*) is a tirelessly voluble and energetic man who does everything quickly, as if eager to get on with something else. He has a photographic memory and a special fondness for Rome, which proves that he knows what is what in the way of good tennis and good living. He introduced me to Rome and I converted him to the grape, an exchange of favours that did both of us good.

Next, from an older school of journalism, the dapper dressers of the 'popular' morning papers. Peter Wilson (*Daily Mirror*) has had a long and distinguished career. Yet as writer and critic he still sets a hot pace for the rest of us, because experience has refined his professionalism without sapping his boyish enthusiasm for sport. Peter is a gentle, considerate man, and unfailingly good company, not least when he is spreading a few chapters of reminiscence before you as one day turns into another. Frank Rostron (*Daily Express*) is another engagingly inexhaustible raconteur: and a smart operator who gets more exclusives than his younger rivals care to think about. A lot of Frank is crumpled—his face (he has an inimitable habit of moving his lips into position well before the words tumble out), his hat, and the bundle of old newspapers that he carries under one arm and sheds around him like autumn leaves. When casting directors think of a newspaper reporter, they think of a man who looks like Frank Rostron. Laurie Pignon (*Daily Mail*) has a hearty *joie de vivre* and a taste for stylish clothes and outrageously effective metaphors and similes. He curls, bristles, and lives vehemently. His response to any conversational vacuum is to pour another glass—or pronounce the word 'Splendid!' as if he had just invented it. Laurie retains a child's wonder and thankfulness for the joys of the world around him, especially if they come from a good vineyard.

To move on to the papers known in the trade as 'heavies', Lance Tingay (*Daily Telegraph*) is another fine raconteur, with a droll wit and a detailed memory for the lore of the game. Lance at work is as amiably bland as Lance at leisure. With a major effort, an obsessive misanthropist might manage to dislike him. But I doubt it. David Gray (*Guardian*) is a burly *bon vivant* who relishes a good phrase as he relishes a good meal or a good concert—and knows how to track down all of them quickly. He is also a rarity among tennis writers in that he not only tolerates the game's internal politics, but dissects them with enthusiasm. The less said about Rex Bellamy (*The Times*) the better. You are already getting to know him far too well.

Two remarkable overseas colleagues are that chic chick from Transylvania, Judith Elian (*L'Equipe*, Paris), who is not exclusively French but looks it, and Bud Collins (*Boston Globe*), who is blatantly American. They have in common an unusual degree of intellectual agility and a capacity to inspire both affection and respect. Judith, bubbling with dark vivacity, has a darting mind. With a bewildering speed of transition, she flits in and out of eight languages and a hundred outfits. Somehow, she manages to be uncompromisingly feminine in a man's world. Bud's clothes, prose and conversation are vividly coloured. Nature designed him for brilliant things. He is a rainbow of a man. A fast talker, a fast writer, and a born comedian, he could—if he chose to do so—report a funeral service in such a way that his readers would fall about with laughter. But he would not choose to do so, because his laughter is never unkind.

All these and many others play important roles in the mutual aid society of tennis reporting. They are good to work with and they know their jobs. Many are regular companions on 'the strawberry circuit' (Rome, Paris and Wimbledon), 'the whisky circuit' (the Dewar Cup series), and a dozen other gathering grounds of the tennis set.

We have had a good look at the writing game. We have discussed the trade and the tradesmen. It is time to put the work in its setting: to move on to the game and the glamour, the players and the places.

2

A Few Trade Names

Like other callings, tennis has a language of its own. Every facet of
the game—its nature, its environment, the character of the men and
women who play it—has been explored by those with a gift for
inventive imagery. The names, words and phrases in common use
are thoughtfully lobbed about in conversation during the long
hours of enforced leisure. They are like apples turned over in the
hand to see if there is more shine or colour on the other side. No
aspect is missed. If there is scope for a double meaning or an amusing
neologism, it is swiftly exploited. So the game's unique and abundant riches have acquired an appropriately diverse vocabulary.

When players gather in dressing room or restaurant, or alongside
the courts, their talk may baffle the uninitiated. This chapter will
not provide all the keys to that private glossary. But it will provide
many of them: and in the process it will help us capture a little more
of the flavour of the game and its players. It should also widen our
understanding and ensure that, even if we do not know much about
the game, the casual listener will be sufficiently puzzled and impressed to give us the benefit of any doubt. . . .

Let us work in three sections—nicknames, jargon, and finally
some fanciful fun with the game's more conventional terms. The
whole should enable us to learn through laughter, which is the best
way to do it. First, with my apologies to those players who think
apologies are necessary, the nicknames:

Addo—Terry Addison (Australia)
Baby—Antonio Munoz (Spain)
Banano—Edison Mandarino (Brazil)
Barkers—Joyce Williams (Britain)
The Bear—Jan Kukal (Czechoslovakia)
Beppe—Giuseppe Merlo (Italy)
Big Bet—Betty Stove (Netherlands)
Big G—Graham Stilwell (Britain)
Bill—Wanaro N'Godrella (France)
The Blond Bomber—Stan Smith (United States)
The Boy—David Lloyd (Britain)
The Boy Octopus—Frank Froehling (United States)
Brun—Richard Russell (Jamaica)
The Bull—Cliff Richey (United States)
The Chief—Alex Olmedo (Peru)
Creals—Dick Crealy (Australia)
Dad—Bob Howe (Australia)
Davo—Owen Davidson (Australia)
Dibbles—Colin Dibley (Australia)
Donald Deal—Donald Dell (United States)
The Egg—Ove Bengtson (Sweden)
Emmo—Roy Emerson (Australia)
Fish—John Paish (Britain)
The Flying Dutchman—Tom Okker (Netherlands)
Frankie—Françoise Durr (France)
Fred—Winnie Shaw (Britain)
Ginny—Virginia Wade (Britain)
Goldfinger—Francisco Guzman (Ecuador)
Gorgo—Ricardo Gonzales (United States)
Gugalong—Evonne Goolagong (Australia)
Hank—Douglas Irvine (Rhodesia)
Hercules (or *Herks*)—John de Mendoza (Britain)
Hesh—Ray Ruffels (Australia)
Hippy—Ray Moore (South Africa)
Honza—Jan Kodes (Czechoslovakia)
IBM—Kathy Harter (United States)
Jay—Jaideep Mukerjea (India)
Johann—John Clifton (Britain)
Jojo—Georges Goven (France)

Joko—Zeljko Franulovic (Yugoslavia)
Jules—Julie Heldman (United States)
King—Peter Curtis (Britain)
Kran—Karen Krantzcke (Australia)
The Leaning Tower of Pasadena—Stan Smith again
Lel—Lesley Bowrey (Australia)
The Little Bird—Giuseppe Merlo again
Lofty—Brian Fairlie (New Zealand)
Lurch—Charles Pasarell (United States)
Mae—Mary Ann Eisel (United States)
Manny—Munawar Iqbal (Pakistan)
Marmalade—Petre Marmureanu (Rumania)
The MGM Lion—Ray Moore again
The Mighty Mouse—Luis Arilla (Spain)
Muscles—Ken Rosewall (Australia)
Nails—Bob Carmichael (Australia)
Nasty—Ilie Nastase (Rumania)
Newk—John Newcombe (Australia)
The Nose—Julie Heldman again
Old Bones—Fred Stolle (Australia)
Old Fruit—Judy Dalton (Australia)
The Old Lady—Billie Jean King (United States)
Omar—Ismael el Shafei (United Arab Republic)
Peaches—Jane Marie Bartkowicz (United States)
Pepe—Patrick Proisy (France)
The Phantom—Kerry Harris (Australia)
Philby—Phillip Dent (Australia)
Pidge—Kristy Pigeon (United States)
Pishti—Istvan Gulyas (Hungary)
Rochie—Tony Roche (Australia)
Rocket—Rod Laver (Australia)
Rolling—Allan Stone (Australia)
Rosebud—Rosemary Casals (United States)
Sam—John Alexander (Australia)
The Shadow—Arthur Ashe (United States)
Slinky—Helga Masthoff (Germany)
Spaceman—Pierre Barthes (France)
The Spiderman—Frank Froehling again
Sputnik—Vladimir Zednik (Czechoslovakia)

The Stork—Frank Froehling, yet again
Superjack—Cliff Drysdale (South Africa)
Superman—Clark Graebner (United States)
Tarzan—Vladimir Zednik again
Tex—Bill Bowrey (Australia)
Tirry Baby—Ion Tiriac (Rumania)
Tup—Kerry Melville (Australia)

Now for jargon and slang. Some words in wider general use are included here because they have become incorporated into the idiom of tennis. But this section is devoted mainly to the unconventional English that is peculiar to the trade. The language of tennis, like any other, is continually renewed. New blood is pumped into it by such droll wits as Pat Pretorius of Johannesburg, formerly Miss Walkden of Bulawayo, who has a smile and a backhand volley of flashing beauty.

Mrs Pretorius is one of the great characters of tennis, makes everyone happy, and inspires deep affection wherever she goes. Much of this book is written in a spirit she should appreciate—and this chapter, in particular, is her line of country. She has not, thank goodness, inflicted on the game the linguistic challenges of Matabeleland or Zululand, though she could have done so had she wished. But she has given new life to such apparently tired and innocuous expressions as 'nothing fancy', 'rough stuff', and 'say nothing'. Above all, she has left her mark on the vocabulary of the game by her gift for verbal shorthand: 'G and D' for guts and determination, 'GGW' for good ground work, and 'R and C' for rugged and casual. We shall be 'talking Walkden' long after she has ceased to grace the tennis set. Meantime, let us dedicate to her this section of terms used by the 'R and C' initiates:

Aggro—Annoyance, fuss, irritation.
Arse—Good luck. Which explains why a player who has hit a winner off the wood may tap his backside as an admission that he has been lucky. An expression not used by the ladies.
The Big Four—Australia, Britain, France and the United States (the only countries to win the Davis Cup): and the championships of these countries.
To blow—To muff a chance of winning a rally, a game, a

set or a match. Most commonly heard as he or she 'blew' it.

To choke—To be afflicted by a nervousness that inhibits stroke play. We may say of a particular shot that he or she 'choked' on it.

To go cuckoo—To become distraught, to lose concentration or mental stamina.

The elbow—When players 'get the elbow' they 'choke' (see above).

Garbage points—Points won by 'pooping' (see below) or by hitting winners off the wood, rather than by striking the ball firmly and cleanly.

The Grand Slam—The feat of winning the singles championships of Australia, France, Wimbledon and the United States ('The Big Four') in the same year. Achieved only by Rod Laver (twice), Donald Budge, Maureen Connolly and Margaret Court.

To hack—To concentrate merely on keeping the ball in play, without having any positive tactical aim.

A hacker—A poor player.

To handle—To beat, to master.

Junk—The commonplace kind of tennis played by hackers; or shots with no pace on them.

Nothing balls—Shots without pace (often looped drives).

Percentage tennis—An investment in the probable rather than the possible. Percentage tennis is the product of a strategic or tactical discipline. The player concerned restricts himself to shots on which the percentages favour success.

To poach—In doubles, to trespass on a partner's territory to play a shot that would normally be his or her prerogative.

To poop—To push or prod the ball, rather than playing a positive stroke.

To press—To play over-eager strokes, usually because of anxiety or impatience. Players who do this are said to be 'pressing'.

Punchy—Punchy players have gone completely 'cuckoo', which means that their nerves have taken all the emotional strain they can stand. The capacity for positive thinking is therefore exhausted.

To rubbish—To tease, banter, mock.

To tank—To lose deliberately. Yes, it happens. Players do sometimes 'tank' a match.

Tennis elbow—An ache in the outer side of the elbow of the racket arm, which may become painful and affect the forearm. It can afflict all those who use repeated rotary movements of the forearm—for example, baseball pitchers, carpenters, fly fishermen, javelin throwers, and pole vaulters. Tennis elbow is a common term for three ailments: epicondylitis, painful annular ligaments, and radiohumeral bursitis.

You may feel that you already have a sound working knowledge of the game's more conventional terms. Let me hasten to confuse you. Plant your tongue firmly in your cheek while we have some gentle fun with definitions. Allow fancy to transform the formal into the incongruous:

Ace—1. The shortest distance between two points. A lucky service which surmounts the net, lands within the permitted area, yet eludes both your opponent and his racket. It is most likely to occur if you serve while your opponent is still bending down. 2. The highest card in the pack, although it is not a court card.

Advantage—1. State of the game when one player has scored at least three points but is one down. 2. State of the game when she has agreed to go back to your place.

Amateur—1. A player who is not good enough to earn money from the game, or is too modest to admit that he is good enough, or finds that he earns more money from the game by pretending he plays only for fun. 2. The one who buys the beer after the match.

Approach shot—1. A means of getting to the point and possibly achieving a set-up (see below). 2. 'What time would you like to have dinner?'

Backhand—1. A stroke played when one player threatens the other with the back of his hand. 2. A distorted form, the backhander, is paid to waiters who work to your rules instead of their own.

Backswing—1. The part of the swing in progress when only a fool would approach the player from behind. 2. A test for the reflexes when you stand too close to swing doors.

Ball boy or ball girl—Energetic youngsters who run about collecting stray balls, roll them to each other, and sometimes let the players have them back if they nod nicely.

Baseline—Base headquarters, from which players who can only run sideways conduct an entire match.

Big game—1. Played almost exclusively by men, this is an

attempt to win a match without playing any ground strokes except the return of service. 2. The dishiest doll around.

Big server—1. A barman who pours without looking because you distracted his attention. 2. The topless waitress with the most top.

Break—You break service by winning a game in which your opponent is serving. This puts you a break up. But your opponent can foul the whole thing by breaking back. The way to win matches is to break back without losing your own service.

Centre court—So called because it is usually in an isolated area a long way from any other court.

Chip—A hot potato in disguise. With luck, your opponent will tread on it.

Circuit—A sequence of linked tournaments in which players meet each other coming back.

Clay—A loose-top surface devised to test the sanity of Americans and Australians. All five-set matches on clay begin at lunch time and last until dinner; because no player can hit a winning shot unless his opponent gets cramp, goes crazy, or falls asleep. One of the three usually happens to one or both. Clay court matches have to be watched carefully, because everything starts happening when nothing seems to be happening.

Continental grip—A handshake used by the French to indicate that they are glad to see you, or glad to see you go.

Cord—1. The part of the net that holds up the rest. 2. A disembowelled apple.

Cross court—You upset the judge by not playing straight.

Davis Cup—A knock-out team tournament played on a zonal basis. Each zone includes one or more nations at least 1,000 miles outside the zone's geographic limits. The competition is not intended to be taken seriously: so players good enough to have contracts with World Championship Tennis have been barred.

Deuce—A mild, old-fashioned expletive uttered by the umpire on behalf of a player who thought he'd won the game but finds out that he hasn't.

Dink—A stroke invented by the Incas and popularized by Jimmy Durante.

Double fault—1. An indication that a player has found his rhythm and is serving to a pattern. 2. When a drunk walks into the same lamp-post twice.

Doubles—1. Form of tennis in which everyone plays half as much as usual, twice as fast. 2. The drinks you order when she's wavering.

Drive volley—Played when you are too early for one shot and too late for another.

Drop shot—Makes the ball drop as if shot.

Drop volley—Occurs when, having considered the potential virtues of a drop shot and a volley, a player compromises by playing both.

Expenses—1. Tax free fees that mean a player will not lose even if he doesn't win. 2. When a player takes a girl out to dinner, expenses are taxable: he will lose even if he does win.

Fault—Occurs when a player does something his opponent wants him to do.

Federation Cup—A communal nervous breakdown by women players, in a peaceful and charming environment specially chosen to aid their subsequent convalescence. The only men admitted are journalists writing medical reports.

Fifteen—See 'Scoring'.

First service—It is a tradition of the game that the server should be given two balls, which is one more than he needs. So he gets rid of the first by hitting a practice service into the net or out of court, usually at a velocity that makes all officials in the firing line check their life insurance.

Flat service—1. Pancakes. 2. A puncture repair kit.

Follow through—1. The part of the stroke that enables you to look good even when playing badly. 2. 'Let's go back to my place.'

Foot fault—When you put your foot in it, or tread on your own corns.

Forced error—When your opponent knew something nasty might happen, but could do nothing about it. Best achieved by making him hit the ball again before he has finished hitting it the last time.

Forty—See 'Scoring'.

Grass—A traditional court surface on which the ball does not bounce. Used only in Australia, Britain, the United States, and places like the Sudan.

Grooved—Turned on and swinging.

Ground strokes—Strokes that can be played only when the ball is not on the ground.

Gut—The part of the racket that fills the hole in the frame.

Gut reaction—The way you really feel.

Half-volley—1. A stroke played to stop the ball breaking your ankle or tripping you up. 2. A half-depression between half-hills.

International Lawn Tennis Federation—The game's governing body, which is concerned with making regulations so complicated that they can neither be understood nor enforced. Its motto is 'the good of the game'. The ILTF lived up to this by forbidding the best players from playing each other, which would be bad for the game because it is what the players and public want. In 1968 the ILTF declared open tournaments legal, which proved its capacity to move forward slowly. In 1971 it declared open tournaments illegal, which proved its capacity to move backward quickly.

Kick service—Religious meeting for chorus girls and footballers.

King's Cup—A European indoor team championship restricted to men who are at least 8 ft tall and hit the ball at 100 m.p.h. or more all the time. Usually played on rally-free courts so that no one has to run.

Knock-up—1. A warm-up period in which the players demonstrate the terrible things they intend to do to each other when the match starts. 2. In a mixed singles, a knock-up may occur when a man (already warmed up) plays a penetrating stroke without precautionary regard for the likely consequences.

Let—'Let's do it again.'

Line judge—Official allowed to doze in a chair beside the court. He sometimes calls out in his sleep. His resting places have such exotic names as Near Tram, Far Tram, Centre Service and Travelling Service. The only line judge who has to wake up at regular intervals is the one who lives at Travelling Service.

Lines—These delineate various sections of the court, notably its perimeter. A shot that hits a line is in court if you played the stroke yourself, but out of court if the other fellow played it.

Lob—An abbreviation for LOng Breather. You achieve this by hitting the ball so high in the air that, on days of low cloud, it brings rain. While the ball is in flight, you breathe deeply, look your opponent straight in the eyes and try to hypnotize him. You hope he will not notice that the ball is about to hit him between the ears.

Lob volley—Played when you are so tired that you cannot wait for the ball to bounce before earning your LOng Breather.

Love—See 'Scoring'.

Love all—Indicates that, as there has been no score, the players are still being civil to each other.

Low volley—A stroke played so that the ball will not knock your kneecap the other way round, which would mean that for the rest of your life one leg would walk forward and the other backward.

Match—The shortest distance between a lot of points.

Match point—1. There is only one more point to go unless the player in front loses the point, in which case there will be two more points to go unless the player who was in front falls behind, in which case the whole business may get a little complicated. 2. She's ready.

Net—A large receptacle for first services.

Net cord—A white band at the top of the net. The strategy of tennis is based on hitting the net cord in such a way that the ball teeters for a moment and then falls vertically—on the other side. When this happens, you utter an apology which everyone knows is the exact opposite of your gut reaction.

Overheads—Noises from the room upstairs.

Partner—In doubles, the one who makes all the mistakes.

Passing shot—You missed him.

Placement—Place meant: the ball went where you wanted it.

Poach—Cook your partner's eggs.

Professional—A self-confessed expert who plays the game for money and admits it, spends most of his time indoors, and plays well only when inhaling clouds of tobacco smoke. He only swears under his breath.

Rally—1. Occurs when both players are hitting and neither is missing. 2. Group therapy.

Receiver—A man who takes a percentage of the profits for selling goods that have fallen off the backs of lorries.

Referee—The man who carries all the cans but delegates all the work. He only appears in public (*a*) after finals, to make sure the winner wipes off the sweat before shaking hands with everybody, or (*b*) to tell the players to break when they start fighting, or (*c*) to stop either or both players from killing the umpire.

Return—Planning a comeback before you go anywhere.

Runner-up—The one who isn't smiling.

Scoring—An outmoded version of the numbers game. Love means nothing (what kind of game is this?), fifteen means one, thirty means two, and forty means three. The point of using this code is to kid the people who do not understand it that the people who do understand it must be very clever. It also deters casual spectators from taking a close interest in what is happening.

Second service—A means of starting play after the first service has been hit into the net or out of court. All players are as good as their second services, which are usually bad.

Seed—A player carefully planted in the draw so that, for a few rounds, he does not have to play anyone who should beat him. Seeds less than 3 ft tall are called seedlings.

Service—A method of starting play when you have been standing around too long.

Service winner—A service which your opponent hits but misses.

Set—The shortest distance between at least six games.

Set-up—You've got it made.

Short angles—1. Even crosser than cross court. 2. 'What about a nightcap in my room?' or 'Do you play any indoor games?'

Singles—Only two can play.

Slice service—Sandwiches.

Smash—1. An attempt to break the racket by hitting the ball so hard that it drills a hole in the ground and lets the worms come up for air. 2. You get smashed by (*a*) getting heavily beaten, or (*b*) drinking until you're as full as a boot.

Spin—Decides whether you win or lose at roulette.

Straight sets—The shortest distance between two pints. One player finishes before the other starts.

Strings—1. Section of the racket used for advertising the manufacturer's initials. 2. 'Will you promise to marry me?'

Thirty—See 'Scoring'.

Throw-up—An occasional consequence of getting smashed.

Tie-break—A polite way of telling two well-matched but probably boring players to get knotted.

Top spin—A means of making the ball travel a long way over a short distance, while kidding your opponent that it will travel a long way over a long distance.

Touch player—A man who never buys the drinks.

Umpire—An official awarded the best seat at a match in return for keeping the score, stopping the players from fighting, and telling spectators to shut up.

Volley—Hitting the ball before it hits you—or before your opponent is ready.

Wightman Cup—An annual women's team match in which the United States beat Britain, and all concerned sweat out the effects of a series of cocktail parties at which everyone talks and nobody listens.

Winner—The one who's smiling.

Wood—1. A rally-free surface manufactured by felling, slicing and polishing trees. 2. The part of the racket that (*a*) prevents the strings from falling off, and (*b*) is used for hitting winning shots.

World Championship Tennis—An independent tennis colony, between Paris and Palestine, administered by Texas and Wales and populated almost entirely by Australians with names like Rocket, Muscles, Nails, Hesh and Sam. The governor, who owns lots of things, is a nice man called Lamar Hunt. He always asks 'Howya bin?' because he can see for himself how you are. WCT became independent in 1967 and prospered in spite of ILTF sanctions; which made the ILTF rather cross.

So much for the terminology of the trade. We have had some fun, and learned a little in the process. Well provisioned and in good humour, we can now turn our steps towards the wide horizons of the tennis set. It is good to start at the top, because it saves the fag of climbing. So that is what we will do. We will start with the tournament that provides the best tennis of the year: the French championships.

3

The French Championships

The French championships are my favourite tournament. The All England Lawn Tennis and Croquet Club, ruminating among the ivy of Wimbledon, may suspect a lack of patriotism. But as Albert Camus put it, 'a man's love for his native soil can be extended to a wider area without perishing'. Moreover, I have French ancestry, though the strain of Gallic blood must now be heavily diluted. In any case, the fact that I like the French and their way of life is of only incidental relevance. On its own merits, their tournament is a pillar of light.

The French championships are the game's finest advertisement. The surface, clay, is gruelling to play on. Yet it provides the toughest, most exacting test of all-round ability: and the most satisfying spectacle. The entry is the best outside Wimbledon. In many ways, the tournament brings the season to a peak that can hardly be challenged—much less surpassed—by Wimbledon, Forest Hills, or the showpiece summits of the WCT and ILTF grand prix circuits.

All is grandeur and pathos. The grandeur is public—the protracted, absorbing exercises in tactics, technique, and physical and mental stamina. Except for strained sinews or attacks of cramp, the pathos is usually private—the spent, exhausted bodies, lumps of flesh on the masseur's table or the dressing room benches.

These are cruelly superb championships. Nowhere else is the aesthetic potential of the game so fully explored, nor the physical cost of it so poignantly apparent. The first weekend of the 1969 championships was a striking sample. All the beauty and drama of life, all its passion and suffering, were mirrored in the small world of tennis. The enchantment of the championships settled upon us like a strange and lovely dream.

There was a great match—played on the new 'show' court tucked away among the trees by the children's playground. John Newcombe, already champion of the German and Italian clay courts, beat Jan Kodes of Prague by 6–1, 6–4, 0–6, 8–10, 11–9. In the fourth set Newcombe served for the match at 7–6. In the fifth, Kodes led 4–1, had two points for 5–2, and was twice within two points of winning. At the end of it all, after more than four hours, Newcombe somehow managed to summon the strength for two pulverizing blows: service aces that won him the match from 10–9 and 30–15. He said afterwards that he hit the first ball as hard as he could—and the second even harder. He was so weary that he talked as if in some far-off dream. And as he talked, this young superman sank back onto the massage table as drained as a Samson whose Delilah had been busy with the scissors.

For pathos, there was Manuel Santana of Spain, playing his compatriot, Andres Gimeno, for the first time in nine years. Santana's game shone in its full splendour: all light and loveliness, caressed by the most delicate brushwork. The gifted but nervous Gimeno was made to look like a craftsman enmeshed by baffling artistry. But at the crux of the third set Santana pulled a muscle. At 0–1 in the fifth, he retired.

In the dressing room, Santana, crumpled and broken, sat on a bench with his head in his hands. Newcombe did not so much lie on the massage table as collapse on it, like a crumbling pack of cards. The bounding bundle of whipcord called Kodes sat silently in a corner, looking as fragile as porcelain, hiding his private pain behind a grim, emotionless mask that told us nothing—but everything. There was hardly a murmur save for the birds outside, trilling their evening chorus to the skies.

What a cruel game tennis can be. But all this was for the public's pleasure. On a day that smouldered with heat, the mighty centre court was suddenly crowded and colourful and fervent after two rain-swept days. Tom Okker, all tiptoe brilliance, frustrated that tough, brave little Texan, Cliff Richey. Zeljko Franulovic and Fred Stolle respectively thrust aside Roy Emerson (who looked as if he had been on clay too long) and Arthur Ashe (who looked as if he had not been on clay long enough). Ken Rosewall and Rod Laver played like the masters we knew them to be.

The whole weekend, indeed the whole game, was summed up by the contrast between, on the one hand, the crowds and the applause, the sunshine and the drama, and—on the other—the quiet pain in the men's dressing room as the birds sang their last songs of the day. That contrast was as sharp as the thrust of a dagger.

Abe Segal, a big man with a heart and personality to match, is more down to earth about Paris. 'On this stuff,' he says, 'you got to work your butt off.' He has been around long enough to know. The gods were smiling on tennis when they gave it Segal. He is a kind and generous man. His language and character are colourful. He is an eccentric of the best kind, because his eccentricity is completely unaffected. He is tough, forthright and inimitable—whether talking, playing tennis, or simply being Abe Segal.

It is in Paris that, meaning no harm to anyone and seeking nothing but a quiet life, we are unfairly assaulted by a programme and an order of play that leave us stuttering in polysyllabic bewilderment. Savour this lot as starters: Szabolcs Baranyi, Massimo Di Domenico, Sever Dron, Harald Elschenbroich, Jurgen Fassbender, Zeljko Franulovic, Wieslaw Gasiorek, Istvan Gulyas, Miroslava Holubova, Jiri Hrebec, Nikola Kalogeropoulos, Jun Kuki, Petre Marmureanu, Alexander Metreveli, Ilie Nastase, Marie Neumannova, Wanaro N'Godrella, Onny Parun, Hans Joachim Plötz, Mieczyslaw Rybarczyk, Junko and Kazuko Sawamatsu, Ion Tiriac, Geza Varga, Vlasta Vopickova, Atet Wijono and Antonio Zugarelli.

In such company, the reporter, copy-taker, sub-editor and printer raise thanks if Mark Cox makes news.

These players are not mugs popped into the draw as first round cannon fodder. True, a few leap from obscurity only during Europe's major clay court tournaments. But in Paris they can all be hard to beat, clinging like limpets to their chance of a fleeting glory. For Eastern Europe, in particular, the French championships are the pinnacle of the game—the ultimate goal of all hope and ambition and endeavour, all the sweat in training and practice, for the other fifty weeks of the year. Musing on the iron men of Eastern Europe, players with faraway faces and strange-sounding names, thus spake Abe Segal in 1970:

These guys are so fit and strong. They're built like tanks and they run like f—— deer. Give 'em a smell of the boodle, and they're off. They should be entered in the Grand National. Some guy, I can't remember his name, was dancing around me like he was Buck Rogers. When you ask your mate who he's playing, he says 'Some bloody Rumanian'. Ninety minutes later he's back in the dressing room. Some bloody Rumanian's beaten the crap out of him.

You hit the hell out of the ball and they still put it past you. Take Lew Hoad yesterday. He hit four or five balls at a hundred miles an hour and still had to come in and hit a volley. He couldn't do it if he wasn't so strong and hadn't been playing on clay for six weeks. But this tournament is bloody important.

Hoad himself told me once: 'You say you don't want to go to the damned place. When you do, your arm nearly falls off. The balls are heavy. They water the courts. You've got to play some guy you've never heard of, and you're out there for three and a half hours. But it's a great tournament.'

Rod Laver was eloquent on the subject of Paris in his book, *The Education of a Tennis Player*. Discussing the Grand Slam, he wrote:

I realized that this was the hardest championship for me to win, and because of that it probably meant more than the other three. The Slam is three-quarters grass, and I wasn't worried about myself there. The other quarter, the French, is something else, more challenging than the others, more difficult to win, more satisfying from the standpoint of having survived a terrific test. There isn't as much pressure, perhaps, because it's early in the season and the prestige isn't as great as Wimbledon or Forest Hills. But in Paris you know you've been in a fight. You come off the court exhausted, looking battle-stained, your clothes and body smudged with red clay.

Paris isn't one of my favourite places, but I look forward to it because the French championships is the tournament I enjoy the most from the standpoint of emotional involvement. I love to watch matches in Paris, grim struggles on that slow clay, beauties for the spectators.

When the 12,000 seats in the stadium are filled and people are hanging from odd ledges, railings, and the scoreboard, as they were for the final with Rosewall, it's a very lively, warm, emotional place. Those people give you a transfusion of élan and it's a great joy to play for them—at least if you're playing well. It's not quite the same sensation as a filled Wimbledon court because sometimes the stillness of Wimbledon can drive you crazy. You keep waiting for a noise, an indication that they're alive. In Paris, there's no doubt. The buzz of humanity assures you this is combat as elemental to the people as a duel or a prize fight.

Paris in the spring may mean love to some, chestnuts to others, but to me it signifies the toughest two weeks of the year.

For the reporter, too, the French championships cannot strictly be classified as fun. For one thing, there is the consonantal clatter of all those ludicrous names, which tend to give reporter and copy-taker mental indigestion before they finish the first 'take'. The tournament also spans fourteen consecutive days, with never a pause to refresh the soul. Then there are the long matches, often spectacles of absorbing beauty—but so protracted that they overlap deadlines and necessitate 'adds', 'rejigs' and 'rewrites'.

During the first week, play often spans eleven hours a day. We saunter about for hour after hour through the rising dust. We sit here and there on stone benches in the heat of the day. We get sweaty and uncomfortable, and wish it were not such an obvious abuse of good will to pop into the dressing rooms and use the players' showers.

By the time the long days have finished, the last stories have been written and dictated, and the confounded telephone delays are to-morrow's threat rather than today's frustration, what is to be done about a meal? It is always possible to eat adequately in Paris, even as far out as Auteuil. The Chez Chaumette in the Rue Gros is first class and often richly sensuous (though the resident dogs have been known to regard the floor as a *urinoir*). The Auberge du Mouton Blanc, in the Rue d'Auteuil, is consistently agreeable. But these and similar restaurants are useful only when open—and occasionally, because of the lateness of the hour, we are driven by necessity to formica-topped tables amid the pin tables of suburban bars. It seems such a shame, such a wasted opportunity, when some of the finest food in the world is only a few miles away. Yet that is sometimes the way it has to be during that crowded first week.

It was the French championships that dispelled any illusions my wife had about the glamour of reporting tennis in Paris. In 1960 she laboured at my side through all fourteen days. In the evenings we hurried back to our hotel near the Place St Michel, in a street once well known to the Resistance and the Gestapo. We recharged our batteries with a shower and a change of clothes, and went out for a meal. Late to bed, and early to rise—for another day's work. Except for a few references to the deficiencies of concrete as seating accommodation, my wife has never said much about those championships. Nor has she suggested a return trip: not as a working wife, anyway.

Which reminds me that when Barry Newcombe reported the French championships for the first time, his wife asked him on the telephone one evening: 'Is this tournament played on grass, or dirt?'

She knows now. Dirt.

But the truth is that reporters, like players, do not go to the French championships for a holiday. We go to work: and how thoughtfully Nature and Man have conspired to cushion the severity of our labours. Granted the best company, the best tennis, the best food and the best wine, who could possibly complain, save for a blind misanthropist whose taste buds have withered?

With the help of Abe Segal, Lew Hoad and Rod Laver, I have tried to convey something of the unique flavour, the transient nuances, of this marvellous tournament. And although the first week tends to be a hard slog for the reporter, the second has its compensations. Unless the weather has unkindly interrupted and congested the programme, there are fewer matches. The working day begins much later and ends a little earlier. It becomes possible to sit down to dinner, freshly laundered, in the sort of places where angels would sing songs of praise if they knew what was what in the way of dining out. Moreover, there is no longer any need to hurry.

Reporters, like players, learn to pace themselves through a tournament. Too many late nights in the first week would leave me jaded for the second. But once the first week is over, the reporter can, as it were, go to town. What matter if he clambers into bed at three or four in the morning, if he can sleep till the sun is high?

In 1971 I returned to my hotel in the small hours with such un-flinching regularity, waking up the bleary-eyed night porter at anything between 2.30 and 3.30 a.m., that a break in the pattern startled the man. He was inspired to progress from his usual terse questions about morning calls and breakfast to a reasonable fac-simile of a speech. The exact French escapes me. But my rough translation is etched on the mind, as is the entire, memorable little scene.

I was early because I had been dining with a player who had a match the following day. I returned to the hotel at one o'clock.

The night porter was still up. In two senses. He was vertical. Leaning against a wall outside the hotel (how gracefully the French lean!), he was puffing a lazy cigarette and looking at the night. Montparnasse had the air of a village that was not yet ready for sleep.

He saw me coming, emerging from the bright lights and strident traffic of the Boulevard du Montparnasse. I walked, and watched, as he stubbed out his cigarette and glanced at his wrist watch. Carefully, he removed his spectacles, took out a handkerchief, and polished them. Restoring the spectacles to the perch for which the optician designed them, he re-examined his watch to confirm his first reading. For a few moments, incredulity plainly struggled with all that habit had taught him. To encourage him to voice the thoughts clearly bursting to be expressed, I greeted him and ob-served that, for a change, I was early. He scrutinized me closely—to confirm, as he had done with his watch, the correctness of his first reading.

'M'sieu,' he said. 'I think I sleep. I dream. It cannot be you.'

In all the years I have known that lugubrious man, he has never come closer to betraying a sense of humour. Which just goes to show how human the French can be, even night porters, when you catch them off guard.

The glitter of the Right Bank has never dazzled me. It is too worldly, in every sense. The Left Bank has always been my milieu. When I cross the river, it is usually to head for the cobbled slopes of Montmartre rather than the glossy opulence of the Champs Elysées. My temporary home in Paris these days is a small hotel in a little Montparnasse community where, each year, I renew acquaint-ance with the same newsagent, the same greengrocer, the same laundress. I know the Left Bank of Paris better than I know any part of London.

French tennis has some charming people attached to it: most obviously such couples as Carolyn and Pierre Barthes and Rosa-Maria and Pierre Darmon. In the press box, Judith Elian is always flashing brightly dark smiles and juggling with languages. On distinguished occasions, Dick Roraback—lean and bearded, with pale, questing eyes and a zest for living—turns up to write one of his vivid features for the *Herald Tribune*.

To arrive in Paris is good: but to arrive at the Stade Roland Garros is even better, because it is to arrive among friends. And where better to meet them?

The championships are separated from the Bois de Boulogne by a highway that is all screaming brakes and tall trees. If you travel by *métro*, you emerge into the sunlight at the Porte d'Auteuil amid a whirling mass of traffic. Across the road is the *jardin des fleurs*. Do not pass it: go in. You will find little plaques scattered about, each offering a few lines of poetry. Each plaque has, as a backcloth, an arrangement of growing things to illustrate the verse. Here, in short, is an imaginative marriage of poetry and horticulture. Your French does not need to be extensive to catch the flavour of the place. In any case, it is a good spot to relax.

On most mornings, you will catch Roland Garros in a warm mood, with little to disturb its drowsy charm except for loud thumping noises from courts tucked away among the trees. It is not the loveliest rendezvous of the tennis set. But it has its own history and character, and there are a lot of trees about, which always tend to lift the eyes and the heart upward. In a rambling sort of way, it offers much solace for the soul—or the stimulus of excitement, whichever you choose.

My mind is not cluttered with dates and facts and statistics. A cluttered mind is often a closed mind. A reporter needs to leave plenty of room for manoeuvre between the ears, so that ideas can dart about freely, and impressions can move in, take root, and blossom. All of which is to justify the admission that I cannot remember when I first reported the French championships.

In that first year at Roland Garros, I busied myself collecting facts and doing all the usual chores. I also spent a lot of time sitting and dreaming, looking at the day, and letting the colour and beauty of it all flood into the mind—while I made little notes and turned them into the phrases that, with luck, would breathe life into the reports. There was time to spare, because hardly anyone bothered me: for the simple reason that hardly anyone knew me. But the years have left a legacy of kind friends: the mutual aid society of the writing game, or players who know what we are looking for and help us find it. Like anything worth while, such a rapport takes time to grow. The friendship that springs up in five minutes has no anchor to hold it firm in angry tides.

The golden era of open tournaments, between 1968 and 1971, is the basis of reminiscence in this book. But a glance at earlier horizons may lend perspective to the view. A few fleeting pictures of 1960, for example, still hang fading in the mind. Paris was making world headlines because of a Summit conference. And a few miles down the Seine from the throbbing heart of the city—from that rich source of news, the Elysée Palace—the world's leading 'amateur' tennis players had their own little summit meeting.

Jaroslav Drobny and Budge Patty were still doing their stuff, though the splendour had gone. Luis Ayala, the muscular Chilean, was dancing around the courts like a rubber ball. The 1959 runner-up, the South African Ian Vermaak, white cap stuck carefully over one ear, was taken to five sets by a highly promising British player, the nineteen-year-old Mike Sangster. A compatriot of Vermaak's, Rodney Mandelstam, who had played through the qualifying competition, lost in five sets to Lew Gerrard amid the grey, echoing vastness of the centre court. The sun and the pace became hotter and hotter. There was time to watch the first set, stroll round the outside courts, have a leisurely lunch, stroll round the outside courts again—and then drift back to find Gerrard and Mandelstam still pounding away, still sweating and straining. Roland Garros is like that. Even the first round losers can play enough tennis to make the trip worth while.

The broad canvas of the French championships gives us plenty to talk about as we sit among the rustling trees. Andrzej Licis ('I am zee smallest,' he told me once, 'but I run quick') gave the fourth seed, Rod Laver, a nasty fright as the first soft shadows of evening were falling across the courts. Laver had a match point against him at 2–5 in the fifth set. But he saved it: and with some new fire of inspiration burning within him, fought back to win. 'I had never heard of Licis before, and seldom after,' says Laver, 'but that afternoon I thought he was one of the greatest players in the world.'

In the next round, Manuel Santana beat Laver in five sets. The championships ran into stormy weather, and play was called off shortly before six o'clock. There were pools on the courts, the weeping willows by the painters' tableau of results were even more lachrymose than usual, and the restaurant was bulging at the seams. But by that time Laver had been washed away. In the same round, Roy Emerson was beaten by that strolling giant from Italy, Orlando Sirola.

Billy Knight, as rumpled as an unmade bed, gave the British some excitement. He lost the first set before beating Wilhelm Bungert. Knight often wore the look of a man whose creditors were closing in. The news slipped along the grapevine. Spectators came flocking in as he set to work to balance the books. But once on top, Knight never relaxed his grip on Bungert or himself.

Some men are happiest with a load on their backs. Knight was like that. After the first set, Bungert had to gather what crumbs he could from the rich man's table. With light rain threatening an interruption, Knight won the last three sets in a trice, acing the German on the only match point that was necessary. The quick kill did not suit everyone. An Englishman, who had watched Britain's Davis Cup tie in Scheveningen and had then walked to Paris, arrived hot foot—in time for the final handshake. But he was philosophical about it. A man who can walk from Scheveningen to Paris is probably philosophical about most things.

In the last sixteen Knight was beaten by Neale Fraser after leading by two sets to one. The third and fourth sets were the kind that put 'nerve-wracking' in the dictionary. Anglo-Saxons inhaled deeply from their Gauloises.

Britain's other survivor, Bobby Wilson, was pounded to submission by the giant American, Barry MacKay, an explosive hulk of a man who roared about the court like a toy tank. Wilson had the sympathy of the vast centre court crowd. In the ninth game of the first set he had three set points. '*Egalité*' was called nine times. The umpire's voice in the drama was like some gramophone record, stuck in a four-word groove. He had nothing to say except '*avantage*', '*égalité*', and the names of the players.

Leaving my wife in charge, I left to check around the other

courts. I took my time. When I came back, my wife had begun a new page in the notebook. But it was still *égalité*.

Other sights and sounds of Roland Garros, 1960, were the shrieking brakes from the Avenue de la Porte d'Auteuil; the blossom swirling down onto the courts on days of sunshine and showers; and, on a hot afternoon, the chic and charming Lea Pericoli. She was wearing what my wife described as a V-necked, sleeveless costume, box-pleated, with a coloured Mexican motif on each pleat, and the whole skirt lined with yellow. Miss Pericoli was winning too.

Well, they do say that when you look good, you feel good—and when you feel good, you play well. Miss Pericoli is still chic and charming. And she is still winning.

One more glance at a few fading prints before we leap to the more recent past. The year was 1961. It marked the first appearance at Roland Garros of one of the great players of tennis history—a woman who later achieved an unparalleled record, had a revolutionary effect on the women's game as a whole and the Australian women's game in particular, and, in spite of her reserve, inspired an ever-increasing depth of admiration and respect both on and off court.

Margaret Smith was then only eighteen years old. But she had already been Australian champion twice. In Paris, she was seeded third. But that was the year when none of the top four seeds (Darlene Hard, Maria Bueno, Miss Smith and Christine Truman) reached the semi-finals. They were beaten, respectively, by Edda Buding, Suzy Kormoczy, Ann Haydon and Yola Ramirez. It was also the year when the sixth seeds, Manuel Santana and Miss Haydon, won their first major singles championships.

Miss Haydon beat Miss Smith 7–5, 12–10 in a thrilling, agonizing test of mental and physical stamina. They were on court for almost two hours of a sweltering afternoon. When Miss Haydon was leading 7–5, 10–all, and 15–love, Miss Smith, suddenly crying quietly, had to stop because of cramp in her feet. Three minutes later she resumed the torrid battle. But she lost the game and, after taking salt tablets, lost the next as well—after saving two more match points (she had already saved three at 9–10).

For Miss Smith, that was a cruel introduction to the ultimate rigours of the chastening clay-court game. It was a fine match, and a harrowing experience for both players. Through the next decade, Miss Haydon and Miss Smith advanced to fame and marriage, to the names Jones and Court. Now we can look back, down the tunnel of the years, and feel that the image of each player is rounded and complete.

The dusty flavour of that day in May 1961 still seemed fresh on the palate when the same players met in the 1969 final. This time, Mrs Court won. But 1961 was Miss Haydon's year. In a semi-final she came back from 3–6 and 0–1 down to beat Suzy Kormoczy. Realizing that attritional warfare from the baseline was not enough, Miss Haydon went to the net more often and became so effectively aggressive that she won eleven successive games. Mrs Kormoczy's game was destroyed. The shift in the psychological balance was remarkable.

With that, the worst was over. '*L'agressive Brittanique*', as the French called her, beat Yola Ramirez 6–2, 6–1 in the final. Time and again Miss Haydon boldly cantered to the net without, it seemed, sufficient cause. But Miss Ramirez, intimidated, could not play the passing shots or lobs demanded. Confident, on her toes, Miss Haydon played drops and lobs so finely measured that the capacity for human error appeared to have deserted her. To a degree, it had. Early in life, she realized that talent was a tender plant which needed the nourishment of work: and she has never fought shy of that.

Those anonymous, painstaking painters, working away quietly at their vast mural of results by the willows, dipped into their fifth different colour on the day Rod Laver and Manuel Santana qualified to meet again, this time in a semi-final.

Santana did so by beating the Australian champion, Roy Emerson, 9–7, 6–2, 6–2. Here were two admirable players with contrasting styles—Santana an artist on slow courts, Emerson a forthright serve-and-volley specialist whose springing stride took us back to the days when a man had to catch and kill his steak before eating it. Moreover, Emerson was good enough on clay to have beaten Laver in the British hard court final a few weeks earlier. But now, except when he least expected it, Emerson was denied the speed on which he thrived. His rhythm was disrupted by Santana's teasing variations of pace and length, arc and angle—by that looped forehand drive, those delicately disguised drop shots and lobs. It was a drop shot that won Santana the match. But long before that, Emerson had been fighting grimly but in vain to escape the tightening net of the Spaniard's wizardry.

Santana beat Laver 3–6, 6–2, 4–6, 6–4, 6–0. Looking back across the dimming years, I can still remember the glow of the occasion, the packed centre court crowd thundering their appreciation. Santana, with the caressing subtlety of his skilfully masked strokes, was up against a player who fitted no mould except the one Laver himself brought to the game. 'There is, and can be, only one Laver,' I wrote. 'His quick footwork and superb wrist make him a difficult player to corner. When all seems lost, he can often pull off a startling winner.'

Santana's sorcery had to be used with discretion. His success was a triumph for self-discipline. Clearly he was living every important point as he slowly pulled himself clear from the perilous position of two sets to one down. At one moment Laver dictated the pattern, at another Santana. The court glittered with colourful stroke play—gentle and violent, short and long, all the angles. This was a thrilling, brilliantly illustrated text book of tennis. The only pity was that one player had to lose.

'I'd had a fine chance to win in four, leading 4–1,' says Laver. 'But I was through, and Manolo wrapped me in a lovely web of shotmaking, 6–0 in the fifth. I believe that's the only time it's happened to me since I've been a world-class player. It happened so fast it was almost painless. Manolo exploded. He rang up eleven straight games and the match. I never got close until we shook hands. Five weeks later I won Wimbledon.'

In the final Santana beat Nicola Pietrangeli, champion for two years running, by 4–6, 6–1, 3–6, 6–0, 6–2. Each stepped from light to darkness in turn as the match followed its curious course. Santana was nervous. That inimitable row of drooping, swooping teeth seemed to jut out farther than ever as he stooped in concentration. But he did not let the occasion spoil his natural game. Here again were all his peerless resources of spin, all his artful versatility.

Often Pietrangeli matched and even mastered him as they fenced for an opening. There were times when Santana's strokes were drawn to his racket as if by magnetism, when the Spaniard's keenest thrusts were countered by winners. But the Italian was never at his best for long. His brush strokes were overlaid by Santana's flickering finesse. The dying fire of Pietrangeli's inspiration had no flame to offer as the wind of imminent defeat grew ever colder.

No one would have predicted that the little, frail-looking Santana, who used to be a ball boy at a club in Madrid, would beat the top three seeds in ascending order—Emerson, Laver and Pietrangeli. It was a moment of unbelievable triumph for a man who still had the awkward bearing of a boy.

The two Latins in the final had established a close rapport with the Latin crowd. Artists and audience were as one. As the last point was tucked away, there was a standing tumult. It was then that Santana's nervous control cracked. He dropped his racket and cried. Pietrangeli, disappointed though he was, knew how the man felt. He put his own racket aside, rounded the net, and advanced into the opposite court. He took Santana in his arms and gently patted him on the back like a father comforting a weeping child. In such a Latin assembly, all passion and sunshine, it seemed entirely right. The soul of Paris, Spain and Italy was laid bare.

That portrait remains as fresh as the day it was painted.

I have dwelt on those 1961 championships not because of a taste for history, but because it was a remarkable year and I remember it well. Doubtless Santana and Mrs Jones do, too. We were not to know, then, that each would later—much later—win Wimbledon. For the sixth seeds who became champions, the trembling crises of Paris, 1961, were complete in themselves.

There is much to tell, in a similar vein, about the next five years. About the triumphs of Laver, Emerson, Santana again, Fred Stolle, Tony Roche, Miss Smith (twice), Lesley Turner (twice), and Mrs Jones again. About 1963, that mighty year for the French when their own Pierre Darmon, a latter-day D'Artagnan, opposed Emerson in the final. About 1966, when the dark and sturdy Istvan Gulyas, a kind and retiring little man who inspires universal affection, was runner-up to the husky and voracious young Roche. About Miss Turner, now Mrs Bowrey, so trim and tidy and tough.

But we will not look closely at those five years. This is not a history book. It merely attempts to catch the flavour of a world game, to offer a few impressions of the tennis set and their setting.

Let us take up the story in 1967, when Emerson, that prancing Peter Pan, won the last of his twelve Big Four singles championships—and Françoise Durr, who makes a virtue of heterodoxy, gave

France their first women's singles champion since Nelly Landry (French by marriage) in 1948, and their first French-born winner since Simone Mathieu in 1939.

There were some stormy early days. When sunshine eventually succeeded rain, the flowers sparkled with a new brightness. But for a while these were damp, drab and frustrating championships—even in the restaurant, where for some unfathomable reason the staff seldom allowed customers to drink wine sitting down or tea standing up.

A violent wind snapped in two a couple of the giant chestnuts, apparently impregnable, that line the Avenue de la Porte d'Auteuil. One glanced off the radiator of a van. The other smashed through the front of a gleaming new coach. It would be understating the case to describe the tennis that followed as a travesty of the game.

The courts had been soaked by rain and were strewn with displaced foliage. The players had spent the better part of two drenching days finding out that there is no pleasure in doing nothing when there is nothing to do. Now they were plunged into a tennis nightmare, with crashing noises all around them and tennis balls behaving as tennis balls were never meant to behave. Air shots were commonplace. Anyone who could play a drop shot into the wind was on to a good thing. To toss the ball too high, while serving, was to risk losing it over the back canvas. In circumstances that mocked the conventions, players were forced to desperate improvisation. Some were close to laughter, others to tears.

Peter Curtis, then ranked sixth in Britain, was playing in the championships for the first time. He was blown to obscurity in the first round by Patricio Cornejo of Santiago, one of the early disciples of sideburns. Ask Curtis about wind players and he will talk about Roland Garros rather than the Promenade Concerts. His frustrations were such that he eventually tried an underarm service: and put it in the net. But the match was played in three phases spanning twenty-three hours. So it may be that Curtis had some kind of record to his name after that first match in Paris.

But sunshine and the heat of battle are seldom far away at Roland Garros. In terms of tennis maturity, the adults were soon sorting out the adolescents. The tournament sprang to life on a day when the dignity of Australian tennis was fiercely assailed. Martin Mulligan, John Newcombe and Bob Hewitt lost in straight sets. Owen

Davidson saved three match points. Tony Roche had to hang on desperately in his fifth set with a Czechoslovak ten months his junior—and in those days the sight of Roche was making his seniors tremble, never mind his juniors.

At last, Roland Garros was hazy with heat, throbbing with drama, glittering with the thrust and parry of often wondrous strokes.

The match of the day, its quality and its shape equally thrilling, was that between the reigning champion, Roche, and that straining bundle of energy, Jan Kodes. They shared the burning eagerness of youth. They also shared that uncommon attacking stroke, a rolled backhand. They fashioned a match that quickened the often gentle rhythms of the clay court game, and raised the pulse rate of all those lucky enough to be perched on the soaring tiers of the centre court.

There were two main crises. When leading by 6–4, 6–2, and 6–5, Roche came within two points of the match and (as Gail Sherriff, later Mrs Chanfreau, observed) had Kodes 'done like a dinner'. But the bulldog from Prague fought his way out of the trap, emerging with blood seeping from his hand and red shale spattered over his clothes. In the fifth set came a shaft of splendour, the sort of stroke that champions play when their titles are rocking. At 5–4 to Roche, with Kodes serving at 30–15, Roche played a cross-court stop volley, a backhand, that died like a whisper in the night.

It was the moment of truth—and Kodes knew it. He made two mistakes, packed his bags, and headed for the dressing room.

Maria Bueno's greatness was then fading, her physical resources afflicted by the wear and tear of the years. But the regal authority of old had not yet exhausted itself. The smouldering fire could still glow with a consuming heat, though its steady flame had gone. On the day she beat Virginia Wade, Miss Bueno's tennis was, for most of the match, irresistibly severe. Her unparalleled flair for the game was in full flow. She was breathtaking to watch. The storm ripped gaping holes in Miss Wade's unwaveringly resolute resistance.

Then came the astonishing day when the top three seeds, the women's singles champions of Wimbledon, France and the United States (Billie Jean King, Ann Jones and Miss Bueno), were all beaten. Miss Melville, only nineteen, had previously survived two match points against Monique Salfati. Now she beat Mrs Jones 0–6, 6–4, 8–6: after taking only three games as far as deuce in that crushing first set. A rising young player tackling a hardened campaigner, Miss Melville went for her shots with courage and confidence whatever the state of the match. In moments of adversity, she seemed to be smiling ('I wasn't smiling: I was snarling'). At 5–all in the third set, Mrs Jones would doubtless have responded gladly when the public address system echoed the referee's demand that she should report for a doubles match (the French seldom carry efficiency to excess).

Françoise Durr beat Miss Bueno 5–7, 6–1, 6–4 and Annette van Zyl, later Mrs du Plooy, beat Mrs King 6–2, 5–7, 6–4. That was a day when we could have written columns. But for some reason space was tight. We mostly had to make do with inches.

Came a sweltering Sunday afternoon that French tennis as a whole, and the Durrs in particular, will long remember. At 4.20 the crowded centre court—its four vast banks ablaze with colour, like giant flower beds—almost burst asunder with noise and movement. A Frenchwoman, born on Christmas Day, had become French champion. Miss Durr, who knows how to apply pressure without using violence, beat the pretty little Lesley Turner 4–6, 6–3, 6–4. An arduously close match lasted 1 hour 35 minutes.

Here was a smack in the eye for the purists, a vindication of all those who assert that character is more important than talent. Miss Durr's sun-glasses and hair-ribbons are distinctive but not elegant. The same applies to her grip and her strokes: especially that sliced backhand that often takes her down on one knee. What binds all the peculiarities together and makes her such a bonny competitor is her ball control and the unfailingly sharp wits that dictate her strategy and tactics. She knows where the ball needs to go: and she has the ball control to put it there.

The crowd's collective heart went out to her at every crisis. When she squeezed a last decisive error from Miss Turner's backhand, the new champion flung her racket so high that it could have brained her on the way down. She has continued to grace the top table. But the wine has never tasted better than it did that day in Paris.

For the second time Roy Emerson completed the second leg of the Grand Slam, which has always eluded him. The historians may recall Emerson as a superb athlete who never stopped running, a bustling, hustling serve-and-volley specialist who won more Big Four singles titles than anyone else: six Australian, two French, two

Wimbledon and two American. But the Emerson whose memory I cherish is the Emerson of the slow clay courts of Paris and Rome. He was not just a fast-court specialist. He was a tennis player. And if we speak of him in the past tense, it is only because he can no longer climb quite so high as he could in his salad years.

Emerson beat Tony Roche, more than eight years his junior, by 6–1, 6–4, 2–6, 6–2. Emerson needed the interval after the third set. But his was a marvellous performance. He was everywhere. When Emerson was leaping and whirling and booming away at the net, Roche must have thought he was playing against a practice wall that was firing back with interest. It was as if every attempt at a passing shot touched off a charge of dynamite.

It was after this match, still thrilling to the beauty of Emerson's volleying, that Barry Newcombe and I decided to watch France and Russia play football at the Parc des Princes. It was the day of the reflexes: Emerson's at one net and the great Lev Yashin's at another. The transition from Emerson to Yashin also had its moments—and two journalists took to heart a lesson that a well-placed expletive can be every bit as effective as a well-placed full stop.

Roland Garros being the dusty, sweaty place that it is, we decided that (between courses, as it were, of our sporting feast) we would return to the cleansing showers of our hotels, so that we might face the evening freshly laundered, and flavoured with such embottled, aromatic lotions as embellished the pocketed recesses of our toilet bags. But first, we had to get a taxi. On such tiresome chores does the progress of life's pleasures depend.

There is a taxi rank at the Porte d'Auteuil. But late on a Saturday afternoon its provision of cabs tends to fall short of the needs of the populace. We had to queue. When our turn eventually came, I nipped into the back, sprightly and impatient to be off, and explained our needs. The driver listened with the mournful inscrutability Parisians usually exhibit when someone else is talking. Then he shrugged, waved his arms sadly, and observed that— grievously though he regretted the loss of our company and custom—he was, for the moment, more interested in eating than earning. He had an engagement for tea and was, he said, late already. *Vraiment.*

Barry, who is a quick lad, never prone to hang about when there is no point in hanging about, caught the drift of all this amiably unproductive chat. Meantime his peripheral vision spotted another likely craft breasting the waves of traffic and coming into harbour. He trotted across to it with such haste as he could muster, aware that French queues are not always mindful of the order of their coming when sorting out the order of their going. But he was beaten to it.

His rival was a tall, lean, distinguished looking chap, immaculately garbed and volubly French. As Barry is burly—but short on vertical as opposed to circumferential inches—they made a pleasantly contrasting picture as they jostled for position outside the open back door of the cab. A sort of Morecambe and Wise duo without the humour.

Now Barry is no slouch at word-swopping. The trouble was, he had no basis of exchange. That dapper queue-jumper seemed intent on rushing through the entire French dictionary in two minutes flat. He was too fast and eclectic for Barry's command of the language, or mine when I joined him. The man babbled on like a mountain stream in flood, a rushing, rumbustious torrent swollen by literary tributaries. Here was a true countryman of Balzac and Dumas, Flaubert and Maupassant, with perhaps even a dash of Gide in his blood.

It was impressive. Yet daunting. Wind up a Frenchman, and he will talk as if he has just learned the trick of it. Full of beans that keep popping out of the can. I was reminded of a day on Exmoor when my wife and I met a lady on horseback, who explained that she was learning to ride the thing but had, as yet, found no means of stopping it. Couldn't find the handbrake.

But it was frustrating. How to answer back, when you cannot understand the questions?

Now Barry's nature is more restlessly combative than mine. Which is to say that he was getting angry. There seemed some danger that the firm nudging of shoulders and hips might erupt, at any moment, into the more bruising impact of what is known to some of my acquaintance as a bunch of fives or a knuckle sandwich. But the Frenchman's cascading loquacity suddenly reached a stretch of still water. He paused long enough to exploit his positional advantage by sliding into the back seat. This was a provocative move, fraught with terrible hazards. Every man has his boiling point: and Barry Newcombe was almost there.

But in the battle of words (or in his case, as it transpired, word) he was not done for yet. He was hopelessly behind on points in a verbal bout for which his vernacular English had not equipped him. But he decided to go for a knock-out in the last round.

He leaned inside the taxi until his face was within a foot of the Frenchman's. Then, nose to nose, he clearly and firmly enunciated a naughty Anglo-Saxon word. It was the only word he said. But its effect was dynamic. The Frenchman's face dropped. It did really: it visibly lengthened. He stepped pallidly out of the taxi and asked:

'*Vous êtes étrangers?*'

'*Oui.*'

'*Je suis français. Montez.*'

And we did. Game, set, and match to Barry Newcombe. Which, as I said, just goes to show what you can do with a well-placed expletive.

Strange how, by some process of catalysis, Barry and I seem to attract trouble in Paris. When we stroll into a café late at night, some sort of fracas tends to break out within minutes. The Place Jean Lorrain, the Place du 18 Juin 1940, the Boulevard St Germain—each has provided the sights and sounds of the primitive man that lurks within all of us. But only once, as I recall, was there any blood: and that was hardly surprising because, at the time, a fashionably dressed young man was bashing some ruffian's head on the pavement. Excitable people, the French.

As Parisian café brawls are apt to be noisy—with all the shouting, and banging about of bottles and plates and falling beer crates—the whole thing gets rather wearing on the nerves. But where else can peace-loving men get their Dubonnet and Perrier, or their coffee and cognac?

Even in the restaurant at Roland Garros, an aproned scullion once went berserk with a carving knife and chased one of his terrified colleagues round the premises (amid much clattering of crockery and cutlery). But that was during the 1968 championships: and that year, everyone's nerves were shaky. In their total impact, that was the most memorable tournament I have ever reported anywhere.

The 1968 championships were the world's first major open tournament. Had the organizers been prudent, the whole thing would have been cancelled. But the championships were gloriously successful. Riots, strikes and sunshine ensured massive crowds: because the citizens had nothing else to do. Roland Garros was a port in a storm. We thought of Drake and his bowls, of Nero and his fiddle. In a strife-torn city, the mighty centre court blazed with colour. Spectators even perched on the scoreboards, which was as high as they could get without a ladder.

The fizz and verve of that fortnight sprang from two sources: a revolution on the courts, and a whiff of revolution in the streets. Roland Garros has seldom been so packed, so animated, so stimulating, so early in the tournament. There was an air of tingling expectancy, because the promoter-controlled professionals, great names of past championships, were returning to active service on these famous courts. The flavour of the occasion was that of a nostalgic reunion. Even Abe Segal (looking slim and fit after training hard to become slim and fit) re-emerged from South Africa at the age of thirty-seven, twenty years after working his passage to Europe to enrich the character of the tennis set. There were colourful and convivial scenes as players streamed into Paris from all over Europe.

The city seemed to be cut off from the world. A few players telephoned to say they were not coming. Other withdrawals languished in the strike-bound postal repositories. There was an early announcement that no one would be scratched until Thursday.

Some of the travellers' tales sounded absurd: but they were true. The four women under contract to George MacCall arrived at 2 a.m. after a nine-hour drive from Amsterdam. That bearded jazz enthusiast from Copenhagen, the blandly serene Torben Ulrich, turned up on a bicycle with a knapsack on his back (a sight that would have been even more remarkable but for the fact that, in any circumstances, it would be no surprise to see Ulrich turn up on a bicycle with a knapsack on his back). Some of the professionals landed at a military airfield after flying from New York. One group came by taxi from Luxembourg. Many travelled by bus from Brussels.

Once in Paris, the players were told they had to move close to Roland Garros, because no transport could be provided to and from the Champs Elysées. Abe Segal and Bob Howe decided that Paris had ceased to be fun. So they tested the rumours that tanks were encircling the city. They set off for England in Segal's Mustang, with a massive drum of petrol in the back. But they neglected to pack a tin-opener. There was no means of unwrapping their cargo: and the garages were closed. They eventually found help in some anonymous French village—and Segal, spitting petrol, sucked up the fuel through a rubber pipe.

But the spectators found petrol from somewhere. The roads around Roland Garros were swollen with cars. And when the sun shines on the Bois de Boulogne, riots and strikes and petrol shortages lose much of their damaging effect on the morale. The first of the Big Four tournaments to be open to everyone was played in the sort of environment nightmares are made of—but the tennis was often like a dream.

Came a weekend of roasting enchantment. The huge amphitheatre of the centre court smouldered with heat. Its steep banks, overflowing with spectators in summer colours, was a dazzling sight. The players must have felt like ants, trapped at the foot of a giant rock garden in full bloom. The promoter-controlled professionals—the old boys coming back to the school of their youth—looked at the brightness and beauty around them and felt, perhaps, that such gloriously open tennis as this was made for the gods.

Ken Rosewall, briefly threatened by Herb FitzGibbon, played some wonderful tennis. The lashing facility of his ground strokes almost stopped the heart. There were puffs of dust as the ball bit into the court like a bullet. The crowd made thunderous noises: and then fell back into those intimidating silences peculiar to vast assemblies.

Even this became a shadow in the memory as Ricardo Gonzales exposed the richest texture of his game in beating Istvan Gulyas 6–4, 6–2, 6–2. The Hungarian had reached the final two years earlier, but he was too modest to fancy his chance against Gonzales. This was a match between a big man and a small man, with Gonzales making tennis look the loveliest of games. He was efficient, but he was romantic. His serving and smashing were explosive. His ground strokes, stop volleys and drop shots had the delicacy of feathers blown by a gentle breeze. At times he seemed to have too much respect for the ball to hit it hard; instead, he whispered to it, like a fond parent lulling a child to sleep. To watch Gonzales was to think in terms of poetry and music. He did not play the game. He composed it.

Then there was the comedy-drama of Ion Tiriac playing Rod

Laver. Tiriac is a swarthy, shambling giant with bulging muscles, black curly hair and long sideburns. There is so much hair on him that he seems to have been zipped into a rug. A Heathcliff of a man, he might have stepped straight from the pages of *Wuthering Heights*. This intimidating Rumanian took three falls, two sets, and—eventually—a hiding from Laver.

To look at Tiriac, you would expect him to play a game to match his size and strength. But he is a slow-court specialist, an expert exponent of lobs and looped drives: in short, a good operator on clay. He was new to Laver. 'The ball was coming at me twenty feet high,' said Laver as he was towelling down afterwards. 'I felt like catching the f—— thing, throwing it back, and saying: "Can't you do any better than that?" '

Laver can be reticent. But that day he had been through the fires of hell and was chattering freely in basic Australian.

The top spin on Tiriac's cross-court forehand set the left-handed Laver awkward problems on the backhand. When the ball did not bounce high and deep (thus depriving Laver of the chance to attack without risk), then like as not it skimmed the net and dipped so sharply that the stooping Laver put his backhand volley in the net. He also found Tiriac's backhand difficult to read. On neither flank was Laver offered the hot pace he likes: instead, the ball came to him in a mostly gentle variety of mesmeric arcs and angles. Laver became tentative and edgy. He was playing from memory in a strange world that recognized none of the conventions of his own. The assurance drained out of him; the errors seeped in.

Meanwhile Tiriac was lunging and leaping, scrambling and stumbling about the court in a disconcerting way. He flung himself headlong in the rally that won him the first set. The centre court seemed to shake with an impact doubtless recorded on the seismographs. Twice in the second set he fell again. When he won that set, his shirt and shorts were strewn with shale, and blood was streaming down his right leg from a cut knee. He was winning, but he looked as if he was losing. Yet for an hour and a quarter his tennis and his expressively menacing character dominated the match.

By the beginning of the third set, Laver was fast losing dignity. He was being drawn to and fro like a puppet on a string. He was running in circles. His legs were getting mixed up. But he kept his head and he kept at work. At the crisis of the third set he played two glittering strokes—a perfect backhand drop shot that spun into the tramlines as it died, and then his pride and joy, a top spin backhand. He was now taking the ball earlier, hitting better approach shots, and visibly gaining confidence. Tiriac, tiring, was beginning to look genially resigned. Laver covered the full width of the court—and more—to win the fourth set with a running forehand, a blazing shaft hit from well wide of the tramlines. In winning the last ten games of the match he played superb tennis against a Tiriac now looking helplessly statuesque. The mesmeric spell had been shattered. In the mind's eye, Heathcliff, still glowering, lumbered back to his brooding moors.

Ricardo Gonzales and Roy Emerson then strode into the dusty arena to delight us. Their match could not equal the melodrama of its predecessor, though the quality of the tennis was higher. With the help of a rain break and a night's rest after the third set, Gonzales won. The busy, fidgety Emerson, covering the court with a predatory, cat-like grace, tried to hustle the older man into error or weariness or both. Up to a point, Gonzales was sucked into the slipstream of Emerson's swift aggression. But Gonzales was an artist—the racket his brush, the court his canvas. For most of the match, his game had a caressing charm that Emerson could not resist. Many of the rallies were as finely woven as some gorgeous tapestry. The sun was shining. Gonzales and Emerson were enjoying themselves. The crowd leaned forward. They roared. They hushed. They burbled with bliss.

Laver played thrilling tennis, repeatedly challenging the laws of probability, to beat Gonzales in straight sets. But Rosewall was taken to five by Andres Gimeno. The tall, stiff Spaniard was at his best only when he attacked—and he did not attack often enough. Rosewall was nearly always the more positive player on the important points. But there was many a trembling crisis to tantalize the capacity crowd, whose bright colours soared steeply towards the tree tops that peep over the perimeter of the court.

Rosewall won the final 6–3, 6–1, 2–6, 6–2. He gave a masterful demonstration of clay court tennis. His ball control was as immaculate as his tactical judgement. He struck a perfect length, peppered the lines, and continually made Laver run and stretch. This was cool, clinical professionalism. Yet often Rosewall showed us the one stroke in which he flirts with the flamboyant—a sharply angled backhand stop volley, played with his back to the net when (logically) the ball has passed him. Laver again became a man Tiriac would have recognized. Rosewall was drilling holes in his game, and Laver's errors were seeping through. Only his service, smash, speed and determination kept him going. He saved seven match points. Then Rosewall nabbed him.

This meant that Rosewall had become the unchallenged monarch of the clay court game. He had beaten Laver by three sets to one in the finals of the first two open tournaments, in Bournemouth and Paris. Rosewall, of course, had been French champion fifteen years earlier. Someone asked him if he was still the same weight: 'Maybe a bit heavier in the pocket.'

In 1968, such men as these had all the attention. They were like returning prodigals, or gods popping down from above to remind mere mortals of the difference between margarine and butter. But the women had some fun, too. Françoise Durr and Rosemary Casals were beaten in straight sets by Gail Sherriff, with her discus-thrower's forehand, and by that cuddly, golden-haired little Mexican, Elena Subirats. Billie Jean King, who was tactically uncertain, lost to Nancy Richey, who was not. In the final Ann Jones misplaced the tenuous thread of authority—and later tired—after making and wasting two chances of a quick advantage over Miss Richey. In the first set Mrs Jones led 5–1, but lost eleven of the next thirteen points and had to work hard to take the set. In the second, she led 4–2 but lost fifteen of the next sixteen points. There was to be no third chance. Miss Richey was as steadfast when facing victory as she had been in the darkness of adversity.

A fortnight earlier—freshly arrived in a troubled, threatening and increasingly isolated city—the tough little Texan had asked anxiously: 'How do we get outa here?' Now she had won the game's first major open tournament. Like the rest of us, she was glad she had stayed.

The personal memories of that fortnight are etched on the memory for all time. A night drive from Brussels in a hired car. Public scuffles, bred from the irascibility of frayed nerves. Electricity cuts. Garbage rotting in the streets. Long walks to and from Roland Garros, because there was no other way of making the trip. Journalists operating the switchboard, taking their own calls from London. The worried players, who had taken a lot of trouble to get to Paris and wisely decided to get out of it as fast as they could. The sundry extraordinary contacts (including an ex-racing driver with an inexhaustible stock of petrol) who turned me into a sort of last-hope travel agent. Most of all, the repeated doses of tear gas, and a night spent in a candlelit garret with four French youngsters—because my bed, a hundred yards away, was in the middle of a battleground.

The Place St Michel had always been my stamping ground in Paris. It is the heart of what, that year, was a riot-torn Latin Quarter. The first night back, I blundered across the square at about 11 p.m. and, at the fountain, was struck by the pregnant silence—by the echoing footsteps (mine) in the deserted stillness. It was usually a swarming, throbbing thoroughfare.

To the left, the helmeted riot police were drawn up across the Pont St Michel. To the right, the Boulevard St Michel was packed with students. Eyes smarting from tear gas, I was caught between opposing forces during some pause in the mayhem. The feeling of conspicuous isolation was chilling. Would they, perhaps, shout 'Fore!' or whatever it is that French golfers use as an equivalent? Anyway, this was no place to hang about. The important thing was not to stop and not to run. The yards seemed long. But the door of the Hotel d'Albe soon closed behind me—and, as if at a signal, the battle resumed. It lasted until three in the morning.

Same scene: twenty-four hours later. I was ambling along the Quai des Grands Augustins, about fifty yards from the Pont St Michel. Again, the bridge was congested with police and supporting transport. A horde of people, clustered round the bridge, suddenly turned and ran towards me as the night exploded with noise. Any discreet man would have taken the hint and cantered along with them: away from the hotel instead of towards it. But some ill-timed whim of the subconscious recalled Guy Mollet's aphorism that fear is always a bad adviser. A fool treading where the angels and the wise would not, I crossed the road (to avoid being trampled underfoot by the stampede) and turned into the Place St Michel. Five yards away, a student wearing a skid lid cried out, reeled backwards clutching his face, and fell in a heap. A white-coated casualty attendant rushed to his aid. Leaping—as on wings—for the scanty shelter of a nook by a café, I took stock of the situation.

From left to right, the riot police were firing or throwing a variety of thunderous missiles. Clouds of tear gas rose from the

road like mist from the marshes. From right to left, students—
brandishing dustbin lids as shields—kept racing into the open to
hurl primitive projectiles at the police.

It was then that, with a lightning shaft of perception, a piquant
feature of the geography was driven home. I was in the middle of a
pitched battle, caught on the narrow margin of the crossfire, and
could not move in any direction. The only other 'civilians' in the
vicinity were police targets: the students in the front line. Ludi-
crously, I was sporting a bow tie and had a copy of *Newsweek*
tucked under one arm. There are moments in life when we feel both
improperly dressed and inadequately protected, like an illicit lover
caught with his trousers down when the husband comes home. But
there was nothing to be done except take a few notes and muse that
the journalists reporting the riots could keep the job. Tennis was
infinitely more civilized.

But they do say that Somebody Up There looks after those who
have not the wits to look after themselves. Or to put it another way,
that if you are daft enough, you will get away with it. Is it the Red
Indians who show kindness to the sick in mind?

In the midst of that banging, shouting, steaming Bedlam of un-
identified flying objects, there came a quiet voice from behind as a
bar was lifted and a massive, grilled door slightly and tentatively
opened. Would I like to come in? It is possible that rabbits get off
the mark faster. But I doubt it.

The door was closed and barred again. A blatant non-combatant
had been rescued by three youths and a girl. This was their home.
By way of introductory chat, I explained that although my hotel
was only a hundred yards away, it was spectacularly obvious that
there was no way to reach it without getting biffed by something
hard and unhealthy. The night shook with the crackling, booming,
yelling din. There was no escape from the noise. Nor from the tear
gas. For a while, we sat in the back yard and coughed, eyes streaming.
As it happened, I was carrying a large cargo of Gitanes. Someone
found a crate of bottled beer. So we talked and smoked—and climbed
to a sixth-floor garret, unlit until one of the youths found a candle.
'*La vie bohémienne,*' he murmured. The Gitanes seemed appropriate.

Through the long night, we looked down on the Place St Michel.
The street lights were glaring on the helmets of the police. Students,
chucking things, sporadically dashed into the open from the

Boulevard St Michel or the Place St André des Arts. The hard stuff was flying in both directions. The rattling rumble of the ugly little mock-war was ceaseless, the tear gas pervasive. There was a crashing of glass. The sirens of ambulances and fire engines. What, I asked, were the riots about?

'Basically, the government.'

At one o'clock the riot police advanced from the bridge and ran across the square, firing from the hip, sweeping swiftly into every dark and narrow street. The students scattered and fled. Behind the police—the infantry—came their lumbering transport. The Place St Michel, an oddly deserted no-man's-land only seconds earlier, was suddenly congested with vehicles and men. The sounds of battle receded towards the Boulevard St Germain.

As we took a last look from that garret window, a man and his dog walked slowly across towards the fountain. It seemed incongruous (like that old story about birds singing to the front-line troops during the First World War). Perhaps they, too, had been waiting two hours and a half. We clattered down the wooden stairs, shook hands, and said goodnight. I picked a way among the police, the host of trucks and grille-windowed coaches, the ambulances, the fearsome assortment of wreckage, and—always—the stinging tear gas. At the hotel, the receptionist smiled and said: 'Tonight, it is not so long.'

In the morning, only the tear gas and the wreckage remained— and the camera-clicking sightseers, recording the heaps of cobble-stones and gratings, the gaping stretches of torn-up boulevard, the burnt-out cars, the barricades, the prostrated road signs, the broken trees, the scattered glass. And that evening, as if nothing nasty had happened or ever could happen, young lovers again shared their private dreams along the banks of the Seine by the Pont St Michel.

I stayed there for the rest of the week. The riots cooled. But then I moved to Auteuil. If you wonder why, try walking from the Place St Michel to Roland Garros—and back—carrying a weighty brief-case through the rain. It happened too often.

The same combination of circumstances—the same unlikely *mélange* of ugly violence and beautiful tennis, the same omnipresent air of crisis—can never occur again. Those 1968 championships were unique. But another fracas, more private, caused a buzz of chat at the beginning of the 1969 championships. Two days earlier, in a Berlin dressing room, Roger Taylor's left fist had collided with Bob Hewitt's left eye. In Paris, Taylor had to scratch. Bruised knuckles and a swollen hand would not allow him to grip a racket. But Hewitt played, and won a couple of matches. It seemed that Taylor had won the war but lost the peace.

A new régime had taken over French tennis. They were bursting with bright ideas for the 1969 tournament. They built a 'show' court and a restaurant by the children's playground. They hustled things along so crisply that, until they slammed on the brakes, it seemed the championships might finish five days early. Their only failure was the half-hearted introduction of floodlighting. One of its aims, clearly, was that their biggest and best entry should be trippingly trimmed by beginning the programme soon after breakfast and letting it run deep into the night. The most spicy of the first round men's matches, between Cliff Drysdale and Manuel Santana, was played under floodlights and ended in a heavy shower. Predictably, the Parisian public had not rushed from the dining tables in large numbers for the occasion.

Rod Laver had to live the 1968 Tiriac nightmare all over again. But this time the ogre on the other side of the net was the towering Dick Crealy—like Tiriac, one of the characters of the game. Crealy is 6 ft $4\frac{1}{2}$ in. tall, with Santana-style teeth, long sideburns, an engaging stream of self-critical asides, and something of a reputation for going cuckoo. He likes belting the ball, and on the forehand he does it rather well. He caught the slow-starting Laver at the end of a day, blew hot while Laver blew cold, and won the first two sets. But towards the end of the second Laver warmed up and engaged top gear. Crealy watched helplessly (and nobody can watch more helplessly) as the winners scorched past him. Laver earned the third set and an interval. Then the lowering sky shed its load of rain and that was that for the day. Laver could not afford another slow start next morning. Roy Emerson gave him a long workout—and Laver won the fourth set easily and went to 3–1 in the fifth. But Crealy lit the fuse again, blasted his way back into the match, and had a point for 5–4. His service was good enough to open up the court; but he blew the chance by trying to play too good a volley. It was out. So, shortly afterwards, was Crealy.

Ken Rosewall and Martin Mulligan, quick little men scuttling about like rabbits, had some fun in line-clipping rallies. Rosewall later beat Fred Stolle in a match interrupted by prolonged whistling and applause as a flagrantly feminine vision in yellow and red, mini-dressed and booted, stepped into a reserved box. Another bewitching but more relevant spectacle came when Tom Okker, hurtling about the premises like a ghost in overdrive, beat John Newcombe 5–7, 6–2, 4–6, 6–2, 6–2. When that delicious but debilitating duel was over, Okker was no longer The Flying Dutchman. He was just a quivering slab of meat on the massage table—a slice of the grandeur and pathos that was Roland Garros in 1969.

It was impossible to feel the pounding pulse of that match with anything as insensitive as prose. It was dominated by earned points, by entrancing rallies in which both men scurried about the court exchanging power and touch, thrust and parry. Newcombe's defeat had three causes. First, Okker. Second, the double-fault that cost him his service at 1–all in the fifth set. Third, Jan Kodes, who had run down Newcombe's batteries with a 61–game match in the previous round. But the shot of the match was Newcombe's. He retreated seven or eight yards behind the baseline to await a smash. When it whistled upon him he smashed it straight back—past Okker and into court—at a velocity that would have perforated the Dutchman had he been in the way. For a moment, both stood frozen in disbelief. But Newcombe enjoys raising a laugh by hamming the role of the virile hero. He grinned, raised his arms, and flexed his shoulder muscles—as if to say: 'Me, Tarzan!'

Maybe. But he was not the king of the jungle this time.

Neither semi-final wore the purple of greatness. The young men, Okker and Tony Roche, began with crackling ambition against the old pros, Laver and Rosewall. But they were consumed by the fires their early audacity kindled. They served merely as foils for two great players. Rosewall was the better man on the big points. His confidence visibly increased as Roche's drained out of him. Okker did take a set from Laver and there were some seductive rallies on the way. One, all touch and subtlety, was full of drops and angles. There was another, also at short range, in which volleys and half-volleys fizzled to and fro at a speed demanding ridiculous reflexes. In yet another, they exchanged a long series of fierce top spin drives (and to hit top spin off top spin is to tamper recklessly with the laws of ballistics). Both men were rich in whiplash flair, and the crowd responded as Latins always do.

Laver and Okker can have crazy spells in which they play like souped-up jugglers and make nonsense of the game. Okker had his when he came from behind to win the first set, dazzling our expectations with all the loveliest colours on his palette. But the match expired like a burst balloon—punctured by a second set in which Laver, whacking everything hard and everything in, was so hot that he swept to 6–0 in fourteen minutes at a cost of only eight points. That was shattering, unbelievable tennis. Okker was not playing badly, but Laver made it seem so. Everything Laver tried—and he tried everything—turned to gold.

Each match had promised to burst into flower. Each had suddenly withered. Somehow that day turned sour on us. It was grey and chilly, dominated by showers rather than sunshine. It was as if some shadow had been cast from distant Mexico by the death in an air crash of the gay little Rafael Osuna, the 1963 United States champion. The flags were at half-mast. We rose for a minute's silence: while beside the net, a lonely figure, stood Osuna's last opponent, Bill Bowrey. He was holding a racket cover without a racket, an accidental yet aptly poignant touch.

Sunshine induced the late Maurice Chevalier to don a cap for the final. The tightly tiered crowd were overlooked by a little group who had clambered out of a skylight to lounge precariously on the roof of a house. Laver beat Rosewall 6–4, 6–3, 6–4. That does not sound much of a match. But it was an astonishing display of clay court expertise, of technical and tactical virtues. To take its measure, you have to consider what it took to beat Rosewall in straight sets in 1969, on clay, when he was playing beautifully. He was very close to his best form. But he never had a chance.

Laver was as quick as a cat, covering the court with such rapacious haste, such fast anticipation and footwork, that even when Rosewall was in charge he had the devil of a job putting the ball away. Rosewall said later that he felt he was playing more than one man: 'Today, he would have made anybody look slow.' Laver began well—and improved all the time. 'I was lucky in that my form stayed all the way through,' he said later. 'I put the pressure on because I got a good length continually, which kept Kenny back. He didn't get such a good length, which let me attack a little.'

A little! The man seemed to spend most of the match volleying winners. Rosewall must have felt the way he did after Laver had beaten him at Boston five years earlier: 'Like a bastard on Father's Day.'

The solidly consistent Ann Jones, her patience always inspired by shrewd and positive thinking, gave clay court tuition to two strong young Americans, Kristy Pigeon and Valerie Ziegenfuss. Miss Pigeon came off looking as bemused as a heavyweight who had been chasing a flyweight for fifteen rounds without landing a punch. Miss Ziegenfuss finally put a smash out of court while a chimpanzee was squealing in a garden a few yards away. If you ask me what the chimpanzee was doing there, I cannot tell you. At Roland Garros, we take such things in our stride. It would be no surprise to see a giraffe in a bathing suit acting as ball boy.

Rosemary Casals and Françoise Durr won nerve-racked endurance tests against Virginia Wade and Helen Gourlay. Miss Wade served for the match three times and had two match points. Then Miss Casals romped through two love games. Santana and Pietrangeli would have enjoyed the *coup de grâce*: the successive thrusts of drop shot, lob, and drop shot again.

In the semi-finals, Ann Jones and Margaret Court beat two more former champions, Lesley Bowrey and Nancy Richey. Mrs Bowrey had avenged her defeat in the 1967 final by beating Miss Durr. She had then arrested the advancing clay court education of Billie Jean King, three times champion of Wimbledon but still a tenderfoot at Roland Garros (a heartbreaking place for impatient Americans). Mrs Jones beat Mrs Bowrey 6–1, 6–2. This was a startling score considering the sprightly efficiency with which Mrs Bowrey slams away on clay. But she did give Mrs Jones a scare with a run of eleven points out of twelve.

Mrs Court recovered from 2–5 down in the third set and was twice within two points of defeat before beating Miss Richey 6–3, 4–6, 7–5. She has seldom given a better demonstration of her ability to raise her game in adversity. At 1–4 down she felt twinges of cramp and decided to 'go in'. It worked. At 4–5 she remembered that, at an identical stage in the second set, she had stayed back and lost the game. She did not make the same mistake again. Whenever Mrs Court is in trouble, her plan of campaign is simple and direct: 'Serve and charge!' The bugles blow, the flags fly, and over the top she goes. She finished the match with a backhand stop volley ('I just threw myself at it') off a fierce forehand that seemed certain to pass her.

She won the final 6–1, 4–6, 6–3, reminding us that we shall be lucky if, ever again, we see such a superb combination of tennis player, athlete and honest-to-God trier. Mrs Court gives 100 per cent only because she cannot give more. Mrs Jones used every scrap of her skill, sense, and determination in an effort to disrupt the Australian's game. But a difference in class was usually evident. Usually. But when Mrs Court was serving for a 5–1 lead in the second set, the confidence suddenly ebbed out of her and the errors flowed in. She was all of a flutter. Four times she double-faulted on important points. Mrs Jones pounced, like the exemplary professional she is, winning six successive games to pump new life into a dying match. But once in charge of the third set, Mrs Court did not leave the door open again.

The last four women and three of the last four men were all former champions. At Roland Garros, there is seldom any substitute for experience. But Laver and Rosewall, who had contested two successive finals, were not to play there again: and the memory of them diminished their successors. In case anyone thought he might be past it on clay, Laver beat Jan Kodes (the French champion of 1970 and 1971) in straight sets in the 1971 Italian final.

In 1970, for the second time in three seasons, the French championships were played amid a rumble of controversy. In 1968 they were the first major open tournament. In 1970 they were the first to be boycotted by World Championship Tennis, whose players have easier ways of earning a living than playing two weeks of five-set matches on slow clay. Relations between the French and WCT were strained anyway—and the French refused to pay WCT anything except the money their players could earn on court. This was a gamble. But it came off. Crowds and receipts were much the same as in 1969. The absence of WCT had no effect except, inevitably, on the quality of the men's tennis. The prestige of WCT suffered. They ducked the toughest tournament in the game, and it managed very well without them. In the short term, at any rate, the event proved to be bigger than the players. The French shattered WCT's ultimate bargaining weapon: that no big tournament could prosper without such players as Laver, Rosewall, Newcombe and Roche. WCT were wrong. Which was a healthy reminder of the old Irish saying that the only thing worse than being indispensable is being dispensable.

The championships were embellished by fresh thinking and imaginative promotional gimmickry. We had *la journée des fleurs*, when nice young ladies pinned roses on our lapels; *la journée des jeunes*, when the young were given a big welcome; and *la journée de l'élégance sportive féminine*, which produced a slightly embarrassing mannequin parade, on the centre court, in weather that must have given the girls goose pimples. But we had to hand it to the French: they were original.

Unfortunately they remained careless about providing such essential personnel as scoreboard operators and ball boys. The tournament was wearing new clothes, but its basic character was unchanged.

The crowds were huge, the sunshine fierce (the mannequins were unlucky). The heat was so merciless that it was a test of fortitude watching tennis, never mind playing it. To sit or stand in the sun was to find out what happens to a steak under the grill. How clement were those evening shadows across the torrid arena! Towards the end, wind blew swirling clouds of dust around the courts. The playing conditions have seldom been as gruelling. By comparison, Wimbledon seemed like a garden party.

Inevitably, the straining, dehydrated muscles protested. Lea Pericoli collapsed, shrieking with the agony of severe leg cramp, when 4–5 down in her third set with Lesley Hunt. A cluster of would-be masseurs (men, of course) rushed on court. It was ten minutes before the Italian could be moved to the dressing room. The 6 ft 3 in. Vladimir Zednik, as massively genial as Tommy Cooper, asked too much, too often, of his mighty muscles. He finally sprained an ankle coming down from a smash, was carted off to hospital and did not compete again for eleven weeks. Bob Howe chipped a bone in a foot, an injury that was to end his run of sixteen consecutive years playing in all three events at Wimbledon. Cramp nearly finished Margaret Court in the second round. And the day before the final, she was struck down by the sort of stomach trouble that can afflict any highly trained athlete who enjoys good food and drink.

It was exciting to see Lew Hoad, thirty-five, and Barry MacKay, thirty-four, back in business. Two ageing heroes, all memories and muscles. Both reminded us that a short ball can and should be punished, even on clay. Against Harald Elschenbroich (an all-round sportsman who had survived a 100 m.p.h. car crash four years earlier), Hoad lost the first five games while active service was lubricating whatever Nature uses in the way of ball bearings. Then he played inimitably thrilling tennis. Hoad won matches in five sets, four sets, and three sets. But just as life was getting easier he came up against Zeljko Franulovic, who disrespectfully kept putting the ball in places beyond the reach of Hoad's creaking limbs.

This was a time rich in nostalgia—with Hoad, MacKay, Santana and Pietrangeli on court, and Jack Kramer among the spectators. MacKay had been top seed in his previous French championships, in 1960. He is 6 ft 3 in. tall and once had his service timed at 110 m.p.h. Like Hoad, he first beat a German, Jurgen Fassbender. Then he ran into Szabolcs Baranyi, the new Hungarian champion, who beat him in five sets that spanned the entire afternoon and a lifetime of hope and frustration. MacKay, 'The Bear', saved three match points before Baranyi tamed him.

Dick Roraback was in good form that day. 'MacKay's serves,' he wrote in the *Herald Tribune*, 'were gouging miniature shell holes out of the red clay surface. He hits like Rocky Marciano, which is to say that anything he can reach is a dead duck. Barry plays the net, though, with all the agility of a Patton tank in quicksand, depending on his Mach-2 serves and smashes to ride him out of trouble. Kramer brought him a cold beer in the dressing room, where MacKay was stretched out full length—which is an awful lot of tennis player. "I got a little tired, a little slow. This clay! You hit a volley and the f—— dust comes under you and you're running and not getting anywhere. He hit a lot of good shots, though, that guy. Who is he?"'

Franulovic and Tom Gorman both had their rackets knocked out of their hands when volleying. The passing shots take some stopping at Roland Garros.

Georges Goven is a wiry, spry, springy little chap with bandy legs and a jerky, swaggering walk. He bounces around the court so fast you wonder what would happen if his brakes went. He is permanently wound up and gaining time. He gave the French something to shout about (not that they need much encouragement) by reaching the semi-finals. On the way he beat Manuel Santana, twice champion but ten years his senior, in a centre court match that was a highly emotional Latin occasion. Noisily stiffening Goven's nerves, the crowd eventually seemed to manage the match rather than watch it. Goven was a bright and breezy twenty-two-year-old. Our minds flashed back to a similar scene on the same court nine years earlier—when the young Santana burst into tears after becoming the first Spaniard to win a major championship.

But Jan Kodes was heading Goven's way. The tight-lipped Czechoslovak was taken to five sets by Tiriac in a tempestuously delightful clay court exercise. It was punctuated by Tiriac's brooding histrionics: and dominated by the fact that Kodes, who has iron concentration, did not let them bother him. Kodes had less trouble with Martin Mulligan, an itinerant, wide-smiling, one-man charm school. At times Mulligan even out-Drysdales Drysdale. He remembers everything about everybody—including the names (and nicknames) of their wives, mistresses, children, dogs, cats and canaries. He has lived in Italy since 1964, suits the climate, and is now known in the trade as Martino Mulligano. Kodes beat him in straight sets.

Terry Williams (Reuter) put a stop watch on this 88-minute match and discovered that the ball was in play for only 28 minutes. Does this mean tennis players should take a two-thirds' pay cut?

Kodes was ready for Goven. Or thought he was. Goven led him 6–2, 2–6, 7–5 and was serving for a 3–0 lead in the fourth set. You can imagine what happens when a dashing young Frenchman—the hero of the moment because he has beaten Santana—plays an important match on the centre court. There was an explosive din whenever Goven won a point, which was often. With Goven darting about and bearing down on him, and the crowd going wild, Kodes sometimes had a look of glassy-eyed bewilderment. He must have felt like an early Christian hauled out of bed and tossed to the lions. Just in time, he remembered that he was the better player.

At the other end of the draw the tennis Cagney called Cliff Richey beat the top seed, Ilie Nastase. The Rumanian is a resourceful, enviably talented stroke player and a superb athlete, his lank hair flopping as he prances about the court with a slightly pigeon-toed gait. But maybe he was jaded by a long run of success. His length was poor and he did not hit hard enough. The chunky and combative little Richey is less well endowed as a player and an athlete. But this dedicated 'loner', an austere introvert with a strong will and a fighting heart, has pushed his abilities to their uttermost limit. He played a fine, well designed, relentlessly aggressive match that gave Nastase the hangdog look of a man who was second best and knew it.

Zeljko Franulovic, so relaxed that he makes Perry Como seem a fidget (Graham Stilwell's comparison, not mine), beat Arthur Ashe in five sets. These are players of class and character, each with his own mannerisms—Ashe pushing up his glasses with an index finger, Franulovic nonchalantly resting his left hand on his hip between rallies. They often played their best tennis simultaneously, which was bad for the blood pressure. Ours, anyway.

Franulovic, who was earning his money that week, took more than three hours to beat Richey 6–4, 4–6, 1–6, 7–5, 7–5. The match had one of the most astonishing volte-face in the history of the tournament. From a set and 1–2 down, Richey sank his teeth into the match and locked on like a bulldog. The pale-eyed Texan, restlessly eager to punch his way to the net, was all bouncing, surging authority. He hardly missed a shot. It seemed that he could do nothing wrong and that Franulovic could do nothing right. The Yugoslav lost his touch and had no compensating weight of shot.

Richey won sixteen games out of twenty. The seeds of his eventual frustration were probably sown when he was 3–1 up in the fourth set and had a furious argument with a line judge and the umpire over a close decision. That changed the climate of the match and put the crowd behind Franulovic. But Richey reached 5–1. He was two breaks up and twice served for the match. The first time, he served two double-faults. The second time he reached 40–15, two match points—wasted by a wayward volley and another double-fault. Franulovic accepted his reprieve just as equably as, earlier, he had accepted his sentence. He regained his touch. Suddenly, his game was sweetly in tune again. Richey lost six successive games—but had a break point for a 5–3 lead in the fifth set. By that time both players had been through so many crises that their nerves must have been numb.

What a match that was, swinging crazily this way and that, with the dust swirling and the crowd roaring—then hushing one another as a fresh point renewed the drama. After those harrowing dogfights with Ashe and Richey, Franulovic was drained of emotional and physical resilience. In Paris a player has to combat both kinds of exhaustion, unless he plays superb tennis or has an easy draw.

Kodes beat him 6–2, 6–4, 6–0 in sixty-six minutes. It was the first time two East Europeans had contested the final. In the absence of WCT, the only Australian in the last eight was the Italianized Mulligan. A year earlier, Franulovic and Kodes had been slapped down by the Australians, who had grabbed five of the last eight places.

Kodes won his first major title and became the first Czechoslovak champion since Jaroslav Drobny in 1952 (this time, Drobny won the veterans' event). The nimble, lusty little Kodes had never played better. He hit fierce passing shots on both flanks, but tossed in a few drop shots to keep Franulovic honest. Yet Franulovic had a chance to get into the match. The crux came in the tenth game of the second set. With Kodes briefly off the boil after an irrepressible start, Franulovic served two double-faults in a loose game that put him two sets down. After that, Kodes was too far in front to worry and Franulovic too far behind to hope: he scored only ten points in the third set.

The big noises in the women's event were big women—in ascending order of inches, Margaret Court, Helga Niessen (now Mrs Masthoff) and Karen Krantzcke. To start at the top, as it were, Miss Krantzcke was confident and bang in form after helping Judy Dalton win the Federation Cup for Australia the previous week at Freiburg (where Miss Krantzcke had not lost a set). She has a brutal forehand and a totally dismissive smash. In Paris she beat Mrs Dalton, Françoise Durr and Virginia Wade in successive rounds to reach the semi-finals, and then led Miss Niessen 3–1. Miss Krantzcke was to score only seventeen more points. She hit the ball all over the place. She had eight successive wins behind her—mostly good ones achieved under pressure. 'The strain of concentrating so hard for so long hit me like a bomb at 3–1. Towards the end I didn't know what was going on.'

Miss Niessen is a languidly leggy 5 ft 11 in. Her glacially composed court presence ('I never get angry—I can't') nettles many of her opponents, but conceals a sharp sense of fun. For years she had been overshadowed by two equally sophisticated Germans, Edda Buding and Helga Schultze (now Mrs Hösl). But late in 1969 Miss Niessen began to use metal rackets and beat all sorts of players she was not supposed to beat. Now she became the first German since the war to reach the women's singles final of a Big Four championship.

Sporting her usual chic line in sun caps, she frustrated Billie Jean King by 2–6, 8–6, 6–1 in ninety-three minutes. They played in an oven called the centre court, amid blazing heat and a wind that had the players spluttering in clouds of dust. Mrs King crisply outclassed her in the first set and had sixteen break points in the second. Three times Miss Niessen held her service from love–40 down. Had the Queensberry Rules been in force, the fight would have been stopped. Miss Niessen had only two break points in the set. But her flowing backhand, a lovely shot, won her the second of them. In the third set Mrs King had a break point for 2–1. But she was promptly afflicted by cramp and hobbled through the rest of the match merely as a formality.

Mrs Court lost only one set in the tournament. That was in the second round, when she twice had to hold her service to avoid losing to Olga Morozova in straight sets. Attacking with unusual boldness for an East European, Miss Morozova kept hustling Mrs Court into error and dashing to the net to hit winning volleys or smashes. Mrs Court was playing only her second match in twelve days. Her legs had lost the habit of running and jumping. Soon she was resisting not only Miss Morozova, but cramp as well. Yet she won.

Mrs Court beat Miss Niessen 6–2, 6–4 to become the first woman since Helen Wills to win the title four times. The match was played in glowing heat and the players perspired freely under their sun hats. They worked each other cruelly hard and the match was far, far more gruelling than the score suggests. In gaining a 6–2, 3–0 lead (she had a point for 4–0) Mrs Court played some of the most resourceful and accomplished clay court tennis of her unparalleled career. She had to. But Miss Niessen won four games out of five to draw level at 4–all. Again we admired her length, her drop shots, her cool tennis brain and her firmness in adversity. But the German lost the tenuous thread of authority with a rash of errors in a loose ninth game—and Mrs Court eagerly wrapped up an exhausting match that had given us some lustrous rallies.

Mrs Court, who should know, considers the French championships tougher, physically, than any other Big Four tournament. It certainly was that year. The playing conditions made sure of it. And it was particularly tough for Mrs Court, who had been keeping two secrets.

She spent a lot of time having treatment from the masseur. Everyone thought the trouble was the injured neck that had kept her out of the Federation Cup competition. But it was her legs she was worrying about. With the masseur's help, she nursed them into condition.

The second secret arose from an evening out, at my suggestion, on the Left Bank. It was carefully planned for the evening of the semi-finals, a day and half before her last match (should she succumb, ever so little, to the pleasures of the good life, there would be ample time to recharge the batteries). I piloted Mrs Court, her husband Barry, and Pat Walkden to a restaurant in a back street behind a back street. With *champignons à la grecque* and *fondue* to be savoured, we dined discreetly well. Then, on to the Alcazar, a noisy, bustling, informal night spot with a continuous stage show that is all bounce and verve and gaiety—the sort of place to wind anyone down at the end of a day's work. Finally, a beer at a pavement table on the Boulevard St Germain.

It was a lucky evening, because wherever we went we seemed to slot into the last vacant seats. Moreover, we were relatively sober. As Miss Walkden would put it, there was no 'rough stuff'—if we may except a chatty drunk on the Boulevard St Germain, who examined Mrs Court's openwork sandals and told her, at quite unnecessary length, that she had the most beautiful feet he had ever seen. Maybe he was kinky about feet.

That was the whole story until almost two days later. Having dictated a report of the final, I popped into the restaurant to raise a glass with the Courts, who were celebrating with the customary beers. They gently broke the news that for most of the previous day Mrs Court had been prostrate with a violent stomach disorder. Something she had eaten, perhaps? Had she lost, they added, they were not going to tell me because I might feel bad about it (even an incidental measure of guilt can weigh a man down).

But no wonder Mrs Court was so desperately eager to win that sweltering final in straight sets. And that, of course, was the year she emulated Maureen Connolly by winning the Grand Slam.

A compromise brought WCT back into the fold in 1971. But Laver, Newcombe, Okker, Roche and Rosewall were missing. Half the WCT stable, including the thoroughbreds, had the strength of will to resist two weeks of physical and emotional torture on slow clay—with not even a tie-break to show them a light at the end of the tunnel. Their main preoccupation, their own championship circuit, was proving rather demanding. They needed a rest before getting back to it, on grass at Bristol, as part of the run-in to Wimbledon. Some also had urgent family affairs to attend to. Their boss, Lamar Hunt, explained with some embarrassment that the dates had been left free, that his men were permitted to play nowhere else during the French championships, but that he could not force them to go to Paris.

What it all amounted to was that the agreement between WCT and the ILTF was not sufficiently binding to get the stars on stage. Which was a lesson for both sides.

So the men's event looked thin on top for the second year running, though the makeshift WCT team did stiffen the competition in the early rounds. There were no Australians in the last sixteen, which gave the tournament the character of a house without a roof on it. In the women's event, true, there was an all-Australian final, but the women concerned were not from the traditional school. Evonne Goolagong has some aboriginal blood and Helen Gourlay is a Tasmanian of Scottish and Irish stock. Their advance to the final provided Australian newsmen with some sensational copy. Because Miss Goolagong was the first player since Althea Gibson, in 1956, to win the championship at her first attempt, and Miss Gourlay was the first unseeded finalist since Ginette Bucaille in 1954.

In the early days there was the usual scope for peripheral humour. Matches started late. There were not many ball boys about. Blank scoreboards seemed to be hanging beside the courts because there was nowhere else to put them. Everyone was complaining about the balls ('It's like hitting a melon,' observed a sardonic Chilean). But there is probably no other big tournament where you can buy a choc ice flavoured with Grand Marnier. As a distraction beside the centre court press box, we also had Titian's reclining maenad—a sunbather who remained glamorously recumbent even when plopping noises and amplified French indicated that players and umpire were on active service. She just wanted a singe, and knew where to get it.

The sensation of the men's event was Frank Froehling, runner-up

for the 1963 United States championship, who had returned to the
big-time after five years as a businessman. Froehling is a sensation
even when he is losing. He is a bony 6 ft 3 in. tall and most of him
is angles: he plays like a mobile windmill and seems to spread
everywhere. When he bends down to receive service, it is like seeing
a lamp post melt. Froehling's forehand is the sort of stroke a farm
hand might use if he wanted to scythe an entire field with one
swing. But he is hugely persistent. Watch what he does to the ball,
rather than the way he does it, and you appreciate that he is a rather
good player.

Froehling won two matches in straight sets. He beat Jan Leschly
in four, though he needed nine match points. That threw Froehling
in with his old sparring partner, Marty Riessen—who is almost as
tall and bony as he is, but better balanced, because there is a lot of
room between Riessen's knees. Neither sees too well in low cloud.
For a time these high, spare men looked as if they were flexing their
trigger fingers from opposite ends of a broad, dusty street in one of
those Western duels. We waited for the bang, the music, and the
credits. Froehling gunned his man down by 1–6, 2–6, 6–3, 6–4, 6–2.

Riessen romped through two sets without any fuss. Then he broke
a string on the first point of the third set, and went off the boil. The
pace of the match declined, its quality improved, and Froehling
played better and better, as if remembering how he used to do it in
the old days. 'I played so well that I thought I could do anything,'
said Riessen. 'I thought it was a game of talent instead of a game of
effort.'

Froehling beat Arthur Ashe 6–4, 4–6, 6–3, 3–6, 8–6, saving a
match point when Ashe was serving at 6–5 in a mighty fifth set.
This was a tense, tempestuous and—eventually—highly dramatic
match, briefly accompanied by the appropriate mood music of a
thunderstorm. Froehling then came to grief against the exuberant
virtuosity of Ilie Nastase, whose fast anticipation and reflexes
blunted many of the American's most cutting blows. But it was a
good match, all light and shade, with each in turn asserting a transient
authority. They were vividly contrasted players.

Come to think of it, most players contrast vividly with Froehling.

Bob Lutz, the Dustin Hoffman of WCT, had some good exercise. Twice he came back from two sets to one down. Ignoring the
fact that it was Gerald Battrick's birthday, he beat the Welshman

in the animated market place called court two. The efficiency of the lightweight's counter-punching was gradually eroded by the assault of a heavyweight who kept coming forward. The other man to lead Lutz and lose was that bouncing, crowd-pleasing extrovert, Jun Kuki. ('He's unbelievable,' said Kerry Harris. 'He's either belting hell out of the ball or putting it in the clouds.') The man who stopped Lutz was the dark and dreamy-looking Patrick Proisy, who is deliberate in all he does. Proisy knows what he wants from life—and from tennis. He has strong nerves, too. He would look the part as a fencer, and that is the way he plays tennis. But in the next round Kodes played it better.

A nice man called Bill Bowrey, who is not supposed to beat anybody in straight sets on clay, beat Ion Tiriac in straight sets. Bowrey said he volleyed and smashed well. Tom Gorman said he moved like a rabbit. Gorman is one of the men whose business affairs are handled by that tennis-playing lawyer, Donald Dell. Another is Charles Pasarell, who was beaten easily by Nicola Pietrangeli: thirty-seven years old and looking slightly the worse for a lifetime of Italian food. Cliff Richey called out to Dell: 'Hey, Donald! One of your boys is getting killed out there by an old gladiator.'

Richey was beaten by our old friend Istvan Gulyas. 'Richey is a bulldog,' observed a French spectator. 'But Gulyas is turning him into a lamb.'

Gulyas is a craftsman and a runner. He seems to have dominated Hungarian tennis since the game was invented. He has the tired eyes, the lined face, and the bulky calf muscles of a man who has spent his life running. He always has a look of quiet suffering, as if he has just cantered five miles and suspects he has five more to go. Which is often true. He lost to Zeljko Franulovic, who calls me 'Beny' because that is the shop where we buy our shirts in Rome. In the third set Gulyas broke to 5–4 with a net cord. Then an obviously wrong call left him poised on set point. So he deliberately served a huge double-fault.

It takes a special kind of man to do that. The crowd liked it. They liked it even more when Gulyas won the set anyway.

Franulovic had been two sets to one down against the well-muscled Pierre Barthes, who can roar through a match like a train unless his opponent tampers with the signals. Then Barthes goes off on a branch line. Jan Kodes had also been two sets to one down against a Frenchman, François Jauffret. But Kodes and Franulovic were now ready for a replay of the 1970 final. Kodes did not find it easy to re-establish his supremacy. They had a better match. But he effectively 'long-and-shorted' the Yugoslav.

Still waspishly persistent, Kodes beat Nastase 8–6, 6–2, 2–6, 7–5 in the final. Kodes never let his concentration slip. Unflinchingly single-minded, he tends to be more solid, less flashy than Nastase—a child of nature, athletic and gloriously gifted, but sometimes a prey to the mood of the moment. You might choose Nastase to play for your delight. But on clay, you might choose Kodes to play for your life. When they are on court together, tennis can look the loveliest of games.

The seedings said the women's final would be between Margaret Court and Virginia Wade. But Miss Wade had to retire (a damaged wrist, prematurely returned to combat duty) after playing one set with Linda Tuero. Miss Tuero wore glasses and looked like some inscrutable archaeologist, roaming the desert for riches and ready to keep on roaming until she finds them.

Mrs Court was beaten 6–3, 6–4 by the slim and fair Gail Chanfreau, who was born in Sydney, married a French Davis Cup player, and has represented both Australia and France in the Federation Cup competition. This was Mrs Court's first defeat in a major tournament since Wimbledon two years earlier. She said she had a cold and felt lousy. She did not move well, failed to strike a length, and therefore could not get to the net. Mrs Chanfreau's inelegant game is based on a heavily rolled, big-swinging forehand, a sliced backhand (sounder and more flexible than it used to be) and an enormous capacity for work. She is the kind who fight until they drop—and then jump up, throwing punches. That was the way it was now. She also played sensibly, and consistently well. 'I decided I had to concentrate on every point and give everything I'd got, even if I died in the second set. If I'd lost the second, I'd have been gone in the third.' This was a memorable triumph and the public were clinging to every available vantage point. They even turned the birds out of the trees.

All this left the doors to glory wide open. One of the players to step in was the winsome Helen Gourlay, a tough competitor with good credentials on clay. She had been winning hearts and matches for a few years but had never managed to break through to a big final. This time, in the early rounds, she went through all the fires of adversity, which can have a maturing effect on anyone strong enough to stand the heat. She came from behind to win thrilling matches with Christina Sandberg (who had done the same to her in 1970) and a jolly Japanese, Kazuko Sawamatsu, who had four match points at 5–2 in the third set. Then, again in three sets, she beat Mrs Chanfreau. Miss Gourlay had so much trouble with her service that she tried serving underhand. But Mrs Chanfreau, and anyone else alert to things that boom and flash in the sun, had good cause to respect her backhand drive and volley—and a forehand which Miss Gourlay often hit so hard that she seemed about to take off in pursuit of the ball.

Miss Gourlay was now playing as if all her Christmases had come at once. She played a dazzling match to beat Nancy Gunter, formerly Miss Richey, by the ringing margin of 6–2, 6–3 in a semi-final. There was some thrilling tennis, especially during the mounting drama of the last four games. Miss Gourlay ('I always take a while to get with it') lost eleven of the first thirteen points and served four double-faults in her first three service games. But she then won seven successive games, the last three of them to love. The match was becoming one-sided. Mrs Gunter was being made to look statuesque—her game disrupted by tennis that was cutely conceived, skilfully executed and illuminated by scorching winners. She was outmanoeuvred, foxed into hesitance, by a lovely demonstration of clay court tennis. Mrs Gunter fought back, but she did not last much longer. 'Maybe I'm growing up,' said Miss Gourlay. 'Nancy is so used to practising with Cliff that you can't outpace her. You've got to break her up. At the start of the second set I had a mental lapse. But I thought that if I lost the second, she would probably have time to work something out—talk to Cliff, and so on. This will be my first experience of a final of this sort. I'm looking forward to it.'

So were her two chums Winnie Shaw and Kerry Harris, who decided they might as well hang around a little longer to keep her game sharp and her nerves in tune. On the eve of the final, Miss Shaw and I had an early dinner with the Tasmanian—to make sure she did not go berserk with the chocolate sauce (if chocolate sauce is addictive, Miss Gourlay is in trouble).

By contrast, Evonne Goolagong was winning so smoothly and

easily that we hardly noticed she was winning at all. She played great tennis to beat Françoise Durr 6–3, 6–0. It was an astonishing result. The highly experienced 1967 champion knows the game inside out. She was still at her peak. She was in form. She was playing before her own people. And she was a difficult test for a youngster because of her heterodoxy—her capacity for doing all the right things the wrong way.

This was quite a challenge. Miss Goolagong's response was always admirable and eventually breathtaking. From 3–all in the first set she lost only twenty more points and had only one game point against her. Her brilliance was such that there were gasps of disbelief from the crowd. Miss Durr was cute and tough. She tried everything, but it was all useless. Every card she played was trumped. Miss Goolagong played an attacking game from the back of the court, swooping on the ball so swiftly and fluently that she had time to turn Miss Durr's keenest thrusts to her own advantage. She drew Miss Durr forward and bamboozled her with a sparkling variety of shots. She took Miss Durr's game apart with a facile assurance that made it seem all the experience was on Miss Goolagong's side of the net. It was a triumph of wits and concentration, as well as skill. Here was a contrast between two finely tuned tennis brains—Miss Durr's trained in the searching fires of experience, Miss Goolagong's instinctive.

'She's got something you can't teach anybody,' said her coach, Vic Edwards. 'You've either got it or you haven't.'

Two of the most delightful people in the game gave us a final full of beautifully designed and firmly contested tennis. Miss Gourlay played every bit as well as she had done against Mrs Gunter. She was brave and positive, went for her shots, and pushed in to the net whenever she could. She varied length and angle and pace, and kept Miss Goolagong on the move. But she was beaten 6–3, 7–5.

Sturdily athletic and unflappably serene, Miss Goolagong raced about at high speed, slid easily into her shots, and did it all so gracefully that she seldom seemed to be hurrying. 'She's the fastest mover I've played,' said Miss Gourlay. 'So many shots that would have been winners just came back.' Miss Goolagong's returns were shrewdly placed, many of them short and low so that Miss Gourlay's penchant for attack was inhibited. In the second set Miss Goolagong was 2–5 down but won five successive games—saving four set points on the way—to win the match. She began slow-balling, so that the ball came high to Miss Gourlay and had to be stroked rather than assaulted. Soon Miss Goolagong was playing flawlessly. 'I was determined not to play three sets, and I find that when I'm down I can bring out my best tennis. I think, well, here goes, I might as well try something.' This fine scrap had an appropriate finish, with the valiant Miss Gourlay in full stride as she cracked a forehand volley just too far across court. Nature designed this honey blonde for wine and candlelight and romantic music. But she had shown us the iron under the velvet.

Vic Edwards, a happy man jingling his francs in readiness, was waiting for Miss Goolagong ('I want a drink!') as she came bouncing and beaming down the dressing room steps. Miss Gourlay popped into the press room for a farewell beer with a couple of friends whose interest had exceeded its strictly professional requirements. The other was Mike Coward (Australian Associated Press).

It was a good year. We saw a lot of marvellous tennis, and some nice things happened to some nice people. Once again, first-time visitors from Britain were babbling with starry-eyed enthusiasm after their first sip of the wine that is tennis at Roland Garros.

'Why don't we see tennis like this at home?'

'Because we can't match these courts and this heat.'

And again we felt that in many ways the season's peak was behind us.

Those are the French championships. We have used Roland Garros for a rendezvous with the tennis set. We have gone into the heat and dust of battle and met the troops. We have assimilated the nature of the game, and of the men and women who play it—because these championships bring out all the flowers of character. We have enjoyed the inimitable splendour of a major tournament on clay courts. The game has no shop windows that are more alluring.

4

The Italian Championships

Rome is a city of narrow streets bulging with cars. Motorists blow their horns all the time, and regard pedestrians as targets. Waggish hawkers stand in traffic jams selling tortoises to the immobile mobile. Because Rome is hell with a sense of humour.

Rome is a dusty Triumph parked in the Via Flaminia, and the clip-clop of a *carrozza* outside St Peter's. Rome is a *pensione* in the Via del Babuino, and the shirts at Beny's. Rome is silence and the Forum, noise and *Da Meo Patacca* (and the patient Roger Taylor eventually suggesting, mildly, that the itinerant musicians blasting away beside him should 'go and play somewhere else'). Rome is an aching neck in the Sistine Chapel, and children playing round a pool in the Villa Borghese. Rome is talking through the night at a bar in the Via Sistina, and going to bed at dawn while the birds are singing. Rome is Bob Carmichael studying a neglected statue, re-cumbently stained and grimy, and observing: 'He looks as though he's had a warm beer.' Rome is Marcus Aurelius looking wise and Tony Roche looking rugged (and carrying five rackets). Rome is sunshine and music, Rosati's and Aurum. Rome is the Piazza Navona with the dancing waters and Mariapia with the dancing eyes. Rome is flowers and the Spanish Steps, love songs and the Piazza Margana—and Mary Ann Eisel drinking 'coke'. Rome is the Trastevere and the Piazza Santa Maria, candlelight and cats. Rome is Frascati and the laughter of friends. Rome is Bertie Bowron, beaming with *joie de vivre* as he exercises his linguistic versatility from the umpire's chair. Rome is all our yesterdays and, if we are lucky, some of our tomorrows. Rome is a nervous breakdown in Elysium, a city where the young of both sexes wear clothes so tight they almost wear them inside. Rome is perfect in its imperfections.

Rome is also the Piazzale Flaminio, a fruit stall, and a bus stop. At the other end of the ride is the Foro Italico, two vast, drowsy hollows that accommodate the Italian championships. Its horizons are alluring. Our eyes rise from the trim hedges between the courts to the tiers of pale marble—to massive statues, peripheral flags and umbrella pines, wooded hills rising from the Tiber, the golden madonna glistening on the skyline, and, finally, to a sky of flawless blue. The hub of the place—commanding a panoramic view of every court except the dazzling white *campo centrale*, where the run-back is so huge that the ball boys should have bicycles—is a restaurant fringed by the clustering mushroom growth of open-air tables and chairs, each little unit shaded by a bright parasol. In shirt sleeves and sun-glasses, spectators dream their way through smouldering afternoons, lulled by the soporific plop of ball on racket. They do not walk from court to court. They saunter.

This is an arena made for the gods—and should they run out of nectar, the ice cream is no mean substitute. The Foro Italico is a tennis paradise. By tradition, the game's leading players converge on it for their annual reunion at the beginning of the European season.

If tennis championships could be divided into sexes, the Italian tournament would be flamboyantly feminine. They look lovely. They have an irresistible charm. They are infuriating. There are times when the botchery is carried so far that it is almost an art form. The frustration of not knowing what is going to happen, or when, becomes too much. The contained anger threatens to erupt. But it gets swallowed again when Gianfranco Cameli (general secretary, an uncommonly nice man) flashes his prominent teeth. Or Sergio Baruti (a flexibly dreamy referee) shrugs his eyebrows as if to say 'Why get excited?' Or the chubby Luigi Orsini (president, all suave *bonhomie*) amiably spreads his hands and launches one of his inimitable assaults on the English language.

At such moments we remember that this is after all, Rome, where more important things have happened—and that there is nothing to be done about the Italians anyway. They are not efficiency experts.

But they have style, even when they try to cheat us. We can't help liking them, damn it.

When in Rome, live as the Romans do: digest your St Ambrose, and you will not go far wrong; even when trying to telephone a tennis report that is nudging the deadline. My first year at the Foro Italico, I had about five minutes in which to make contact with London. The situation teetered between the ticklish and the desperate. As is the English way, I put my case to the telephonist, observing with quiet courtesy that the call was rather urgent, and would she please do what she could to hurry it along? She did not get the message. But I did: different tactics were necessary. Afterwards, whenever a similar small crisis occurred, I put on a little act appropriate to the occasion—stamping, shouting, pacing up and down, and pounding the tables. And it worked.

Not that we have problems at the Foro Italico. The operators are firm friends and fast workers with plenty of initiative. When it comes to getting telephone calls, they stand at the top of the overseas ranking list.

In that press room we once discovered a stranger—to us, and to the game. We did not know his difficulties, and he was too humble to seek advice. The following day we came upon his story and such improvised solecisms as 'Nastase made some good shots from his back side'. So we took our new colleague gently by the hand, before he could further embarrass the profession and make a fool of himself by rewriting every cliché in the game's vocabulary.

The championships are played on slow clay, which is trying. But this is merely one of many darts that lodge in a player's soul and fester (especially if the player happens to be a hustling, excitable American who has not been to the Foro Italico before). The programming is often illogical, the line calls often bad, the ball boys often undisciplined (they play a private game, taking off their caps for use as butterfly nets, but catching balls instead). The foot-fault rule is disdained. Cameramen swarm about like gnats. The crowds are emotional, noisy, and blatantly partisan. If an Italian is on court, his fight is theirs. They do not just watch: they participate. They yell their man on, they call the lines, they intimidate the umpire, they take the match over: or at least they try. Umpires, line judges and ball boys smoke on duty. The umpires and line judges wear straw hats or sun caps. They can be sent packing if they are too much of a nuisance to the players (especially the Italian players). When a match finishes, the court is watered immediately—and some player next door, who may be tautly poised at match point, suddenly hears a splutter at his elbow and observes a spraying arc of water, wobbling about in his line of vision. To be drawn even slightly wide is to risk a cold shower.

Which reminds me that Graham Stilwell was once swinging into his service when he heard a clunking noise close behind him. He turned and perceived, two yards away, a groundsman wandering absent-mindedly across the court toting an enormous block of ice on his shoulders. 'I could have done with cooling off,' said Stilwell, 'but if he'd dropped that thing he could have broken a leg.'

That sort of thing happens all the time. It often happens on court three, which is dominated by shadowing trees and is sometimes called 'the circus court' because the things that go on there have to be seen not to be believed. That court was once invaded by a crowd of spectators and journalists who gathered round a befuddled umpire to help him sort out what was afoot. That was the court where Frank Froehling, a new boy with his mind and his sun hat askew, sprawled on a line judge's chair (he sprawls memorably) and mused: 'These guys are trying to con me out of it. . . .' He was bewildered and incredulous: because, as I said, he was a new boy. That was the court where one day—no matter what time it was, no matter whether we were savouring morning coffee, lunch, or tea—Jiri Javorsky was always playing Thomaz Koch.

That was also the court where Roger Taylor and his friend Lew Gerrard had a sharp exchange of one-liners.

Gerrard was going through one of those spells when a player feels as though his wife has left him, the house has been burgled, and the bank has turned nasty. Nothing was going right—and the nagging irritants of the Foro Italico were no comfort. Throughout the match he was muttering angrily, to himself and anyone else who would listen. This irascible chatter finally provoked a sympathetic yet terse comment from Taylor, standing with hands on hips at the other end of the court:

'Lew. Stop moaning.'

Gerrard glared.

'Roger. Get stuffed.'

A good place for newsmen, court three.

John Oakley tells a good story of the 1963 championships, in which Ian Crookenden and Tony Pickard sweated and strained through five sets. Came the crisis—and Crookenden hit a forehand well over the baseline. But there was no call. Pickard had already suffered from plenty of bad decisions and he turned irritably on the young line judge:

'What about that, stupid, what about that?'

Back came a torrent of Italian from the line judge, who had spent most of the match dozing but was now alert.

'What did he say?' asked Pickard, baffled.

A spectator translated:

'He said he couldn't give a decision on that rally, because he was leaning over the fence buying an ice cream.'

John Oakley was himself an actor in a 1964 comedy. He was up in the restaurant, contemplating with disappointment (as a British journalist) the prospect of Mike Sangster's defeat in the first round. Sangster was two sets to one down against Ray Senkowski and they were taking a break. John had never heard of Senkowski (outside Michigan, not many people had). Who should appear at his shoulder but Senkowski himself, drawling to an uncomprehending waiter: 'Tea with lemon, and make it snappy.'

John made the mistake of offering his services as interpreter.

'Great,' said Senkowski. 'I'm beating this guy Sangster and I've got to get back to the centre court in a hurry. Bring the tea down.'

There was no time for the reporter to point out that he was not a travelling caterer. Senkowski had gone—downstairs and into the long tunnel that leads to the *campo centrale*. John was left to pay the bill and carry the can: specifically, the tray. He set off on his errand of mercy, treading carefully so that he would not spill his cargo. Gunga Din would have been proud of him. At the end of the tunnel he came upon an official who seemed a likely candidate for the role of anchor man in a relay.

'Tea for Senkowski. You take it in.'

But the Italian was a solid trade unionist.

'Not my job.'

So that day a reporter reluctantly emerged into the sunny splendour of the centre court, where the match had already resumed. Could he, perhaps, nip out, slap the tea down on the drinks stand, and beat a hasty retreat before being spotted?

No chance. He advanced, unloaded his freight, and was making a smart about-turn when Senkowski hit a winning volley and yelled:

'Pour one out. Two lumps.'

Up in the stands the late George Worthington, who was then Britain's national coach, spied Fleet Street bringing succour to the enemy. He shouted cheerfully:

'Bloody patriot!'

Sangster looked puzzled. John went red. But he poured out the tea, submerged two lumps, and made a fast exit. As far as Rome was concerned, the story ended there. But it had a sequel at the French championships a fortnight later. Senkowski, losing to some South American, suddenly saw John Oakley walking past the court. He promptly waved and called: 'Two cokes!'

But John had learned his lesson. He made an appropriate gesture, and left.

In 1959, at the age of eighteen, Christine Truman (now Mrs Janes) had her finest season: she won the Italian, Swiss and French championships and was runner-up to Maria Bueno in the United States. Ann Jones, in her book *A Game to Love*, observed of Miss Truman during those precocious peak years: 'Unlike some judges, I thought she was even more formidable on clay than grass.' Certainly the 1959 Italian final was one of Miss Truman's most astounding performances. She beat Sandra Reynolds 6–0, 6–0 in twenty-eight minutes, losing only nineteen points.

'I wondered at the time how it happened,' says Mrs Janes, 'and I remember thinking: if only I could play all my matches this afternoon.'

Mrs Jones, housewife, wit and raconteuse, was the 1966 champion—and like Miss Truman before her she beat a South African in the final. This time the player was Annette van Zyl, the score 8–6, 6–1. 'I've never seen her play with such command on a hard court against a player of the class of Miss van Zyl, whose style is both unusual and original,' said Dan Maskell, the British team manager.

For a decade Mrs Jones impressed us with her capacity to push her talent to, and apparently beyond, its logical limit. We admired her concentration and courage, her physical and mental stamina, her will of iron. She was so shrewd that she seldom missed a trick,

especially on the big points. She assessed the strengths and weaknesses of everyone's game, including her own. She worked hard in
preparing for her matches, and in playing them. She was never an
enchanting player (that is a gift of Nature). But she was a great
competitor.

After discussing that final, I rounded off the day's report with a
note about the organization: 'It takes an unusual degree of bungling
to make a tournament overrun after a week of glorious weather in
which one event (the mixed doubles) was cut out of the championships altogether. But this is Rome: with centuries of history around
us, what difference does a day make?'

The tennis at the Foro Italico is inimitable. It is served hot, and
spiced by exotic flavours. Let us assemble a few fragments that may
show us the shape and substance of the whole.

The eyes and ears of the mind retain a moving picture, complete
with sound track, of a match played on 10 May in that year of 1966.
Laughter and tears, passion and fury, storm and silence—all this and
more ebbed and flowed around us in the echoing Roman circus of
the *campo centrale* as Nicola Pietrangeli beat Roy Emerson 3–6, 6–1,
3–6, 8–6, 6–1 in a semi-final. Pietrangeli—twice champion of Italy,
twice champion of France, once champion of Germany—was
thirty-two years old and had not won a major title for five years.
Emerson, reigning champion of Wimbledon and Australia, was
twenty-nine. They entertained us for almost two hours and a half:
an hour and three-quarters of tennis succeeded by forty-five minutes
of melodrama in which the crowd did not so much watch the match
as conduct it.

To write of statistics amid such a surfeit of drama is to eat bread
and water at a banquet. But a taste may do us no harm. The first
three sets spun away quickly and, on the whole, uneventfully. In the
fourth Emerson reached 5–3 and came within two points of the
match at 15–30 on Pietrangeli's service. At 5–4 Emerson served for
the match and got to 30–15. Then he was beaten in turn by a cross-
court forehand and a forehand passing shot that clipped the net
cord on its way down the line. Finally he was forced to volley too
deep. . . . Pietrangeli was level, and it seemed that the noise within
it would burst the arena asunder.

From that moment, the rot set in for Emerson. Pietrangeli broke
through for the set in the fourteenth game and romped through the

fifth set, the shortest of the match, in twenty-three minutes. A lob and a drop, successive shots, took Pietrangeli to match point. A forehand down the line finished the job.

The court was slower than usual after rain, and Emerson took some time to adjust his game to it. He accepted the obvious challenge by getting to Pietrangeli's drop shots and playing plenty himself (two in one rally). For the rest he played the game that had served him so well for so long—hard hitting to make the openings and acutely angled volleys, like the lashes of a whip, to take them. To all this he added his superb athleticism and speed of reflex, playing some wonderful stop volleys as Pietrangeli tried to pass him.

This was the Emerson we knew, a swordsman with a wrist of steel. Though sick at heart, the crowd amply acknowledged the sudden splendour of his winners. And as thousands of pairs of hands moved in applause, the whole stadium seemed to heave like an ant-hill. When Pietrangeli made a counter-thrust, it was as though someone had opened a door on Bedlam.

So it went on, with brief breaks in the pattern, until Emerson, twice, was just two points from what seemed an inevitable victory. Then came that sadly grand finale, with Emerson stepping from the sunshine to the shadows, Pietrangeli spreading his wings with passing shots and drops, and the soaring concourse taking the match in their keeping and shaping it as they pleased.

It would be appropriate, but untrue, to say that the genius Pietrangeli once commanded burst into flower again amid the hothouse of the *campo centrale*. True, the surging waves of sound that crashed and boomed round the packed arena stiffened his spirit in the succeeding crises of the fourth set, when logic insisted that he was beaten. True, the shrieked appeals to 'Nicola!', the roars of 'Bravo!', the continual hubbub, inspired him to hold his form, regain his confidence, and flaunt some of the golden colours of his game in the shadows and the sunlight.

Yet all this might have been so much chaff swept away on the cooling breeze but for the pathetic and bathetic decline of Emerson ('I just threw it away'). In the fifth set this fine athlete looked at the end of his physical resources. Mistakes flooded into a game that had become strangely naïve and tentative. A great weariness seeped into the man. No one, not even Emerson, could be sure whether it came from the mind, the heart, the body, or the din around him. But for

Emerson to let a man off the hook was like Olivier forgetting his lines.

Few knew or cared what was happening on court four. The tough and vastly improved Tony Roche, beaten by Martin Mulligan at Wimbledon, was taking his revenge in the cruellest way—on the Roman courts that little Mulligan, the defending champion, had made his own. But a mere tennis match, good though it was, could not compete with the opera on the *campo centrale*.

Still a few days short of his twenty-first birthday, Roche beat Pietrangeli to gain his first major title. The butcher's boy from Tarcutta was a popular new champion. He is a good man, and thoroughly Australian. He also has an interesting face. Under the stress of playing tennis, it seems to fold, dip and heave, like a handsome crag subject to violent mutations because of disturbances somewhere beneath the earth's crust. The lines on that rubbery and mobile face have deepened since then. Roche moved on to Paris and won the French championship as well. There is a theory that any man who wins these two clay court titles in quick succession will never be the same again: that in terms of physical cost, the accounts can never be settled. Roche won both. So did Rod Laver. But they had to keep on paying for it—in the currency of pain.

In 1967 tennis and breakfast were served simultaneously, in such scorching heat that cool characters from northern Europe lurked in shadows or sheltered under ridiculous hats. Roger Taylor was disguised behind a drooping black moustache and Mark Cox sported a rather dashing beard which chicken pox had imposed on him. They looked like a scratch doubles pair from South America and Scandinavia, and must have shattered many preconceptions about the British. Cox was touring the world, learning about life, after graduating from Cambridge. He was given a teasing tutorial by the neatly diminutive Beppe Merlo, who was still ranked fourth in Italy at the age of thirty-nine.

We called Merlo 'The Little Bird' or, more obviously, 'Merlo the Magician'. He was an original, a delightful eccentric in an age of uniformity. His racket was loosely strung, as if the manufacturers had used spaghetti instead of gut. The ball rebounded with an apologetic plunk. His service was no more than a means of getting the ball into play. He used a short, two-handed grip with no discernible backswing, but he was a master of chips and slices, spin

and subtlety. He did not hit the ball. He nudged it. He had a fondness for such strange flora as drop-shot service returns.

Amid the blazing heat of a golden Roman day, Cox was thus
plunged into action with a man who made nonsense of every text
book ever written about the game. Cox was forthright and tena-
cious. He ran and sweated and swatted until the strength drained
out of him. All his conventional notions about tennis came tumbling
around his ears. (Merlo almost took a tumble, too: chasing a wide
backhand, he suddenly came face to face with an equally startled
line-sweeper.) Two years later Merlo was still good enough to
induce Gerald Battrick to break a racket in two by treading on it,
in full flight. But by that time Merlo's legs had gone and his ball
control was fast going with them. Which is why I write of him in
the past tense.

While Cox was suffering, so was Bobby Wilson. He never had
much liking for the treadmills of Rome and Paris. He lasted only
eighty minutes against the bandy-legged Francisco Guzman, who
serves like a clockwork toy. Vlasta Vopickova, sister of Jan Kodes,
beat Winnie Shaw in a match remarkable for the fact that a line
judge was reading a letter when he should have been making a call.
That was the year, too, when for twenty minutes a long-limbed
Californian called Kathy Harter startled herself, Jan O'Neill, and
everyone else by playing like Ricardo Gonzales. A touch of the sun,
perhaps.

During a weekend of swarming crowds and remorselessly grilling
heat, the price of a 'coke' went up from 120 to 150 lire.

'Why?' asked Barry Newcombe sternly.

'Because they ees so many people,' said the itinerant salesman,
grinning shamelessly. 'I make lotta money.'

'You're a liar, a cheat, a thief and a crook.'

A big beam, an expansive sweep of the arms.

'That's ri'. . . . You wanna coke?'

Even when it did rain, the *gelati* merchants swiftly switched to a
new line—plastic rain hats. We had to admire their resilience.

But again, the organization of the championships was not the
kind that makes efficiency experts redundant. After seven days of
unremitting sunshine and the fortuitous additional aid of twenty-
seven walk-overs and four retirements, the referee still had sixteen
matches to get through in two days. In its own way, that indicated

a kind of genius. So did a stroke Martin Mulligan played against Ion Tiriac. Mulligan has a fine and faithful forehand, and during a long rally, with the crowd eagerly urging him on, he repeatedly aimed at a loose ball resting between Tiriac's service line and baseline. When Mulligan hit the bull's eye (the ball shot off at right angles to earn him the point) the public gave a rapturous roar and Tiriac glowered with a huge and menacing rage. Thus did Jack taunt the giant before clobbering him.

The brawny Roche, with his crunching backhand volley, thundered through the draw like a one-steer stampede. He did not lose a set until he played the final, on his birthday. Then he was beaten by Mulligan, the man he had tossed out of the tournament a round and a year earlier. Posterity will remember Mulligan because he was Italian champion three times and married a girl born in Vatican City—which is an uncommon record of achievement for a man from Marrickville, New South Wales. Come to think of it, posterity would remember Mulligan anyway.

Courts five and six at the Foro Italico are as far as you can get from the *campo centrale* without climbing over a hedge and leaving the premises. On the other side of the hedge, buffeting your eardrums, there are usually hordes of schoolchildren whose day seems to be divided between playtime and band practice. Let us say that if a player has to select a suitable environment for concentration on great deeds, neither of those courts would start favourite.

But it was to court six, on a grey afternoon, that Lesley Turner and Maria Bueno were banished for the women's final.

Miss Turner, 5 ft 4 in. tall and pretty with it, won 6–3, 6–3. She had been runner-up three times, which was too often. She was a bonny baseliner with twinkling feet, exemplary ball control, a sound tactical sense (in her variation of length and pace and her use of the long and short angles), and a competent forecourt game. She had an inexhaustible reservoir of 'G and D' and she reminded us of the prime importance of footwork. A decent stroke demands a decent set-up, a decent set-up demands decent footwork, and decent footwork demands a Lesley Turner. Hers was the basic grammar of the game. And if I write of her in the past tense, it is only because she is now concentrating on Bill and the baby, rather than tennis. Anyway, her bouncing virtues were too much for Miss Bueno.

In 1968 Miss Turner married Bill Bowrey and they set off on a honeymoon tour. In Rome she was refused admittance to church because they said her dress was too short—and it was so decorous as to be almost staid. It made the 'mini' look like a scarf. But she did manage to get into the *campo centrale*, which is no mean distinction for women at the Foro Italico. Moreover, she retained her title by beating Margaret Court in an arduous and absorbing final played in a crowded arena, with the flags fluttering in a benign breeze, the scorching sunshine relentless, and the sky a cloudless, burnished blue.

Mrs Bowrey had a point to make. She was ranked second in Australia but had been omitted from their team for the Federation Cup competition. She found this 'a bit hard to take'. So she was restlessly resolute and made cruel demands on her trim little physique. The punch and precision of her passing shots eventually made Mrs Court indecisive about leaving the baseline: and from the moment she was induced to play Mrs Bowrey's game instead of her own, Mrs Court was on the hook.

In successive matches the burly Bob Hewitt beat Allen Fox, Manuel Orantes, Jan Kodes, Nicola Pietrangeli and Alex Metreveli. In heat fit to toast a bun, he then took Tom Okker to five sets in a final that lasted more than three hours. Both showed a facile flair for the splendours of the clay court game. The *campo centrale* glittered with sharp yet silken stroke play. Okker's astonishing speed enabled him to ride some of Hewitt's heaviest blows and rebound from defence with resilient winners. He was quick at the net, too. While Okker was whizzing about the court like a firecracker, Hewitt was making the ball do much of his work for him. There were times when Hewitt almost made the ball talk. He masked his variety of forehand strokes with baffling legerdemain. But he was the heavier and older man. In the fifth set he reached and passed the limit of his resources and was reduced to leaden-footed helplessness.

We should remember the irascibly brilliant Hewitt for matches like this: not for the inexcusably petulant court manners that have often caused embarrassment. He can play lovely tennis when he is not languishing in a private torment of peripheral grievances. In an angry match during the 1970 French championships he beat David Lloyd, who is never at a loss for a few hundred words (using friends in the crowd as a verbal practice wall, he gets through more words per set than any other player). Lloyd later made a shrewd comment about Hewitt: 'He's such a perfectionist that if he doesn't hit the ball on the lines he gets upset.'

Few tennis players believe their luck, unless it is good: Hewitt tends to have more difficulty than most in living with the other kind.

The 1969 championships began in dreary weather, like a radiant beauty with a briefly grey-faced hangover. There were other departures from the norm: this was now an open tournament; and programmes were available from the start and contained the mischievous innovation of betting odds on the day's matches.

But the championships were instantly recognizable. Virginia Wade beat that bouncing bundle of fun Alena Palmeova, who lives by the principle that if she keeps smiling, everyone will wonder what she has been up to. Miss Wade chased a drive deep to her backhand—and almost hurtled into a clinch with a diligently indiscreet ball boy from the next court. In the next round, Miss Wade was more relevantly confronted by the straight and severe Peaches Bartkowicz, who has a look of haughty disdain but is really rather fun. Miss Bartkowicz is so attached to the baseline that, by her own admission, she goes to the net only to measure it or to shake hands. Miss Wade was apprehensive and tetchy. She swore. She screeched at a ball boy. She lost. She has taken some terrible emotional punishment at the Foro Italico. But she keeps going back for more.

By contrast, Christina Sandberg is an erect and equable Swede with a serenity from which every kind of adversity rebounds like a ping-pong ball from a table. But she was beaten by Christine Janes—who deserved some compensation for a trying morning in which she was squeezed between the closing double doors of a bus, banged her head on an iron rail, knocked over a flower pot, and mislaid her handbag. Sometimes, life is like that.

We enjoyed a taste of prime and pure Lea Pericoli, whose recherché doubles partnership with Silvana Lazzarino has done for the lob what Heinz did for beans. Miss Pericoli was beaten 6–1, 6–2 by Ann Jones. But it took ninety-five minutes. The stroke count during individual rallies often went into three figures. One game lasted fourteen minutes. Miss Pericoli is one of the few players inclined to follow up a deep first service with a lob. She likes to rest and prink and preen between strokes—strokes, not rallies. Having launched the ball on a steeply parabolic path, she flutters her eyelashes, tidies her hair, and chats with friends and dogs (poodles, of course) by the court. She always has friends and dogs by the court. Miss Pericoli is maddeningly charming. In terms of age, she and Beppe Merlo should have stayed as they were about the time Ian Smith took over Rhodesia, so that they might delight us for all time.

Julie Heldman is almost as patient as Miss Pericoli, and more resourceful in her cunning. She came from behind to beat Lesley Bowrey and Mrs Jones (still in a post-Pericoli coma?). Then she baffled Kerry Melville and became the first American champion since Althea Gibson in 1956. Miss Melville could not win from the back of the court, and could not go to the forecourt without paying for a reminder of the difference between the bold and the reckless. She was boxed in a tactical quandary from which there was no escape. But she blinked beautifully.

That was the year the stocky and stoic Graham Stilwell emerged from anonymity. News from the place they keep having to rebuild, Catania (you turn left at Etna), had warned us he was up to something. Because in successive rounds he had beaten three slow-court specialists, Wieslaw Gasiorek, Ion Tiriac and Istvan Gulyas. In Rome, he played with a purring smoothness to beat Manuel Santana and Fred Stolle in the span of twenty-six hours.

Stilwell's aptitude for the game came to full flower against Santana on the sweltering *campo centrale*. The disbelieving crowd came to hail Caesar and stayed to bury him. With Santana serving at the edgy crisis of two sets and 3–5 down, a baby cried: which in the immense silence of its context sounded like a burst of the Hallelujah Chorus. As Stilwell served for the match and reached 30–all, a salesman dropped his clattering cargo of soft drinks down the marble steps. There was juice and noise all over the place. The echoes must have reached the Piazza del Popolo. Santana promptly won two fine rallies to break service, and his game surged with renewed hope. But Stilwell swiftly snuffed the sudden flame. Against Stolle, he had to come from behind on a pine-shadowed court. But Stolle could not put his volleys away and was submerged in a flashing stream of passing shots. The party was fun while it lasted. But Tom Okker showed Stilwell the door.

The mighty grandeur of the centre court throbbed with a passionate response to a superb semi-final between Okker and Tony Roche. Their sparkling stroke play carved luminous patterns across the arena. Okker is slim and supple. His fluent facility almost pulled him through in straight sets, but at a high cost in energy. Roche resisted with all his strength and lion-hearted courage, his face creasing with effort. And the big guy finally got to the little guy.

It was a similar story over on court four, where another whippy welterweight, Jan Kodes, was ground into weary submission by the unyielding proficiency of a robust Australian: John Newcombe. Baring his teeth and stretching his pectoral muscles, Newcombe looked fierce enough to lick any man alive, and eat his meat raw. Time and again he had Kodes on the ropes. Time and again the elusive Kodes slipped away and counter-punched with a tattoo of passing shots. But Newcombe finally nailed him. In the final New-combe stuck closer to his best form than Roche did, and played the big points better. That meant he was champion of the German and Italian clay courts. A monarch of the serve-and-volley game was extending his empire.

Newcombe's natural gifts are for the heavy stuff: the rapid-fire rallies of fast surfaces. But he is a good professional with a proper pride, a determined man reluctant to admit that anything is beyond him. Over the years he mentally disciplined and trained himself to master the technique and tactics slow clay demands—to familiarize himself with the delicately fine balance between jockeying for an opening and, at the right moment, making a burst for the net. He is, in short, a self-made clay court player ('It takes ten years to learn how to play on this stuff').

The hero of 1970 was Lew Hoad, taking time off from his tennis ranch in Spain. He turned up by chance and was drafted into the draw at the last minute. He had not played at the Foro Italico since he was champion in 1956, the year he won everything until Ken Rosewall stopped him at Forest Hills.

Hoad has the presence of a champion. He looks the part. A hand-some chap with piercing eyes and striking golden colouring, he could have served as a model hero for ancient Greece or the upper sixth. With his casual, easy-going nature, he is the epitome of the strong, silent man. Hoad is the Robert Mitchum of tennis, the kind of man's man women adore. On court, he has an air of almost arrogant authority. But he is always human, never mechanical.

Margaret Court—'Serve and charge!' (*Tennis World*)

Rod Laver *(World Tennis)*

A row of Richeys—Nancy (now Mrs Gunter), George and Cliff
(Ed Fernberger)

Lesley and Bill Bowrey at San Juan on their honeymoon tour (*Ed Fernberger*)

Donald Dell and a few clients in the Champs-Élysées—left to right, Tom Gorman, Dell, Charles Pasarell, Stan Smith, Arthur Ashe, Bob Lutz (*Richard Evans*)

Roger Taylor with his wife Frances (*Ed Fernberger*)

Pierre and Carolyn Barthes (*Ed Fernberger*)

Kerry Melville—blinks
beautifully *(Tennis World)*

Lea Pericoli, who did for the lob what Heinz did for beans *(Ed Fernberger)*

Helen Gourlay—fond of
chocolate sauce and chutney
(Tennis World)

Pat Pretorius—gift for verbal
shorthand *(Tennis World)*

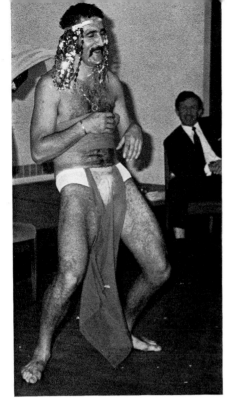

Ion Tiriac performing the Dance of the Seven Veils for charity, at Torquay (*Tennis World*)

Betty Stove and Françoise Durr (*Ed Fernberger*)

Ken Rosewall, Jack Kramer and Tom Okker (*Ed Fernberger*)

Mike Davies, executive
director of World
Championship Tennis
(*Richard Evans*)

Teddy Tinling, couturier, on court at Philadelphia (*Ed Fernberger*)

Angie and John Newcombe (*Ed Fernberger*)

Ilie Nastase and Evonne Goolagong, two of the most exciting personalities in the tennis set *(Tennis World)*

Virginia Wade, who won the first and last open tournaments—in April 1968 and January 1972 (*Tennis World*)

Ann Jones (*Ed Fernberger*)

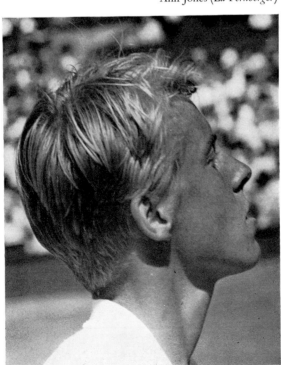

Bud Collins, companion in the writing game (*Ed Fernberger*)

Sherlock Holmes and a beauty queen (John Barrett and Lew Hoad) at a players' cabaret (*World Tennis*)

The Emersons (*Russ Adams*)

Winnie Shaw relaxes at San Juan (*Ed Fernberger*)

Tony Roche, who is always carrying rackets and looking rugged (*Ed Fernberger*)

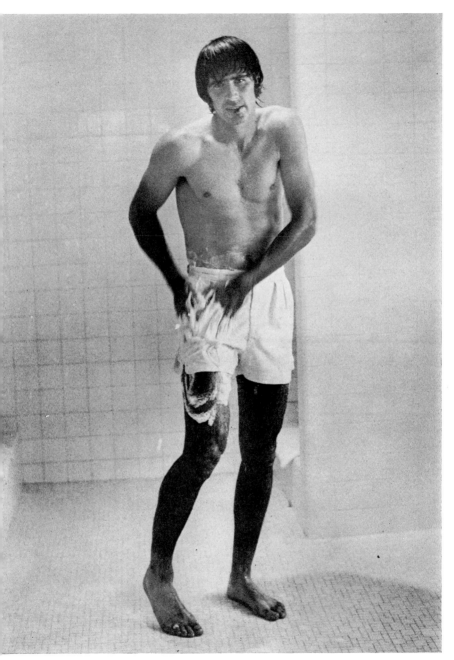

Marty Riessen washing his shorts the easy way (*Richard Evans*)

Chris Evert keeps her eyes on the ball (*Ed Fernberger*)

He made a creaking start but came back from two sets down to beat a Roman called Massimo Di Domenico. The match began on a sunny afternoon, straddled a series of vacillating crises, and ended in the shadows of evening—with one of the greatest of players giving us a thrilling reminder of the majesty he once so casually commanded. Then the same thing happened again: Hoad came back from two sets down against Manuel Orantes. At two sets all, the match was interrupted by the dramatic gloom of nightfall on the *campo centrale*. That evening Hoad revived all our memories, all our favourite sporting dreams, by playing some breathtaking tennis. The crowd gave him a lingering ovation for a dynamic display in which yesterday met today for the nostalgic pleasure of the gods. The middle-aged felt younger. The young regretted all the splendour they had missed, and were grateful for the little that was left. Because Hoad finally played as if mind and muscles alike had recaptured all the glory of the past. As the electric scoreboard flickered its statistical messages through the twilight, he forgot he was a thirty-five-year-old part-timer. Suddenly he was back in the past—a champion in a champion's environment. He rose to the *campo centrale*. He rose to his own legend.

When Hoad served an ace to reach 5–all in the fourth set, the umpire announced that only two more games would be possible. Hoad broke service with a leaping, flashing forehand volley. Then he held his service for the set with two backhand passing shots, an explosive smash from behind the baseline, and a forehand passing shot—played on the run when he was under pressure. It chilled the blood to watch the years fall away from the man so marvellously.

Next morning Hoad spent forty minutes warming up with Owen Davidson, and then won the fifth set easily. Later he was beaten by Alex Metreveli before a swarming, sweating, volubly pro-Hoad crowd who knew they were in the company of genuine class (there was not much of it about, that year). For much of the day Hoad moved well and played beautifully. For a set and a half Metreveli was overawed and overwhelmed, perhaps conscious that Hoad was Wimbledon champion before a Russian had competed there. But the longer the match lasted, the better Metreveli played. He needed to. Hoad reached out for the old glory and grasped it—but lacked the youth and fitness to hold on to it. The spring went out of his game as he tired. So he showered and changed, lowered his aching muscles into a wicker chair, and wrapped his fist round a beer.

'How do you feel now, Lew?'

'Buggered.'

Jan Kodes survived a hot streak by Mark Cox, whose composure and concentration were eventually shattered. Cox had to use five rackets, one of them borrowed from Françoise Durr. His wife Alison, praising the Lord and passing the ammunition, dashed to and from the professional's shop to hasten the supply of restrings. Whenever Cox changed ends, he examined the stock with desperate speculation, like an anxious shopper turning up late for the sales and wondering what was left. No man playing Kodes can afford to worry about anything except Kodes.

If Sir Henry Irving ever watches tennis from Up There, he watches Ion Tiriac and Nikola Pilic, actors both. Pilic, indeed, is often in touch with Sir Henry's Manager: he sometimes prays on court, standing up or even kneeling down.

Pilic is tall and temperamental, lean and lissome. He brings to his matches a gloomy, melodramatic panache. If his play displeases him, he will at least make the plot theatrical. He says he has to express himself somehow. Pilic expressed himself clearly enough in Rome. He came back from two sets down to beat Phillip Dent. He also beat Zeljko Franulovic. The news of this unusually private match must have echoed round the Dinaric Alps, causing an excited buzz in such settlements as Klis, Sinj, Omis and Solin. Because Pilic and Franulovic—and, of course, a lot of other ics—both hail from the Dalmatian resort of Split (which grew out of Diocletian's palace and boasts a statue of one Gregory of Nin).

Pilic also came within two points of beating the eventual champion, Ilie Nastase. Remarkably, the last four men were all from the mysterious cloak-and-dagger area between the Caspian, the Adriatic, and the confluence of the Eger and Elbe. Kodes had no bother with Metreveli. In the final, Nastase had a little to spare against Kodes.

This was Nastase's first major championship. He beat Georges Goven, Graham Stilwell, Istvan Gulyas, Nikola Pilic and Jan Kodes: a list which suggests that the title itself had more distinction than the resistance he overcame in winning it. But Nastase was still on the way up, and indicated that already the comedian was capable of playing Hamlet. He has since become the most exciting player in

the game. Late in 1971 he took a long stride forward by beating
Rod Laver and Stan Smith in the decisive matches of the Embassy
championship at Wembley and the Pepsi masters' tournament in
Paris.

Nastase's shots are relatively lightweight. His first volley and
second service tend to be only moderately punishing. When he can
afford to, he often plays from the heart rather than the head. But he
drives with top spin, and has the capacity to long-and-short his
opponents. His touch, his command of spin, and above all the speed
of his reflexes and footwork, make him an uncommonly gifted
player, with a flexible repertoire and a talent for instinctive improvisation. This superb athlete with the rubbery build is sometimes
embarrassed by his abundance of ability. Given a situation in which
many men would have only one shot to play, he may have two or
three—and miss his chance by choosing the wrong one, or not
making up his mind in time.

Nastase also has some of Cassius Clay's consciously conceited
showmanship. After beating John Newcombe at Wembley in 1971,
he observed: 'I am too good for these guys. Too much talent.' At
times he dances up to the net on a half-pace, three-quarter length
approach shot, as if defying his adversary to hit the obvious passing
shot—just as Clay, when feeling mischievous, drops his arms and
leaves the target wide open. For Nastase, life is an adventure or it
is nothing.

For years this flamboyant character has been inseparable from
his older compatriot, Ion Tiriac. Always the dominant personality,
Tiriac has been friend, mentor, rival, father figure and interpreter.
For a long time he was also the better player. And when Nastase
caught and passed him, Tiriac seemed somehow rejuvenated—as if
feeding on Nastase's growing skill and rumbustious zest for
tennis and for life. They are a team, as essential to each other as
Rowan and Martin. When Nastase is playing a big match, his
Svengali is usually a still and brooding figure lurking quietly in the
crowd. Their eyes often meet: there is a transfer of will.

Tiriac has provided the emotional and tactical cement in the
partnership, though he shares Nastase's liking for histrionics. They
slouch about, with much expressive 'arm talk'. They discuss every
controversial detail like two merchants haggling in a Balkan
bazaar. In the tradition of the great clowns, they slip swiftly from

joy to sorrow and back again. Off court, they never arrive anywhere quietly, be it airport, hotel or clubhouse. There is always
some funny business, some *badinage*. They have never learnt how
to be dull.

Tiriac's behaviour is the more calculated, Nastase's the more
spontaneous. Nastase is a man of moods, most of them playful.
('He's got a funny approach to the game,' said Ken Rosewall once.
'He jokes around a lot.') The ebullient Nastase is usually inoffen-
sively naughty, engagingly cheeky. He is the life and soul of any
party, though he has his moments of silent, isolated introspection.
On court, his conduct often transgresses the Anglo-Saxon code that
has come to be regarded as the conventional norm in tennis. It remains to be seen whether he will ever completely conquer the
enemy within. He is still digesting the lesson that talent is not
enough: that a consistently disciplined effort of will is necessary if
he is to play his best tennis and command both himself and a
match.

At Torquay in 1970 he caused a fuss by banging a loose ball into
the crowd and hitting a spectator. He can make mountains of
drama out of molehills of dissent. He can simmer fretfully about
adverse decisions which he believes to be wrong: and without being
malicious about it he can taunt the line judge who makes them. He
probably thinks a stiff upper lip is a reinforced balcony. He has
sometimes teased and taunted his opponents, too. Cliff Richey
showed astonishing forbearance during the 1971 Pepsi masters'
tournament. Clark Graebner saw that match—and remembered it
when he played Nastase during the Rothmans tournament at the
Albert Hall, London, a month later. After five games Graebner
stepped over the net, walked up to Nastase, and gave him a menacing, finger-wagging warning. Nastase did not win another game,
and after the first set he walked off court. He was scared, he said,
and could not play because his hand was shaking. At the time,
Graebner's intimidating action was hardly justified. But perhaps
Nastase had it coming to him.

Back to Rome in 1970 and to the women, in all their rich variety.
To Maria Nasuelli, whose dress could not have been shorter without
being a blouse (on and off court, her clothes do not so much disguise
her figure as exaggerate its lack of anything even remotely angular).
To that exploding box of fireworks, the tiny Monica Giorgi,

scurrying about the run-back and carving a network of skid marks in the clay. To the comprehensively estimable Pat Walkden, who came from behind to beat Kerry Melville and Rosemary Casals and, in a semi-final, advanced within two points of giving Julie Heldman the same treatment.

Billie Jean King also beat two fine players after conceding them a set start: first Helga Niessen, then Virginia Wade. Mrs King survived two match points before beating Miss Wade 3–6, 7–5, 6–3. Responding to the inspiration of the centre court, they enthralled the Romans for 2 hours and 10 minutes. Much of the match was played in a gusty wind that encouraged errors—and for almost two sets Mrs King made most of them. But in the crisis this great competitor attacked with desperate courage. She won the crucial second set in an extraordinary game which lasted twenty-two minutes and contained twenty-one deuces, sixteen game points to Miss Wade, and seven set points to Mrs King (who won the last of them with a top-spin lob). After that, Miss Wade went off the boil. Even the players on the terraces felt exhausted.

A day later Mrs King tossed her racket high in the air and jumped joyously in pursuit of it after beating Miss Heldman 6–1, 6–3 in the final. Mrs King had good cause for delight. She had won all the major grass court championships: Wimbledon three times. Now she proved what she had long wanted to prove—that she could also 'win big' on clay.

Buffeting breezes again played tricks with the ball. Mrs King is a good player in a wind because she can hit through it. She also played lobs and drops as if Californians were weaned on them. The crafty Miss Heldman plays tennis as if it were chess with muscles. But she needs calm conditions if her gentle persuasion is to be at its most effective. She was finally frustrated by two shots that hardly bounced.

Miss Wade was back again in 1971, like one of those Marciano-type fighters who keep going forward, soaking up punishment, on the assumption that sooner or later they will get in close and land a big punch. She had endured so much agony of spirit in Rome that at times her nerves must have seemed knotted. She had been petulant, even tempestuously cross. As Sir James Barrie put it, the gladness of her gladness and the sadness of her sadness are as nothing to the badness of her badness when she's bad.

But she gradually learned how to play on slow clay. She gradually bridled her mettlesome temper. And in 1971 she kept on winning until there was no one else to play.

True, the field was only sixteen strong, and half of it was weak. Miss Wade's worst match turned out to be that against Marie Neumannova, who has an unorthodox first service and hits the second left-handed (which means that expectation is twice confounded). Miss Neumannova led 6–1 and in the second set had a point for 5–3. This was awkward. Miss Wade needed her strongest nerves, her best form, and all her competitive experience to prize that trap open, win the tie-break, and then take the third set from 4–5 down. But the machinery of her game was now working smoothly. She won her last two matches in straight sets against those formidable exponents of the clay court game, Helga Hösl and Helga Masthoff, formerly Miss Niessen. Both provided severe tests for Miss Wade's character and match-playing ability. Her response was consistently firm and accomplished. She looked ready for anybody. But there was nobody left.

So Miss Wade let her hair down, slipped into something more comfortable, and passed round the champagne: 'I've learned how to play on this stuff.' Presumably she meant the clay.

But the women's event was a sideshow. What mattered at the Foro Italico in 1971 was the return of the game's upper crust, because the tournament formed part of the inaugural World Championship Tennis circuit, besides attracting the leading professionals from the national associations. Except for Ken Rosewall and Ilie Nastase, all the lions were loose. The sacrificial meat tossed their way was the best Italy could muster. Backstage, the slick WCT promotion team did their stuff. It was hardly surprising that the tournament was one of Rome's best organized, most exciting, most successful sporting shindigs since Honorius closed the Colosseum.

Mind you, there were mixed feelings about some things. Take Rome itself. A lot of people were on strike, including the garbage collectors, and for a few days water was rationed (luckily the Foro Italico has a private pipeline to the Tiber). Then there were reminders that WCT refuse to be shackled by conventional thinking. The early matches were reduced to the best of three sets. The tie-break was introduced. A few of the WCT men did their bit for brighter men's fashions by wearing their garishly coloured 'television' outfits. They soon had their feathers ruffled: Italians dismissed six of the Texan group in the first round and two more in the second. That was good box office, and led to one reverberating din after another from the huge crowds.

It was a time of high temperatures and high drama. The milling thousands flocked from court to court to watch seven Italians competing for places in the last sixteen. By the time John Newcombe and Vincenzo Franchitti started slapping balls about, the excitement had reached a peak—and when the excitement reaches a peak in Rome, the sound waves echo along the *autostrada del sole* in the Sabine Hills.

Newcombe's nervous system was almost wrecked when he finally beat Franchitti 6–4, 6–7, 7–5. Franchitti, a fair-haired Roman, had nothing to lose except his inhibitions. Newcombe, the top seed, had won a lot of big tournaments and knew all about pressure. Or thought he did. He had come across nothing more intimidating, in its own way, than the emotional tightrope he walked amid that barrage of noise. His opponents seethed high and low on every vantage point round court two, which is tucked in a corner below a long promenade. The hubbub was deafening. The populace were willing Newcombe to defeat. They held up play with their chants of 'Vincenzo! . . . Vincenzo!'

Vincenzo looked like Stan Laurel doubling for Errol Flynn. But the overwhelming ardour carried him along—and finally found a crack in Newcombe's concentration. The first time he served for the match, Newcombe missed three volleys and put an easy forehand in the net. The uproar suggested that Franchitti had taken Burma.

The mighty Newcombe, of all people, looked as if he might get the shakes at any moment. He could not have been more pale and strained if cannibals had been preparing him for the pot. But again he broke through—and this time his booming services (never did he need them more) finished the job without need of volleys. But if you want to know what a man can go through at the Foro Italico, ask Newcombe about the afternoon he played Franchitti.

The public dominated that day, not least when they rushed rapturously on court and lifted Ezio Di Matteo shoulder high as he beat Marty Riessen.

But order was quickly restored. Only two Italians reached the last sixteen, and those two went no farther. And out of tumult came splendour. If they play tennis in Valhalla, they play it in such places, on such days, in such ways as it was played in Rome on 6 May 1971. Sunshine streamed through the trees into that seductive setting. Famous players were scattered about the courts designing a responsive beauty of their own—and as is often the Italian way, the best match was dismissed to the shadows. To court five.

The terracing of every court within sight, however remote and microscopic the view, was congested with clamorous citizens engrossed in a match of high quality and thrilling tension. Two masters of the clay court game were in action: Jan Kodes and Tony Roche, both unyieldingly combative. Each in turn achieved a marginal authority but could not maintain it. The beefy Roche almost cut chunks off the ball in making it pursue puzzling courses. Little Kodes bounced about like a rubber ball and biffed buzzing drives down both flanks. His last bounce took him over the net for the handshake. He won 6–4, 5–7, 7–6.

The restless Tom Okker beat the unflappable Zeljko Franulovic, who won a set and, in the second, surged from 1–4 to 4–all. The imperilled Okker took a nasty tumble as he struggled to stay in the match. His prospects flickered like a dying fire. But he rekindled the flames and Franulovic wilted in the heat. There are times when the Yugoslav seems to lack whatever it is that tennis players use in the way of overdrive.

The Peter O'Toole of tennis, Cliff Drysdale, whose manner and mien lend elegance to his unconventional game, confirmed the evidence of recent good form by beating Andres Gimeno. Roy Emerson mastered Nikola Pilic in another good match. We had all these and we had Rod Laver and John Newcombe too, bursting through at the expense of Di Matteo and Bob Lutz. The sixth of May was quite a day.

Emerson lost a fine match to Arthur Ashe. It ended with a disputed call that left both players standing doubtfully in mid-court while the crowd howled around them. It was characteristic of the sportsmanship of both men that Emerson was the first to the net for the handshake. Off court, Emerson was flashing his gold fillings and baffling the Italian staff daily with his hearty but—to them—utterly unintelligible 'Howya goin', Blue?'

Laver quelled a bold challenge by Stan Smith, who won a set by gambling on taking the ball early. Later Laver's touch was beautifully assured. In the third set he broke to 5-2 with the help of two facile top-spin lobs: as Smith is 6 ft 4 in. tall, these indicated an impish confidence. In the next game Laver played a volleyed drop shot that died like a bird killed in flight. Oddly, Laver played only one of his WCT colleagues (Ashe) in the entire tournament. His opponent in the final was Kodes, who had left behind him exclusively WCT wreckage—Fred Stolle, Roche, Newcombe and Okker.

Against Newcombe, the tight-lipped Kodes was a David challenging a Goliath. In the final set Newcombe was serving at 5-3 and 15-love. But the public, sweating and shouting, stiffened the little man's ambition—and Newcombe went into one of those curious dazes that an overtaxed concentration can sometimes inflict on a man. Suddenly tentative, he lost thirteen successive points, eight of them on his own service. First his forehand let him down, then his volleying. And Kodes pounced. The Czechoslovak thereupon joined Okker in tracing some graceful patterns in the sunlight. Kodes's best tennis was not as good as Okker's. But Kodes played his best tennis more consistently.

Laver beat Kodes 7-5, 6-3, 6-3 to regain a title he won in 1962 (the year Laver took the Australian, Italian, French, Wimbledon, German and United States championships, a sequence without parallel). Kodes had done terrible things to WCT. So Laver was not playing merely for himself. He was playing for the dignity of the contract professionals—as he did against Mark Cox at Bournemouth three years earlier, after Cox had beaten Ricardo Gonzales and Roy Emerson in successive rounds of the first open tournament.

Kodes did all he could. But Laver's length was superb and his touch was so good as to make the impudent shots look easy. He masterfully commanded lobs and drops—all the crafty clay court stuff. Nothing was more impressive than his capacity to hit winners from apparently defensive positions outside the court. He was glorious to watch: fierce, foxy, sometimes florid. He seemed to be putting on a special show for his parents, who were up in the packed terraces.

Before we leave the Foro Italico, let us stroll back to join a group of players at the top of the terracing beside court four. It commands a view of all six outside courts. This is the day of the Newcombe–Franchitti festival of sound. But that has not yet burst upon us. It is early on a sunny, dreamy, drowsy afternoon. The watching players are in a light-hearted, bantering mood as their colleagues sweat it out:

'What's happening?'. . . . 'Everybody's a set up and losing the second.'

'Who's Charlie Parasol playing?'. . . . 'Zugarelli'. . . . 'Who?'. . . . 'Zugarelli'. . . . 'I think I've just had two of those for lunch.'

'Roy Tub's run about six miles in this set. And he's got one game.' (Roy Tub—Roy Barth.)

'Shaff's hit a boomer'. . . . 'Zeljko doesn't look too confident. I practised with him yesterday, but I packed it in. Every time I hit the ball back, he went for a winner. And he made eight out of ten.'

'Lutz is playing well over there'. . . . 'Majoli's only a weekend player'. . . . 'If I could play like that at weekends, I wouldn't bother playing Monday to Friday.'

'That's one of my drop volleys—hit the service line and bounced shoulder high. I'd say this guy's in a lot of trouble.'

'A drop shot. . . . Followed by a lob. . . . Followed by a bad call. . . . That's what it's all about in Rome.'

It is indeed. For tennis, as for most things, there's no place like Rome.

5

The German Championships

The German championships have lost their separate identity as the European season's end-of-term party. In 1971 they were brought forward from August and assimilated into a streamlined clay court circuit running from April to June. They no longer have to compete with the American tournaments that serve as an approach to Forest Hills. The change makes sense. Tradition should always be a guide rather than a master. But the heart has a logic of its own, and this tells us that the change of dates plucked something of genuine though intangible value from the structure of the European game.

After the long weeks of shared summer pleasures, farewells are inevitably sad. At the friendly Club an der Alster in Hamburg, they were at least relaxed and romantic.

Those of us with time to dream can cruise across the lake (chugging gently along with housewives and shopping bags and children), and then stroll to the courts through the leafy loveliness of Alster Park. Or we can burrow into the Quaternary crusts and travel by subway to the Hallerstrasse.

The championships have a drowsy charm. The green and gracious grounds are splashed by the russet rectangles of the courts in their sleepy hollows. The three main courts, hedge-hidden and steeply tiered, are each self-contained, with no distractions from next door. The crowds—sometimes so dense that it is difficult to find standing room—are brightly banked against a backcloth of tall trees, themselves etched elegantly against a burnished sky.

We can quietly digest a match while children romp across the sunny lawns around the clubhouse on a sweltering afternoon. We can refresh ourselves at a counter colourful with juicy peaches, pears and plums: an array that attracts public and players as the sweet stall does at Wimbledon. Or we can nibble one of those interesting hot sausages. Or munch cheesecake. Or savour an ice cream. Or take our ease with a cold beer in the restaurant, where everyone seems to know everyone else. That was the restaurant where, once observing some unemployed player brooding with massively solemn introspection beneath a ridiculous hat, Judy Dalton sadly tapped temple with forefinger and generalized about the tennis set:

'He's not well, you know. . . . We're all the same. . . . Not well.'

And if we have any small problems, they are quickly sorted out by the dapper and infectiously genial 'Happy' Görnemann, an unfussy trouble-shooter who never needs a gun. Or by Karin, the girl in the post office caravan. She looks after our telephone calls, wears a smile that comes from inside, and is clearly the type Nature designed to wake up cheerful and never get cross.

Come August, we miss all that.

Then there are the rosy evenings of wining and dining. Our Hamburg hosts know their stuff. They are aware that tennis players like to have some fun organized for them, but also enjoy a few free evenings so that they can go their own way. So there is a dinner at the club, or down by the lake, or perhaps on a moored liner. And there is a dance at which the young exercise their limbs (Ilie Nastase can make the teenagers look like statues) and the not-so-young exercise tongues and beer muscles.

There is time, too, for a look around thriving Hamburg. While the attractive modern shops open their doors to the day's trade, soberly dressed men sit at pavement tables drinking beer with breakfast—they should know better. For evening delectation, there are a host of fine restaurants: including, when we can find it, one with a name that hangs heavy on the tip of the tongue, the Mühlenkamper Fahrhaus. Its fish is superb. The reverential ambiance of the place tells us we must take the food seriously, and not titter over our lobster.

Come August, we miss all that, too.

Small groups of players and camp followers have also been known to invade such beer halls as the Zillertal, where plump men in *Lederhosen* play jolly Bavarian music. Or to expand their education in unusual directions during the hours of a discreet darkness. For the deprived, the curious, or those with a special taste in the way of entertainment, St Pauli has outrageous facilities. In one of those courtyards officially set aside for such negotiations, a young lady whose erection and demolition services were for hire was not amused when asked by a playful journalist if her rates included breakfast. The clubs on and around the Reeperbahn offer spectacles that doubtless delight the discerning eyes of connoisseurs of obscenity. Things are done that should probably not be done, and should certainly not be seen to be done. And the examining critics submit their reviews at the tennis club next morning.

At the championships, as at St Pauli, fashions change. During the four seasons of open competition the German event acquired a status similar to that of the Australian championships—but behind that of the Wimbledon, French, United States, Italian and South African tournaments. They rank third in the hierarchy of the clay court game but lead both France and Italy in terms of organization. True, they are easier to manage because the fields are smaller. The draw is always neatly assorted and padded out with players of polysyllabic mediocrity, so that there is elbow room for a few Germans to go a long way and attract profitably large crowds.

An essential element in the championships' eminence is the nature of the courts. These are not as slow as those of Paris and Rome and therefore do not turn tennis into quite such an enchanting spectacle. But they have the basic virtues of clay and, at the same time, offer serve-and-volley specialists a fair chance—as long as the violence is applied with precision. Their pace is an ideal compromise between the extremes of Paris and Rome on the one hand and Wimbledon and Forest Hills on the other.

The line judges, and often the umpires, are unusually young. On the whole they competently sit in judgement on their elders. But I have seen such well behaved players as John Newcombe and Istvan Gulyas in blazing tempers after decisions that seemed to stray from the narrow path of justice. In 1968 Newcombe angrily grilled a line judge and in 1970 Gulyas furiously swung his racket at a box of balls on the umpire's chair and scattered them—box and all—across the court. But all that was uncharacteristic of Newcombe, Gulyas, and Hamburg.

In Paris and Rome we have already scrutinized the broad canvas of clay court tennis. We must not be greedy. So in Hamburg we will make do with a few miniatures. My favourite was painted in 1968, when a once-famous exponent of the big game reminded us that he could still do his thing supremely well, and without overt brutality.

In 1957 Mal Anderson became the first unseeded player to win the United States championship. In 1958 he was runner-up for the Australian and American titles. In January 1972 he popped out of the box to reach the final of the Australian championship, the last open tournament. Anderson is such a fluently clean striker of the ball, such a facile athlete, that although he never goes in for fancy shots he is the sort of player we can watch for hours. His game has the uncomplicated charm of a Strauss waltz. His is the art that conceals art. He plays tennis as if born to it. The one flaw may be that he is too highly strung for the ultimate challenges of his calling. But for that, the impression he made on the records might have equalled the impression he made on the memory.

He married Roy Emerson's sister. He is from the same vintage as Emerson and looks and plays so much like him (though Anderson's style is smoother and less punishing) that he combed his hair forward so people would not mistake one for the other. He also favours cigars, which is a distinctive preference for a tennis player.

In 1968 Anderson was not originally entered. But he filled a gap in the draw thanks to the intercession of Newcombe, whose local connections include the winsome Angie—formerly Fräulein Pfannenburg of Hamburg (the citizens may presumably be described as Hamburgers). This was only Anderson's fifth tournament in fourteen months: and in 1968 the weather varied mercilessly between hot and hotter. It was enervating merely to be exposed to the sunshine, never mind prancing about on a tennis court. The only umbrellas in use were serving as parasols. Yet one day Anderson beat two of his Australian compatriots, finishing the second match six hours and a half after he had begun the first.

Soon after breakfast, when several players were feeling old and grey and full of sleep (which is Yeats, not Bellamy), he beat Bob

Howe. Anderson spread his arms wide and bowed low in gratitude as Howe served a double-fault to lose a 28-game set. The next victim was the springy little Barry Phillips-Moore, whose hyphen has mysteriously survived in a country where they are almost extinct. Anderson played lovely, gossamer-steel tennis to come from behind in the second set.

Then fate almost pulled a joker from the pack. Because when Anderson was serving at 6–4, 6–4, 6–5 and 30–all, he came within two points of beating Newcombe. It seemed that he was about to toss out of the draw the man who had got him into it.

Both were former United States champions, though they had won the title ten years apart. They had not played each other until they met in the oppressive heat of Hamburg's crowded centre court. For two sets, almost three, Anderson was marginally the better player: not least in the astonishing ease with which he banged his fluent service into the corners. But when the crux came, Newcombe played the big points better. The rest of the match told us what we already knew. It was a hot day. It was a long match. Anderson was thirty-three. Newcombe was twenty-four.

Newcombe later came back from 3–6, 4–6, and 2–4 down, to beat Marty Riessen, who played beautifully until he missed a few volleys and lost thirteen successive games. But after all this bother, Newcombe won his first important clay court title by beating the willowy Cliff Drysdale in straight sets. Newcombe found a perfect blend of stealth and strength—drop shots, short angles, and all the usual heavy stuff. This was not his habitual game. But he wore borrowed clothes as if they had been made for him. In the women's event Annette du Plooy won the most important championship of her career.

The 1969 titles went to Tony Roche and Judy Tegart (later Mrs Dalton), who are perhaps more vividly Australian than anyone else in tennis. Whether winning or losing, the big and boisterous Miss Tegart has brought a lot of hearty laughter to the game. There is no nonsense about her, and her tennis is true to her nature. She plays with booming zest and gives the ball a healthy whack. Now she carefully worked her way up through the German ranking list, celebrated her first big championship by winning both doubles as well, and even found the time and energy for a stint of canoeing in the twilight.

There was an extraordinary scene on the centre court. Jan Kodes, who was having trouble with his back, was a set and 2–4 down to Wilhelm Bungert but recovered to lead 5–4. At this crisis Kodes had two bad calls. So he collected his gear and prepared to walk off. Whereupon Bungert, as straight and stiff as a door, strode to the umpire's microphone. In his role as uncrowned king of German tennis, he addressed Kodes and the public: players had bad calls all over the world, said Bungert, but they did not walk off.

Kodes was doubtless startled by this probably unprecedented reminder of what was what in the way of emotional fortitude. He must have been tempted to demand his share of time for an amplified debate on the philosophy of sportsmanship. Instead, he played on. And lost.

Come August, we miss all that.

Tom Okker was the 1970 champion. In his last two matches he beat the French and Italian champions, Kodes and Ilie Nastase (who played that tournament with his racket hand so severely blistered that the beginnings of a hole had appeared in the palm). Kodes had previously been 0–3 down in his fifth set with Owen Davidson, who has been known to use strong terms about clay court tennis but can play it well if he is in the mood and wants to work up a thirst. When Kodes beat Mark Cox, John Ballantine (*Sunday Times*) referred to the Czechoslovak's 'steamroller strategy' and to 'the psychological emasculation that accumulates to rush one to defeat at the hands of a slow court master like Kodes'. That was neatly put. There are players who express the same thought in more homespun English.

The nervously intelligent Helga Hösl beat the statuesque Helga Niessen in the first all-German women's final for twenty-two years. Mrs Hösl had reached the French semi-finals six years earlier. But she had to acquire a husband and a daughter before reaching her first major singles final. Had she known the trick of it, she might have done everything sooner.

Perhaps for the last time, the championships had written the closing chapter in the story of the European season. It was not a good year. The ratio of sunshine to showers was wrong. The sky was often grey. The breezes that blustered through the entire summer were still baiting us. This fickle weather, plus the absence of

Germany's Davis Cup team, doubtless had much to do with the decline in attendances. Even those delectable sausages seemed to have more gristle in them than usual. In short, some of the magic had gone out of the tournament. Even at St Pauli, obscenity had apparently nearly exhausted its most ingenious permutations.

In 1971 the championships were moved to May. They produced a memorable reminder that Hamburg gives the slow-court savant and the serve-and-volley specialist an even chance. The two schools were represented, respectively, by Juan Gisbert and Dick Crealy. Gisbert is a solemn and sensitive Spaniard who has dabbled in bull-fighting and the law. Crealy we met in Paris. His is a name to bring out when some fool tells you there are no characters in the game these days. He is a rawboned giant with a daunting display of teeth and the head-jerking, rooster-type walk affected by a few stage comedians. He is also a scholar and versifier, hot stuff on economics and politics. In 1971 I caught him reading *Martin Chuzzlewit* one day and Yeats's poems the next. One way and another, an unusual chap. On court, his nerves can take so much and no more.

Crealy was leading 6-3, 6-2, 5-3 and had a match point. But he lost the third set 7-9, the fourth 6-8, and eventually cracked. He led in all five sets. Time and again he had Gisbert wrapped up and ready for posting. But poor Crealy raced around so much that, as they say in the trade, he ran himself into the ground. When serving at 7-all and 40-15 in the fifth set, he had two game points. He dashed to the net each time, but lost both rallies. By now he was twitching ('I couldn't control any muscle at all—everything was jumping around'). There ensued a remarkable scene.

Instead of retreating from net to baseline to serve again, Crealy went over to a bench by the umpire's chair and sat down. He was locked in a world of private anguish. He had the glassy-eyed look of those who dream.

'Come on,' urged a sympathetic spectator. 'You can do it.'

Crealy went over to the drinks box, took out a bottle, and sat down again. Gisbert now approached, with his air of gentle puzzle-ment, and pointed out that the score was only deuce. What was wrong?

'I'm gone,' said Crealy. 'You got me. I got cramp in my feet, cramp in my legs, and cramp in my hands. . . . I got cramp in my stomach and cramp in the back of my head. . . . And when I got cramp in my head, you got me. I'm gone.'

He could hardly pick up his gear. But he managed it—and walked off. Game, set, and match to Gisbert.

That is Hamburg. That is clay court tennis. Above all, that is Dick Crealy.

6

Wimbledon

The Wimbledon championships are the game's best shop window. They are also one of its worst. They are the best because of the sublime splendour of the setting and the sense of tradition that casts a glow within it; because of the size and nature of the crowds; because of the huge and eclectic entry; because of the slick organization; and because the courts (and indeed, the grounds as a whole) are smartly maintained. They are among the worst because the courts are grass, which does not induce the players to paint the game in its loveliest colours. In the select gallery of great tournaments, Wimbledon is a picture of thrilling, awesome beauty—with a flaw in its central subject.

This is not to suggest that its grass courts should be torn up and replaced by something better. Variety is essential. Uniform playing conditions would breed a uniform playing style, and that would strip the game of the joyous contrast between slow-court and fast-court specialists. But in terms of variety, an accident of history gave Wimbledon the worst of the deal. In every respect except one, its supremacy is unchallenged. But we see better tennis on clay and on at least two of the new synthetic courts.

The faster surfaces are losing favour. Grass is a minority surface that seems slightly eccentric—and is coming to be regarded as an anachronism—in the context of the international circuit. The players mostly reckon that, at the highest level, Wimbledon will be the last sanctuary of 'lawn' tennis as we used to know it.

Wimbledon produces the best tennis only within the technical and tactical restrictions grass imposes. The courts tend to be peopled by big men with muscles and small men with problems. Rallies are short. Two strokes, the service and volley, are often tediously dominant. All is split-second timing. In its own way, this powerful game can be laudable, even exciting. But it can also be a crashing, bashing bore. Grass courts exalt strength and reflexes: both admirable qualities, but not to the exclusion of the more imaginative tactical pleasures of the game. In tennis, as in painting and music and drama, the fact that a task is technically difficult does not necessarily make it good entertainment. When a men's event on grass is pared to the pounding expertise of the later rounds, the lure of women's matches and the dreamland of clay court memories becomes ever more appealing.

In reducing a richly coloured game to stark black and white, Wimbledon does not even offer the players their most rigorous test of all-round ability. From a physical point of view it is not the toughest tournament to win.

Nor is it the richest. And in 1972 it could no longer pretend to its former status as an unofficial world championship. Because in 1971 the International Lawn Tennis Federation made the daft and damaging decision to exclude World Championship Tennis from all events that recognize the authority of the ILTF's constituent national associations. In such a situation, Wimbledon was bound to suffer.

To put the worst interpretation on all these factors, it is possible to foresee a time when Wimbledon will no longer draw sell-out crowds and inspire massive international publicity. Because the sporting public have only a limited appetite for a sub-standard dish, however well served.

It is not a habit of mine to take such a pessimistic line. I have done so now in order to lend perspective to our view of Wimbledon, and to remind us that we should not take it for granted. It has always been the supreme festival of world tennis. But it need not necessarily remain so. Its soundest insurance for the future is the admirably forward-looking All England Club, which has acquired the habit of success and is unlikely to be satisfied with anything less.

Wimbledon is a sporting and social occasion that makes news all over the world. It is a time of reunion for players of the present and the past. It brings together teenage enthusiasts and grizzled connoisseurs. It is an annual meeting of world tennis held in a pervading air of tension. The tradition of the tournament inspires everyone's endeavours. The mystique of royal patronage is itself a bond with an old glory that hangs like a sunlit mist over those green lawns in the land where tennis was born. Ghosts flit about the courts. Because in the mind's eye the giants of the past are still with us: indeed, many are there in the flesh.

The graceful grounds give the international game a beautifully designed spiritual home. The setting is lovely, with hydrangeas brightly patterned against a green backcloth of grass, trees, hedges, and those famous ivy-clad walls. The year-round labours of the staff keep the place in perfect condition: or as near perfection as it is humanly possible to get. Christine Janes told me once: 'Even when I went there in the winter, to practise, I sort of put on my best things and made a real do of it. There's something special about it. I think it's the fact that everything is in tip-top condition. So much care is taken there, even off season.'

Wimbledon can be old-fashioned in its bland urbanity, yet is modern in the hard-headed professionalism of its players and administrators. Months of preparation precede the championships. On the first day the staff is swollen to the dimensions of a small army, and the organization slips back into gear as if it had never been in neutral. The work is painstaking. No detail is overlooked.

The players are cared for with such consideration that they have nothing to worry about except their tennis. They even have shining, chauffeuse-driven saloons to carry them to and from the grounds. They must feel like gods and goddesses as the polished procession of smart cars purrs slowly along the crowded promenade. The public line the route and watch the players get out, clutching bundles of rackets. Kerry Melville recalls how it felt the first time: 'They're waiting for you to hop out. Then they can't figure out who you are—and you see them pass on to the one behind. They say "That's nobody" . . . even though you've got about four rackets in your hand to try and look good.'

The players feel cosseted, important, eager to do their best.

'There's no other tournament quite like Wimbledon,' says Margaret Court. 'It's the atmosphere. Tension and everything. The crowd's quite sensitive. And everyone is treated equally. Everyone who plays at Wimbledon must feel good. Just to be playing there. It's tremendously well organized.'

Merely to play at Wimbledon is, for many players, to realize a life's ambition. The emotional strain of the qualifying tournament at Roehampton can be a shocking revelation to those reared in the belief that tennis is a genteel game. Geoff Bluett of Middlesex, who beat Nicola Pietrangeli at Wimbledon in 1968, qualified four times. He knows all about Roehampton: 'Almost anything goes. The language gets really bad. Rackets fly. Balls fly. I've seen rackets thrown yards from the court, and hurled against the dressing room wall. I've seen men players crying. One chap smashed two rackets across his knee. When you get to match point, you suddenly realize what's at stake. And you go to jelly.'

To win Wimbledon a player must be at a physical and mental peak, with a hot game and a cold brain. Because Wimbledon is an intimidating test of nerve and confidence and maturity, of the specific skills grass courts demand, and of strength and fitness. Elsewhere, men can rest after three sets, women after two. There is no rest at Wimbledon. 'The guy who is in the best physical shape has got a hell of an advantage in the second week,' says Arthur Ashe.

But when a player has a Wimbledon title among his references, his reputation is secure. This, above all others, is the tournament they want to win—because of the character and prestige of the event itself, not because of its prize money or off-court benefits (a Wimbledon champion is prime bait for manufacturers who want a 'name' to endorse their products).

'The money isn't the object when you're playing Wimbledon,' says Rod Laver. 'It's the number one tournament in the world, and if you're in tennis it's the most important one to win.'

And while the Lavers are on court, the Bluetts are up in the players' seats: 'It's a privilege to watch. You learn more about tennis in an hour than you do in six weeks of ordinary tournaments. You see the way the champions play the big points when they're fit and keyed up and really going for it. And every now and then you see one of the Wimbledon classics, like a champion going down to someone who's playing out of his mind. At the end, even the players rise in their seats, some with tears in their eyes. Those moments I treasure almost more than playing at Wimbledon.'

The force that knits all these separate strands together and makes Wimbledon such a vivid occasion is the swarming enthusiasm of the sophisticated crowds who pack the grounds every day. For many of these people, as for many of the players, merely to be at Wimbledon is fulfilment in itself. Some spend hours queueing in tunnels beside the courts of their preference, and do not look discontented. Others cluster on the promenade, watching the electric scoreboards and echoing the roars from the centre court and court one.

'The thing that struck me most about Wimbledon when I first saw it was how beautiful it was,' says Cliff Richey. 'And there are so many little things that are different. Bowing to the royalty. I didn't know what to do when I walked out, and there was royalty in the box. And it's sort of embarrassing when everybody stares at you when you come in the car. But if it wasn't for the keenness of the crowds—year in, year out—it wouldn't mean anything. The biggest single fact is that you have fantastic crowds. People are so mad about tennis. And that means a lot to the players.'

Evonne Goolagong brought her exciting talents to Wimbledon for the first time in 1970, and was beaten by Peaches Bartkowicz.

'A really great sight—all the people, the flowers, and the colours. I was surprised to see so many people standing there, waiting to see the players get out of the cars. And to see so many waiting outside. Just walking about, when I wasn't playing, I could feel myself getting butterflies. When I found out I was playing on the centre court, I got nervous straight away. When I got out there, I looked up once and saw all those people: I'd never played in front of so many. I didn't look up again. I just wanted to get off. I rushed everything.'

For tennis, Wimbledon is the greatest show on earth. There is a tingling flavour in the air that enters the bloodstream and quickens the pulse rate. Going through the gates on the first day is a moment to catch the hearts of starry-eyed young players who have not been there before. One said it was like going into a cathedral, and that was an apt comparison: because to the tennis sect, Wimbledon is sacred ground.

Because of its grass courts and its diversified yet continuous pressure on the emotions, playing at Wimbledon is a unique experience —inspiring to some, distressing to others. Virginia Wade, additionally burdened by the weight of her compatriots' expectations, has played some of her worst tennis there. She has been pitiable to watch, her highly strung nerves jumping around as if an imaginary dentist was going berserk with the drill. Billie Jean King, by contrast, is famous as 'a good Wimbledon player'. So was Bobby Wilson. Wimbledon drove his game to peaks he seldom attained anywhere else.

In 1967 Wilhelm Bungert beat Wilson in a memorable match on the centre court. And as if the match were not enchantment enough, the whole wide setting was perfect. A gem of an afternoon cast a lustre on the actors who trod their various stages, and on the fans who flocked to watch them. It was a day bright with colour, drowsy with warmth, yet throbbing with excitement: a Wimbledon in all its glory. Yet compared with Bungert versus Wilson, the other men's matches were as water to wine.

To assess the contest in terms of statistics would be like ordering porridge as an hors d'œuvre while dining out in Paris. All that needs to be said on that score is that Bungert took 2 hours and 25 minutes to win in five sets after being within two points of defeat, and that he raced up the home straight with a masterly sequence of three games in which he lost only two points.

The quickly shifting patterns of light and shade fell first across one man, then the other. What left such a delicious, lingering flavour on the palate was the style and grace, the flair and feeling, the wrists and reflexes, with which Bungert and Wilson took hold of a sport and turned it into an art form. There are times, as with the mosques of Isfahan, when men create a beauty beyond the apparent capacity of their tools and materials. So it was with Bungert and Wilson.

Gorgeous rallies flickered with the shining bladework of two fencing masters happy at their work. The first two sets were among the finest Wilson ever created. Play was interrupted by a swirling swarm of bees: sniffing something good, they descended on the court and caused a flutter in the crowd. Then Wilson, too, came to earth after playing those two sets in the clouds. Bungert has a wrist of steel. His chief weapon, as always, was that whipped forehand, a stroke that at times seemed to exist outside the world of human error. But the result seemed irrelevant, because the match was perfectly designed—beautiful in its content, dramatic in its form.

That was the year Roger Taylor rose from the ranks by winning a three-hour match with Cliff Drysdale, who always looks as if he has strolled on court from a film set—or from charming the customers at a plushy Texan tennis resort called Lakeway, where he reigns as king. Reading Drysdale's two-fisted backhand is like trying to solve a Chinese crossword puzzle when you are pushed for time. He is smart, too. But that Wimbledon he was not smart enough for Taylor, who reached the last four and later earned a contract with World Championship Tennis and—as player and dashing young hero—acquired a reputation even Drysdale had to respect.

Taylor is tall, dark and handsome. The cliché fits. He is a characteristic Yorkshireman in that he is something of a loner, a man who takes an independent line without making a fuss. He comes from industrial Sheffield, where a youngster learns to use his fists as soon as he can walk without a harness. Two of the most impressive things about Taylor are his shoulders. When he comes into a room, you notice the shoulders first. Then Taylor. He is a good man to have in your corner when the trouble starts. Bobby Wilson tells a story of a tournament they played once in Istanbul.

Wilson is a cat-lover. On that part of the earth's crust there were plenty of feline friends to engage his affections. They looked pathetic. But they kept the rats and mice in line. A venturesome little bag of bones walked across the dance floor, and a young Turk picked it up by the front paws and swung it around as if dancing with it.

Wilson did not regard this as a genuine contribution to the cat's health and happiness. Indeed, he thought the creature might be damaged. He saw red, he says. And he rushed off on an errand of mercy. Nothing more constructive coming to mind, he grabbed the Turk by the throat to make him let go. Which the Turk did (squeeze a man's windpipe, and he drops whatever he is doing).

But three or four of the Turk's chums converged on Wilson and started shouting. The situation looked fraught with painful possibilities for the gallant, if reckless cat-lover. Start strangling a Turk, even in a good cause, and the tribe tend to turn nasty.

It was at this delicate crisis that Taylor rose from his chair. He removed his jacket. The stuff inside his shirt was obviously not padding. And he strolled across.

'That quietened them down,' says Wilson. 'The bloke said he was sorry and in the end I think he gave the cat a saucer of milk. But without Roger's muscles, I don't think they'd have been quite so sympathetic.'

But the racket-swinging Wilhelm Bungert, who had it in for the English in 1967, was less impressive than the cat-swinging Turk. Bungert had packed his bags and booked out of his hotel four times, partly as a superstitious insurance against defeat. But he beat Taylor in five sets to become the first German to reach the final since Gottfried von Cramm in 1937. On the morning of the final (which coincided with von Cramm's birthday) one of Bungert's business associates flew from Düsseldorf with Bungert's evening dress suit, in case it should be needed for the Wimbledon Ball. It was never unpacked. Indeed, since the injured von Cramm had been crushed 6–1, 6–1, 6–0 by Fred Perry in 1936, no men's singles finalist had won fewer games than Bungert did. John Newcombe beat him 6–3, 6–1, 6–1.

This was Newcombe's first major championship, and he told Princess Marina he was going out to get drunk. In his speech at the Ball, Newcombe was equally honest when he thanked Nikola Pilic for putting Roy Emerson out of the running.

Ann Jones won an eventually nerve-racking match with the tiny Rosemary Casals, who is related to the great cellist, Pablo. ('He's my great-uncle. So what? I never met the guy.') Miss Casals is all bouncing audacity. She plays a wonderfully versatile game compounded of Latin flamboyance, American know-how and a bursting wealth of talent. She is a quivering assembly of muscles who does everything except travel in two directions at once. She plays as if she is wearing something that itches.

Billie Jean King does not hang about, either. Enviably assured on her low volleys, she beat Mrs Jones 6–3, 6–4 and became the first woman since Doris Hart, in 1951, to win all three titles. In the men's doubles, Bob Hewitt and Frew McMillan (all sombre dignity under that voluminous cream cap) did not lose a set.

Every title changed hands except the women's championship. In the singles, eleven unseeded players beat seeded opponents. Then Wimbledon lost its momentum. The singles finals were such an anticlimax that one jaded reporter muttered about 'the mourning after the frights before'. But tennis had reached a stage when new blood was needed at the top—and this was the year when the pack caught up with the leaders. Such famous former champions as

Emerson, Manuel Santana and Maria Bueno were nudged out of the way by rising players: Pilic, Charles Pasarell and Miss Casals. It was an exciting tournament, and the attendance was a bulging record. Yet towards the end, this choice conversational morsel was overheard:

'But my dear, I haven't seen *anyone* at Wimbledon this year.'

In those days an open Wimbledon was just a dream. When it happened, in 1968, we thought it was a mirage.

Many famous players had deserted their national associations and the 'Establishment' tournament circuit in favour of a more honest and exclusive brand of professionalism. In 1968 it was agreed that this need not disqualify them from competing with their inferiors. The decision made sense, because tennis had outgrown the need for petty distinctions. But if you live with sophistry long enough, it becomes a habit. Tennis could hardly believe its luck when the outlaws rode back into town as law-abiding citizens.

There were fourteen former singles champions in the field: nine men and five women. Plus Ricardo Gonzales and Ken Rosewall, who had each, in turn, been recognized as world champion. All these were among the great players of past generations who returned to Wimbledon. We could see again—or perhaps for the first time—some of the heroes and heroines of our childhood. It was as if some time machine were at work, taking us back to the magic that was yesterday.

Most of the living legends had no real hope of winning. They entered because history was being made in the sport that meant so much to them, and they wanted to catch the flavour of the occasion. So they were willing to play bit parts on a stage where they once had starring roles. To a degree the same applied to many younger players (the men, anyway) who were pushed out of the limelight that had been theirs a year earlier. The reigning champion, John Newcombe, was seeded only fourth.

To all of us, life grants a few rich experiences that will never recur: experiences that are unique, complete in themselves. The 1968 Wimbledon was one such. There had been nothing like it before: there can be nothing like it again. The first open Wimbledon could only happen once. Beppe Merlo beamed and summed it up:

'It's lovely. The friends of twenty years—all at Wimbledon.'

That tournament had the eyes and ears of the world. The information services—press, television and radio—were swamped, as never before, by news of the supreme tennis festival.

The hard men of the professional circuit gave depth to the men's field and lifted the standard of play to a sometimes dazzling level. The competition was more intense. But we were reminded of the general truth that the better a man plays, the better he behaves. It is a misconception to assume that the strain of conflict is bad for a man's principles: it merely puts those principles to the test.

That 1968 Wimbledon was memorable because of its significance in the history of the game. But it was not a great tournament. Shangri-La turned sour on us. The first five days were wet, which had undesirable consequences. Attendances fell. The inevitably congested programme meant that strength and stamina, youth and fitness, were more important than ever. Rain and heat in turn produced absurd variations in playing conditions. And a little of the laughter went out of Wimbledon as the stern expertise came in.

Because of a transport strike, it was difficult for the public to get to Wimbledon on the first day—and because of the rain, the effort was hardly worth while. There was a late start, play was twice interrupted, and some of the tennis we did see was ludicrous: players were tumbling across the forecourts, sliding along the baselines, and generally teetering about as if taking part in an ice show.

But as the days went by, the damp lawns were gradually warmed by humanity and drama. A dog called Brandy, owned by Alison and Mark Cox, spent a long afternoon in a car; because while Alison watched and Brandy missed all the fun, Cox played a match that—including a 2-hour rain break—spanned 5 hours and 10 minutes. It was Cambridge versus Princeton on the centre court. Cox saved three match points before beating Herb FitzGibbon.

Next day came the one great match of the tournament. Ken Rosewall beat Charles Pasarell 7–9, 6–1, 6–8, 6–2, 6–3. Three interruptions carried the match over a span of four hours. They may also have helped Pasarell to maintain the velocity of his service, and Rosewall to keep those little legs twinkling to and fro on urgent errands. The match seemed an interminable delight, and we wished that it could be. Come grey skies come blue, come rain come sunshine, come tea come Martinis, Rosewall was always playing Pasarell—and it was getting better all the time.

For two sets it was a good match. In the third the purple of greatness fell upon it and stayed there. It had all the necessary components. Its content was of the highest class, its course attained a thrilling crescendo, and its protagonists offered a perfect contrast in style and personality. A climax fit for the theatre was played by actors from different schools. Rosewall is quick and quiet, neat and careful—so cool and calculating that even his strides between rallies seem to be measured to an inch. Pasarell has a straight back and broad shoulders. He is splay-footed and walks with a drawl, repeatedly pulling at his trousers as if adjusting a gun belt. His arms swing menacingly and seem to itch for a challenge to a fast draw. He has the slow, casual assurance of those poker-faced heroes in films about the old West. And his game is a gambler's, with explosive services and ground strokes. He gambled now, and he often won.

The match caught fire in the third set. In the fourth, an interruption was succeeded by sunlight and by a drama so tense that actors and audience were suddenly at one as Wimbledon echoed to the collective heart cries of the centre court. Even when Rosewall prepared to serve for the match, there was still some exciting tennis to come—and two break points. When Pasarell put a last backhand out of court, we could not believe—we did not want to believe—that such a match was over. Nor was it: because we shall tell our grandchildren about it. Rosewall and Pasarell gave a corner of the memory a sheen of gold.

It was during this match that, getting on for seven o'clock on the fourth day of the tournament, sunshine graced the gloomy centre court for the first time. Bud Collins was ready:

'Does the sun always rise at this time of day over here?'

And then, as an alternative one-liner:

'Hey! Would someone douse the house lights?'

Rosewall and Andres Gimeno were on leave next day. Only four of the old regiment—the professionals past thirty—were in the front line. Ricardo Gonzales, Lew Hoad and Alex Olmedo were wiped out. Olmedo's sacrifice enabled Roy Emerson to survive. Reporters dined heavily on the corn grown from nostalgia. Clichés flowed from tongue and typewriter: there were curtain calls and swan songs as the old soldiers faded away, the bugles sounded *The Last Post*, and the cognoscenti agreed that 'they never come back'. All that was the sentimental heart of an eventful day.

Gonzales was beaten by that cheerful Georgian, Alex Metreveli, who was only three years old when Gonzales first won the United States championship. It is hard to deny that sort of arithmetic. But the old lion with the silvering mane roared with defiance before he was tamed. 'A few years ago,' said Metreveli, 'we in Russia thought of Gonzales as such a great player that it was unthinkable that any Russian could ever beat him.'

Hoad was beaten by Bob Hewitt, who had escaped the peril of four match points when playing Thomaz Koch the previous evening. A nice contrast they made—moody ball-coaxing from Hewitt, silent power from Hoad. For a while Hoad's form was almost embarrassing. Then he won five successive games, his fair hair flopping about as he bobbed to and fro on the high tide of a manly challenge. He did not merely hit the ball. He hurt it. His smashes threatened to create tunnels. But he was beaten because he was not quick enough to cope with repeated thrusts that used the full width and length of the court. The spotlight was not on the youngsters that day. It was on the men of the old regiment, cruelly cut down while on active service.

On the second Monday, the temperature and the speed and quality of the tennis were all high. On the main courts, the mercury soared to the middle 90s. Players wore neckerchiefs and spectators fainted. Some famous competitors melted away: Ken Rosewall, occasionally disguised beneath a large white cap; John Newcombe, who walked so slowly between rallies that at times he hardly seemed to be walking at all; and Roy Emerson, whose speed was trumped by Tom Okker's. In the doubles, Francisco Segura (47), Abe Segal (37), Gordon Forbes (34) and Alex Olmedo (32) played a set of 62 games, a Wimbledon record. Did somebody say tennis was a young man's game?

The joy drained out of the men's singles as the last eight withdrew behind the towering walls of the main courts. They stripped the game to its grass court essentials. They mostly looked jaded after the hard labour imposed on them by the congested programme. The lambent rallies offered fleeting moments of splendour. Here and there came the promise—but never the fulfilment—of a dramatic denouement. The material was combustible. But there was no spark to ignite it. This was a day when the applause was often desultory, when spectators yawned—or walked out on the big matches in search of a little more charm and gaiety.

Rod Laver and Tony Roche advanced to the men's final. They come from the sort of places (Rockhampton and Tarcutta) that only Australians have heard about. They are both left-handed, which made their final the first of its kind since Neale Fraser beat Laver in 1960. Roche had benefited from missing the French championships, which are not an ideal preparation for Wimbledon. He spoke for many when he said: 'To win Paris, or reach the final, takes a lot out of you.'

Roche played well. But his was an impossible task. Laver took only an hour to gain his third championship, a feat that had been matched only by Fred Perry since the challenge round was abolished in 1922. Laver was in form, so it was unreasonable to expect a memorable match. He pulverized the ball. Everything he did was done fast—anticipation, reflexes, footwork, strokes (even faster in their effect, because he took the ball early).

'It's like playing a doubles team,' said Bud Collins incredulously.

Laver won 6–3, 6–4, 6–2. He was very good in the first two sets. In the third, when a lesser player might have relaxed a little, he was marvellous. He went for the kill as if fighting for his life. He tore about the court like lightning. All Roche could do was stay out there and take it.

In a women's semi-final, Ann Jones served for the match at 5–4 in her second set with Billie Jean King. But some psychological gremlin perched on her shoulder at the moment of truth. We had seen it happen before. Mrs King flicked her glasses into their most effective viewing zone, stuck out her chin defiantly, and came back to win. We had seen that happen before, too.

Judy Tegart beat Nancy Richey in the other semi-final. Miss Tegart is all bounce and bash and laughter: yet discreet in her court candour. As an earnest of her intentions, she had not had a beer for almost four weeks. She was blowing through this sternly professional Wimbledon like a gust of fresh air. Champions were swept aside: first Margaret Court, and now Miss Richey. Miss Tegart had a green stripe down her dress and a green ribbon in her hair. She wanted everyone to know she came from Australia. Having dealt with Miss Richey, she swaggered off court and winked towards the players' seats, as if to say: 'Bit of a lark, isn't it?'

She had never before reached a major singles final. It was enough.

It had to be. Because Mrs King won her third successive Wimbledon singles championship. In the mixed doubles, Alex Metreveli and Olga Morozova became the first Russians to play in a Wimbledon final.

The 1969 tournament began under a cloud of tragedy: the former Maureen Connolly had died of cancer. Less than three weeks earlier another one-time United States champion, Rafael Osuna, had been killed in an air crash. As if to encourage an appropriate mourning, the first day was washed out by a grey, misty, autumnal sort of rain that looked as permanent as the ivy on the walls or the church spire peeping above the trees. We heard only subdued voices and the soft rustle of rain—instead of the sound of ball on racket, the staccato statistics of the umpire's call, and the roar of the crowd. Our sympathy went out to those for whom this was a first and possibly a last visit to Wimbledon. They came to the royal court and they saw the damp trappings of majesty: but they could not enjoy its warmth and substance.

After a wet day and a cool one, Wimbledon was consistently sunny. There were huge crowds and record receipts. The standard of play in the men's events was probably the highest the championships had ever known. The overall quality of the entrants had risen so sharply that, in future, arduous matches in the early rounds would clearly be the rule rather than the exception.

That was a Wimbledon dominated by mini-dresses, maxi-sets and Ricardo Gonzales. He beat Charles Pasarell 22–24, 1–6, 16–14, 6–3, 11–9 in 5 hours and 12 minutes. It was the longest match in Wimbledon history and eventually became one of the greatest. In the fifth set Gonzales was twice love–40 down on his own service. He survived seven match points. Yet he won the last two games to love. There had been more protracted matches elsewhere, but none in which a man of forty-one showed such resilient powers of endurance. This was one of the supreme individual achievements in tennis or any other sport.

The match was suspended overnight after two sets that lasted 2 hours and 18 minutes. Gonzales reacted angrily to the worsening light. He shouted with rage. He whirled his racket about as if desperately fighting off an adversary he could not see. Twice he flung his racket at the umpire's chair. He was like a wounded, tormented animal who had lost his way in some sepulchral jungle. A noisy section of the crowd erupted in sympathetic response: 'Stop play!' Then 'Off! Off!' There was a slow handclap. The light was bad. But so was Gonzales's behaviour. He was booed from the court.

That was quite a day: cool and breezy, but with banks of sartorial colour around the courts, drama everywhere, and, in the evening, a whiff of gunpowder from a greying grandfather who had become a legend.

The next day, Gonzales won three sets in 2 hours and 54 minutes and earned a tumultuous ovation. The villain was transformed into a hero. Behind the beast of prey we saw the artist, behind the lion the sporting surgeon with a wondrous delicacy of touch and an enviable economy of effort. Gonzales was born to greatness and did not scorn the gift. He is one of the few who have dominated Wimbledon's centre court instead of being dominated by it. The man smoulders with character: there are dark, brooding depths in his intense concentration. He has the loose-limbed ease of the natural athlete, the mannerisms of the well-rehearsed actor treading a familiar stage—the fingers of his left hand flicking away the sweat and tugging his sodden shirt back around his neck. He has all the 'business'. No one upstages Gonzales.

Pasarell, as we have noticed, is also a man of presence and pertinacity, with a knack of being on stage for big scenes at Wimbledon. The pounding power of his assault was relentless. Gonzales bent before it, but never broke: and the pressure finally swung from one man to the other. When that happened, Gonzales was like primitive man pouncing on his first good dinner for a month. One match point was enough. Gonzales was beaten by Arthur Ashe, who observed: 'It was 60 per cent age. If you can't get to the ball, you can't hit it. If he was one step quicker it might have been the other way round.'

The bony, bland, bespectacled Ashe had some bother with Graham Stilwell, who was causing a fuss everywhere that year. Stilwell saved five match points in the fourth set and served for the match himself at 9–8 in the fifth. Whereupon Ashe played four ferociously uninhibited shots: the kind the game's upper crust tend to produce when harassed.

There were plenty more, especially on the backhand, when Ashe took the first set 6–2 in his semi-final with Rod Laver.

'He was hitting winners at will,' said Laver. 'I got embarrassed at one stage. I was picking up balls at the back of the court, ready to serve, knowing that he would hit another winner back.'

It was that sort of match. Laver and Ashe played in a blizzard of their own making. Each seemed to regard the other's carefree violence as a challenge, as if to say: 'First to baby a shot is a sissy.' To any rational human being, controlling a tennis ball at that speed seemed impossible. Laver, of course, eventually turned out to be better at it. He usually does. He had been taken to five sets by Premjit Lall and Stan Smith, who both discovered that Laver does not stop playing great tennis. He just pauses occasionally.

Ken Rosewall was beaten by Bob Lutz, who has a flopping fore-lock and always looks slightly surprised. Lutz is big and beefy but moves well. Rosewall is little and wiry and moves better. But the busy environs of court three did Rosewall's concentration more harm than they did Lutz's.

Tom Okker lost the first two sets to that facile stroke-maker Ron Holmberg, who later became coach at West Point. The wraith-like Okker continually has to fight out of his weight. He took a hiding from the shrewd John Newcombe, who is far more than a blud-geoning Tarzan with good ball control. Okker is all concentrated nervous energy when waiting to receive service. He twirls his racket. He sways from one foot to the other, pawing the ground like a frisky colt eager for a gallop. That day he ran like a deer and once finished poised, arms akimbo, on the wall separating court from crowd. He was all dash and flair. He also lost ten successive games.

But an odd thing happened. Newcombe led 8–6, 3–6, 6–1, 5–0 but lost the next five games, missing four match points. The alarm call of 'five games all' woke him from the nightmare. He lost only four more points. Then he told us something about the centre court: 'I thought I'd won. That was the trouble. There's an electri-fying atmosphere at Wimbledon, in which you can get caught up if you're not careful. I seem to lose concentration, and when you do that on the centre court you can go into a daze. I don't remember much about the five games that slipped away. I was hitting balls. I wasn't playing tennis.'

Newcombe's sparring partner, Tony Roche, ran into even more trouble. Clark Graebner won the first two sets and had three match points. But his concentration and confidence were sapped by the irritant of light rain on his glasses—and in any case, Roche was finding his best form when he most needed it. Roche won with one of his crunching backhand volleys. Up in his stand, his father (who had travelled all the way from a telephone listed in the directory as Tarcutta 1) almost bent his neighbour's ribs in the bear hug of a well-muscled butcher.

But Graebner hit the shot of the match to win the first game of the fifth set. He was driven deep in defence, with Roche lumbering to the net to punch away what apparently had to be a weak return. But Graebner turned and slashed a forehand with such effectively primeval violence that it sang past Roche as if it had come out of a gun. Roche dropped his racket in astonishment. Even Laver does not play that sort of shot often (that day, Laver hit some scorching winners against Cliff Drysdale, who had won their last two matches on grass and needed calling to order).

Newcombe broke Roche's resistance in a 26-game third set, but was beaten by Laver in one of the best men's finals for many years. They played a thoroughly professional match with the measured care of two business efficiency experts. Newcombe mixed his game artfully, teasing Laver with lobs and short angles. He seldom nourished Laver's insatiable appetite for speed. It was a bright and brave try, but it failed. Laver played some marvellous strokes, including two memorable forehand passing shots—the first delicately controlled when he had no right to be anywhere near the ball, the second a full-blooded drive off a full-blooded smash. It may be a long time before we see another champion of Laver's quality.

Virginia Wade and Pat Walkden reminded us of the terrible things the centre court can do to the nervous system. At first Miss Wade was all bouncing assurance, ribbons bobbing as she launched one fierce attack after another. But from 5–3 up in the first set she lost nine successive games and, shortly afterwards, the match. The cause was chiefly internal. The score became a gauge of nerve rather than skill. Both players were as jumpy as kittens on Bonfire Night. But Miss Walkden retained a greater capacity for keeping the ball in court.

Judy Tegart had another go at Billie Jean King and came within two points of beating her. Lesley Bowrey led 6–3 and 5–3 before Rosemary Casals wriggled off the hook. Somebody once said that Miss Casals had a bag full of jewels but did not know how to wear them. Her abundant talent has seldom been properly harnessed.

She won only 18 points from Mrs King in one of the shortest semi-finals on record: Miss Casals seemed mesmerized, as if mentally beaten before she went on court with her friend and mentor.

Nerve, will, maturity—all these count for a lot at Wimbledon.

Christine Janes led 2–0 against Margaret Court but did not win another game ('I kept looking at her across the net and she looked so fit, I thought: Crikey!'). Mrs Court was offered a much closer challenge by Julie Heldman. Behind the shrieks and the 'body talk', behind the flashing grin and the stooping gait, Miss Heldman has one of the most finely tuned tennis brains in the business. Mrs Court frustrated her but, sensationally, could not frustrate Ann Jones, who played the finest grass court match of her career. Mrs Jones lost the first set from 5–2 and 40–15 up, yet rebounded to win 10–12, 6–3, 6–2 in just over two hours. 'That's the best I've seen Ann play,' said Mrs Court. 'I thought she might crack after the first set. But she didn't. She worked me pretty hard.'

Mrs Jones was modest: 'If she plays well, there's not a lot I can do about it. She's the greatest player I've ever met. But not the greatest match player. On the very important occasions, she can tighten up. She stretched me so much that I don't think I had one easy shot in that first set. But I got used to her serve. And suddenly my short chips and my backhand cross-court began to go in, instead of missing.'

There was a mighty roar as a lob and a succeeding volley squeezed a last error from Mrs Court. There was another as the players left the court. Mrs Jones was a national heroine who had reached eight semi-finals and, now, her second final.

Inevitably, this turned out to be an emotional patriotic occasion, not least because Mrs Jones exemplified the qualities for which the British were once called the bulldog breed. On one of the loveliest of English days, a military band occupied a corner of the sunny centre court until the players came out with their brilliant bouquets. Mrs King was not opposing a tennis player: she was opposing the will and the aspirations of the United Kingdom. The royal family were present in strength.

The tension in that packed arena was almost tangible. The match was not as good as that with Mrs Court. But Mrs Jones won 3–6, 6–3, 6–2, which was all that really mattered. Mrs King played an imperious first set and had two points for a break to 2–0 in the second. But her service declined and she began to make the marginal errors born of anxiety. Mrs Jones raised her game, played some of her finest tennis, and was the firmer of the two in the crises. Mrs King lost the match with a double-fault and told us later: 'Ann is the most underrated player in the history of British tennis. The only thing is, all the great players have had one great stroke: but this isn't the case with Ann. It's her ability to manœuvre you about the court.'

So it was that, in Park Lane the following evening, two left-handers opened the Ball. They were both thirty years old.

Another left-hander, Roger Taylor, kept the Union Jack flying proudly in 1970. But on the first day (breezy but sunny, with the banked crowds sporting such gay plumage that we had to look hard to find the hydrangeas) the British troops took a hammering and mostly went down in straight sets. 'They're not taking any prisoners,' said Taylor, who himself had a lot of bother before beating Brian Fairlie. Taylor was inhibited by a back injury and while barging past Fairlie and Jaideep Mukerjea he nursed his service power. But he could withhold nothing from Charles Pasarell. Taylor was in there with another heavyweight, and with 14,000 people willing him on he was in no mood to pull any punches. He had to let his service go, and his back must take its chances. Taylor won 8–6, 17–15, 6–4. The tennis was brutal and the second set alone lasted 1 hour 36 minutes. Playing Pasarell is like that.

This parked Taylor in the last sixteen, which should obviously have been the end of the road because his next opponent was Rod Laver, a man he had never beaten. Laver had not been rebuffed at this stage of the tournament since 1958. He had played six finals and won four of them. He had won thirty-one successive singles matches at Wimbledon.

Taylor beat him 4–6, 6–4, 6–2, 6–1. It was the best result any British man had achieved at Wimbledon since the war, and one of the most astonishing in the history of the championships. The centre court crowd were rather pleased.

It was a thunderously thrilling scene—all over the premises. Thousands of people around other courts and on the promenade were watching Taylor's progress on the electric scoreboard and adding their lung-powered rapture to that of the multitude within. The noise was particularly distracting on court two, where Winnie

Shaw was beating Kerry Melville. 'It was a bit off-putting,' said Miss Shaw. 'Everybody kept cheering and cheering, and it obviously wasn't for us.' When Taylor won, the tumult was explosive, someone threw a coat in the air—and Miss Shaw double-faulted.

Wimbledon needed shaking up, and it happened that afternoon: all four men's singles and three of the eight women's singles confounded the seedings. But Taylor's *lèse-majesté* was all that seemed to matter.

Laver, unusually sharp when Wimbledon began, had probably reached his peak too soon. He was not at his best, especially when serving. But Taylor was. Agile, foxy and resourceful, he seldom offered Laver the ball at a pace and height the champion liked.

'We all imagine he's invincible,' said Taylor later. 'But he has the same frailties as the rest of us. I felt I kept him under a lot of pressure. All the little bits and pieces fell together. I'm starting to move well and play well. The fellows in the massage room have done a great job. I've been having treatment every day, and they've loosened me up a lot. But there's still a long way to go. It's almost disappointing—only being in the quarter-finals, after beating him.'

But Taylor beat Clark Graebner 6–3, 11–9, 12–10 to reach the seni-finals for the second time in four years. The stiffly muscular Graebner has a first service that seems designed to blast divots out of the turf. He is a hard man to break (unless he turns sulky and forgets to concentrate). Taylor needed two match points one day, and eight the next, before winning a grimly powerful exchange that raised Wagnerian echoes. Taylor emerged from the turbulence into the dangerously deceptive calm that surrounds a player who keeps coming back like a song—a man who is 5 ft 6½ in. tall, weighs 10 stones or less, takes a size 7½ in shoes, and answers to 'Muscles'.

Ken Rosewall had already been in the news. An unsung hero from Seattle, Tom Gorman, who is more Irish than many of the Irish, first caused a stir by nudging Cliff Drysdale into a temporary obscurity. Though he did not really need them, the little people were working for Gorman that day. His volleys and half-volleys clipped and surmounted the tape so often that he said later: 'Cliff couldn't believe it and neither could I. But that's the best I've ever played.' Gorman then made his centre court début. He took the third set from Rosewall and, at 5–4, served for the fourth. He lost that game to love. 'Four quick points in about twenty-five seconds,' said Gorman. 'I guess it's the difference between the really great players and the others.'

Rosewall beat Tony Roche 10–8, 6–1, 4–6, 6–2. These are players of touch, flair and imagination. Their first set, the finest of the championships, had a marvellous beauty. They spread gorgeous patterns the length and width of the court. They played cat and mouse. If they had as much fun as the rest of us, they had the time of their lives. When Roche was serving for the first set at 5–4, Rosewall played an unbelievably great game. Having taken the set, Rosewall won seven games in a row ('I don't think I missed a ball'). His form throughout the match stamped him as part magician, part ordinary mortal, and all tennis player. Towards the end, someone rummaged among the recesses of his memory and murmured: 'I haven't seen a backhand like that since . . . since . . . since Rosewall.'

'That,' observed Rosewall, 'is as good as I can play.'

He then beat Taylor to reach his first Wimbledon singles final since Lew Hoad defeated him in 1956. For the public, there could be no loser—because a national hero was on one side of the net, a sentimental favourite on the other.

The court was worn, rough, and powdery. ('It's playing a little slower,' said Rosewall, 'which has helped my style of game a bit.') A gusty wind tossed the ball about, sometimes in clouds of dust, to a rattling accompaniment from the billowing awning over the royal box. Again we admired the quickness that enables Rosewall to create the time for a proper stroke when returning service, whereas others can often do no more than block the ball back into play. Again we admired that lambent cross-court backhand, a shot that eventually gave Rosewall a place in history as the first man to play two Wimbledon singles finals sixteen years apart. At thirty-five, he was the oldest finalist since the thirty-seven-year-old Bill Tilden in 1930.

'It's always a let-down, losing,' said Taylor later. 'I'm sitting here trying to pretend it doesn't hurt. But it hurts a lot. Yet there were 128 fellows in the tournament. I was struggling in the first round and could have gone. Who thought I'd get to the semi-finals again? I didn't. So from that point of view it's been a great Wimbledon.'

One morning that hearty and wise coach, Vic Edwards, gave

Bob Hewitt some advice about his service and backhand. Hewitt then beat Tom Okker in straight sets. Hewitt was assured and re-sourceful. But straight sets! We had come to know Okker as The Flying Dutchman; but the breeze had gone out of his sails. For the cause, we could only put his slender physique in the context of his rigorous schedule of tennis and travel. He looked like a sprinter in a stayers' race. Hewitt later recovered from two sets down to beat Bob Lutz. But he could not win a set from Bob Carmichael.

Bob who?

Carmichael. He is a Victorian who lives in Paris and is known in the trade as 'Nails' because he is a hard man and was formerly a carpenter ('I used to get up at six and work, out in the hot sun, lugging timber about'). He lost only five games to Zeljko Franu-lovic, the gentle Dalmatian, who is an expert on clay but never fancies his chances on grass. Then Carmichael stopped Hewitt.

Carmichael is an honest workman and a self-made tennis player. He had some discouraging experiences in his first few seasons on the circuit. 'But even in the couple of years when I wasn't making any money, I was still living well—staying in good hotels, with all expenses paid. I thought: This can't be too bad—it beats carpentry. I've had to work hard, because the game does not really come easy to me. I've got to concentrate like the dickens and try my guts out. Some days it doesn't work and I might as well play with a cricket bat. But I was happy with the way I played today.'

Against Andres Gimeno, it didn't work.

Fred Tupper, of PanAm and the *New York Times*, epigramma-tized a wet and windy day, grey in every way, with his drawled: 'Riessen's playing Scott. . . . Things like that are happening all the time.' But there was also a golden day that began with a buzz of expectancy, a tingling feeling that we were down to serious business at last. John Newcombe served seventeen aces that afternoon against Owen Davidson, who may have reflected that with a friend like Newcombe he had no need of enemies. Newcombe then came from behind to beat the mettlesome Roy Emerson 6–1, 5–7, 3–6, 6–2, 11–9 in a combat so consistently fierce that Emerson dislodged a trouser button and had to borrow a safety pin from a spectator.

Newcombe's tennis ambitions had been stirred seventeen years earlier when he listened to a broadcast of a Davis Cup challenge round in which Ken Rosewall was playing. Now he beat Rosewall in the first five-set final since 1949. Basically it was a question of Newcombe's service—his second was admirably reliable—and forehand volley against the teasing versatility of Rosewall's returns. Newcombe won because he played the big points better. Yet the match had a rum wobble to it. Rosewall was down 7–5, 3–6, 2–6, 1–3, and love–30. But he won twelve successive points and five successive games. That strange centre court affliction, let us call it 'Newcoma', had struck again.

'I lost concentration completely and went into a bit of a daze,' said Newcombe. 'If I hadn't had the experience of being in the final before, I might have lost. The crowd maybe upset me. They were a little over-sympathetic to Ken. I thought: What have I done? Why do you hate me?'

Soon after Wimbledon there was a tournament in a public park at Hoylake on the Wirral peninsula, where the wind roars in from the Irish Sea to keep tennis players honest. It is one of those remote corners of England that no one ever goes to by accident. But it achieved stature in tennis because a quiet visionary called Alan Morris did for Hoylake what Bill Riordan did for Salisbury, Maryland. While playing at Hoylake, Newcombe was interviewed on a local radio programme. He dedicated a record to all the people who were on his side at Wimbledon: 'There weren't too many of them.' The memory rankled.

But the Wimbledon crowd had nothing against Newcombe. They simply had a special affection for Rosewall, an affection enhanced by their natural support for an underdog who had never won the championship and was running out of time. So Rosewall won sympathy—but Newcombe won the championship. Newcombe and Roche then took the doubles for the fourth time and the third year in succession, a feat unparalleled since the days of the brothers Laurie and Reggie Doherty at the turn of the century.

The eighth seed in the women's event was Helga Niessen, who had not played a tournament on grass since she lost to Helen Gourlay in the second round two years earlier. The Thursday before this 1970 Wimbledon, she wandered into Queen's Club during a tournament most players use to adjust their games to grass, though they do not take many risks with their muscles. Miss Niessen, who was not competing, was turned off a practice court after ten minutes. So she gently loped twice round a court on a miniature training run, and then did three press-ups. Deciding that enough was enough, she went for a shower. Miss Niessen is thrifty with her ergs. Next day she had half an hour's practice at Wimbledon. Amid all the frenzied and fanatical preparation for the big event, all the nervous hustle and bustle, she then strolled nonchalantly into Queen's Club sucking an ice cream. Watching Rod Laver in full flow against Cliff Richey, she observed with cool detachment: 'Perhaps tomorrow we practise.'

Would that there were more like her. I have never come across a swimming pool in the Sahara. But to meet Miss Niessen three days before Wimbledon is a reasonable analogy.

In retrospect, the mobilization of her physical and mental resources was adequate if not excessively rigorous. She showed Wimbledon something new in the way of style and character, especially on the day Margaret Court beat her 6–8, 6–0, 6–0.

Mrs Court had beaten Miss Niessen in the final of the French championship—on clay, which is Miss Niessen's métier. So there seemed no logical grounds for expecting that they would have much of a match on grass, which is Mrs Court's métier. But Miss Niessen rose to the challenge of her first match on the centre court. For a long time she volleyed more often, and far better, than we (or she) had believed possible. She demonstrated her powers of anticipation, her capacity to use the length and width of the court, and her fluent ease on the backhand. Through it all, she remained thoroughly and inimitably feminine. Her elegant languor suggested that she felt it improper even to appear to hurry. She was the coolest, most composed competitor left. The closest she came to showing emotion was that characteristic flick of the skirt after a tough point had gone the other way. Between rallies, she rested hand on hip and took up a cross-legged stance as if arrested in the middle of a *pas-de-deux*. Her personality alone dominates many opponents. It did not dominate Mrs Court; but it worried her. Unbreakable assurance always worries the fretful: and for a set, Mrs Court was fretful.

The forty-one-minute first set cost Mrs Court as many games as her three previous matches. The umpire once told the crowd: 'Please keep quiet during the rallies.' But she romped through the next two sets in thirty-one minutes. Wonderfully athletic and aggressive, Mrs Court punched winners in all directions and maintained a pace and pressure Miss Niessen could not withstand. The only anxiety for Mrs Court was her left ankle. She hurt it in the thirteenth game while stretching wide on the forehand. Later she put on an elastic bandage.

Miss Niessen said she was tired after the first set: 'Because I run too much to the net, I think. On clay, I never run to the net after each service.' She confessed that she was so surprised to win the first set that she may have been suffering from shock for the rest of the match. Tongue still tucked firmly in her cheek, she added that in future she intended to double her competitive programme on grass—a tournament every year, instead of every two years. 'I like to play on grass. But in Germany there are no grass courts.'

Mrs Court scratched from both doubles events. She had the ankle strapped. She had pain-killing injections. She beat Rosemary Casals 6–4, 6–1.

'The doctor said I wouldn't feel anything. I didn't. Half my leg was numb. The injury slowed me down a bit, which is good. I've been rushing a lot, lately. Today I played better than at any time in the whole tournament. I had nothing to lose. So I had a go.'

The mind plays strange tricks on us. It could be that Mrs Court's nothing-to-lose attitude, her ankle, and the need to tread more carefully than usual all combined to thrust aside the nervous tension that had sometimes afflicted her at Wimbledon. She played beautifully, never more so than in using the lob to exploit the tiny Californian's tendency to crowd the net.

'I was conscious of her trying to finish the match as quickly as possible,' said Miss Casals. 'But that's Marge. You have to make sure you put the ball away and don't give her a second chance. She's got the arms. . . .'

Until that afternoon, Miss Casals had been flitting about the courts like a bird on the wing and had not lost a set. At the opposite end of the draw another Californian, a girl who is crazy about horses, was causing a stir at her first Wimbledon. 'The atmosphere makes you wanta play,' said the powerful Sharon Walsh, United States junior champion. 'I wanta do well here more than any place else.' She beat Patti Hogan and Helen Gourlay in straight sets, which is not a respectful thing to do when you are only eighteen and fresh out of San Rafael. She led Françoise Durr 5–4 and 40–love. Then she woke up from the dream: 'All of a sudden I realized where I was.

I got nervous. Court one was a bit scary. I'd never played before a crowd that big. Plus the fact that she came up with some great shots.'

Miss Durr became the first French player to reach the last four since the war. Billie Jean King beat her 6–3, 7–5. But Miss Durr was so effectively unorthodox that the watching coaches must have been apprehensive: if she does too well too often, she could put them out of business. The important thing is where Miss Durr puts the ball, not how she does it. She never stops thinking, she thinks quickly, and her game is packed with teasing questions for her opponents. She also shows us the Gallic trimmings—the ribbons, the decorated skirt, the stamping and shrieking and snarling, and the expressive 'body-talk' (she can make even Julie Heldman seem inhibited) as she wills the ball onto the course she has chosen for it. Miss Durr is kind, too. It is doubtful if anyone in big tennis inspires more affection.

That day she was on court with another extrovert. In her early years Mrs King was one of the all-time court chatterers. She still handles her press conferences with a fluently articulate good sense most players would envy. On court, she has learned to keep her beans in the can, to mutter to herself rather than thinking aloud. She is a superb player, with a memorable facility for swooping on the low volley and kidding us that it is an easy shot. She has an assured touch on the lob. But we shall remember her best for the services and backhands that create her openings, for her twinkling footwork, and for the volleys and smashes with which she punches her chances home. To all this she adds the sharp wits of a grimly unyielding competitor with a true champion's capacity for playing her best tennis in a crisis. Like some portrait hanging on the wall, she has been around for so long that we tend to take her for granted. Instead, we should be grateful that the Kings and the Courts are still with us.

Mrs King played the big points better than Miss Durr. She made the forecourt game look child's play. She was cool. She was calm. She collected. And she joined Mrs Court in one of the greatest women's matches ever played.

Mrs Court was in the running for the Grand Slam and therefore had more at stake. The effect of her ankle injury on her mobility and mental approach were incalculable. Again she had the ankle strapped and took pain-killing injections ('I would have stayed there until I'd fallen over'). For her part, Mrs King knew that she would soon need an operation on her right knee. Ailing and anxious, these two women went out and played powerfully majestic tennis—the right stuff for a King and a Court to offer a crowd including three princesses and the Prime Minister.

Mrs Court won 14-12, 11-9 in 2 hours 27 minutes. It was the longest women's singles final in the history of the championships. The first set was the longest played by either sex in a Wimbledon final. The match had a thrilling beauty that chilled the blood and, in retrospect, still chills the blood. Here were two wonderfully gifted players at their best, or so close to it that the margin was irrelevant. Theirs was a marvellous blend of athleticism and skill, courage and concentration, experience and wit. They moved each other about with remorseless haste. The match was punctuated by rallies of vivid enchantment, but the bright colours were never meretricious. Every stroke, every tactical shift, was neatly tailored to the need of the moment. This was thoroughly professional tennis, the best the women's game could provide.

There is a temptation to look for a flaw in the texture of all great deeds—sporting, literary, artistic, or what you will. To succumb to that temptation for a moment, the only thing this match lacked was a sharp contrast in style. It had everything else in abundance. It was so good that it challenged belief. It still does.

The last crisis came when Mrs King was 6-7 down in the second set. Desperate, she tried a gambler's throw: a spate of backhand drop shots. These were designed (at considerable risk to the designer) to finish the rallies quickly. They cruelly taxed Mrs Court's mobility and thus asked the only question that remained on the examination paper—could she take the punishment? She could. This crucial question-and-answer routine must have told both players all they needed to know. Mrs King fought on, still challenging an authority that had always been precarious. She saved five match points before losing a contest that, in the enduring beauty of its flashing steel, will live long in the memory.

By a happy coincidence of names, Princess Margaret presented the trophy.

Mrs Court had never been seeded lower than second at Wimbledon. Her unique tally of singles championships included three Wimbledon, four French, four American, three Italian, three South

African, ten Australian, and three German. Hers was an extra-ordinarily consistent record on all surfaces. She was a great player—I say 'was' because she has passed her best and has no new ambitions to inspire her. This was all the more remarkable because she was the first Australian woman to reach the summit. She had no one's shoulders to climb on—but she climbed to the top.

All else was subservient to tennis. Like all Australians, she enjoys a beer. She knows when and how to relax. She is the kind who enjoys a party but would rather not be the centre of it. Because she has never lost the modesty and reserve with which she emerged from Albury. Forthright and independent, with an iron will, she is a paradox—a loner with many friends. To these her loyalty is firm but never effusive.

As a player, she is a professional in the best Australian tradition. She does the best job she can. If it is not good enough, she loses with grace—and learns from her defeat. She behaves well because she is a champion by nature, which is to say that her personal pride, and her sense of responsibility to the game, are not restricted to the function of clobbering tennis balls. There are plenty more Australians—for example, Rod Laver and Ken Rosewall (both smaller than Mrs Court) and that extrovert trio, Roy Emerson, John Newcombe and Tony Roche—who mirror similar qualities every time they step on court.

The basis of Mrs Court's excellence, and Emerson's too, is a highly trained athleticism and a studied aggression. She has height and strength, mobility and agility. To be granted such gifts is one thing; to use them wisely is another. Given her physical resources, plus her courage in adversity, her supremacy also demanded dedication and an enormous capacity for work. No one trained and practised harder. No one tried harder. No one achieved as much. Because she always set herself the highest standards, she pushed her remarkable talent to its limit. That limit was her 1970 Grand Slam.

The 1971 tournament was a landmark in the history of the championships because Laver, Rosewall, Mrs Court and Mrs King—who between them had graced Wimbledon singles finals twenty times—were all beaten in straight sets. Three Americans, Stan Smith, Cliff Richey and Tom Gorman, pushed their names forward for future reference: all were born in 1946 and had therefore reached

an age when youth and experience combine to lift a man to his peak
as a tennis player. John Newcombe, a relatively wise old fox of
twenty-seven, precariously defied the challenge of young America
and became champion for the third time in five years. In the
women's event a fresh flower, Evonne Goolagong, burst into
bloom. Her bursting promise was swiftly fulfilled: on her second
overseas tour she became 'world champion' on clay, in Paris, and
on grass, at Wimbledon. Billie Jean King and Rosemary Casals,
who play like a couple of jumping beans, won the doubles for the
fourth time in five years.

Another feature of the 1971 tournament was an experiment with
the tie-break. It was so seldom important as to be almost irrelevant.
But the limited influence it did have was healthy. It abbreviated
the monotony of some service-and-volley exchanges, kept matches
within a reasonable time limit, and added a little artificially dramatic
garnish to the dish. In short, it did some good and no harm.

On the first day, the party was slow warming up. But by tea
time it was swinging. Tom Gorman beat Cliff Drysdale again,
though Drysdale had a match point which Gorman saved with a
volley considerably less than masterful in the manner of its playing.
They were on court a long while, which the ladies appreciated. The
gentle Andres Gimeno, who strokes the ball with the stylish flourish
we expect from a bullfighting breed, is a high man whose back
seems to have been starched. But his resistance was softened by the
deceptively languid John Paish, who plays in glasses and always
looks sleepy. From 1947 to 1955 Tony Mottram and Geoff Paish
were the heart of Britain's Davis Cup team. Now their sons,
'Buster' and John, are shaking off the paternal shadows and making
reputations of their own.

The other talking point on opening day was that Charles Pasarell
became the first man since Manuel Santana, in 1963, to beat Tony
Roche in round one. Roche was having a bad year and was hurt in
most of the places where tennis players like to feel particularly
robust. That plastic face, as rugged as a map of Australia, did not
tell us much about how the man felt. But the empirical errors were
obvious. Four months later he had an operation to repair a pinched
nerve in his elbow, which had bothered him since 1967.

Pasarell has a habit of walking tall at Wimbledon. We have
already noticed that in build and looks, gait and manner, he is like

one of those characters in Westerns who stroll up to a bar, tip their hats over their eyes, and regard monosyllables as the reasonable limit of conversation. His tennis, too, is staccato, laconic and entirely to the point. Hit or miss, he shoots to kill. He was too sharp for the ailing strong man from Tarcutta. But he was not sharp enough for Adriano Panatta, the rising young giant of Italian tennis.

Jan Kodes, Ilie Nastase and Zeljko Franulovic, the triumvirate of East European professionals who dominate the clay courts of the Continent, were swept to obscurity in two days. They won only six sets between them. Nastase was taken to five sets by Ray Keldie, a handsome man heavily disguised by a lot of hair, and was then beaten in straight sets by the nimble little Georges Goven, who tries hard to refute the irrefutable fact that no man can be omnipresent. Nastase gave the impression that he thought talent alone should suffice for his purpose.

The champion of 1952, Frank Sedgman, subdued the hard young ambition of Robert Maud over five sets strongly flavoured with nostalgia. Sedgman always seemed to be grinning, even when he was not (he grits his teeth a lot). As worn and weather-beaten as the veteran of a hundred gunfights, he still had the heart of a young man—a spirit of adventure that prompted him to volley past the incoming volleyer. His game was immaculately conceived, if some-times imperfectly executed because of ageing limbs. His backhand, his low volleys and his half-volleys were played with charming assurance. He won the match with a low forehand stop volley of such beauty that it almost stopped the blood. The clock said 4.18. The sun was shining. The world was kind.

Jaroslav Drobny had been looking on from the players' balcony. Sedgman, sipping a drink during a change-over, had glanced up at the centre court scoreboard to see how Ricardo Gonzales was getting on. It was like a reunion in Valhalla.

Gonzales was beaten in five sets by Pierre Barthes, who had temporarily lost his singles place in the French Davis Cup team and therefore had a message for France and for the world. He delivered it with aristocratic élan. But Gonzales, a man for all seasons, showed us some warming glimpses of bygone summers before the wintry greyness of defeat was forced upon him. Lew Hoad considers Gonzales the greatest player he ever met: 'It didn't matter where you played, what time you played. It didn't matter whether there were no lines on the court, no lights. Gonzales went out there—and that was his life. He always gave 100 per cent effort and no less.'

Bob Lutz survived two match points in his fifth set with the lanky Frank Froehling. These two look interesting; Lutz because of his solemn serenity (he is a camouflaged swinger) and Froehling because he covers a lot of court even when standing still and just waving his arms about. Lutz won because he was good and lucky, which is better than being either. He saved one match point with a flicked half-volley lob that soared over Froehling like a bird—and birds start thinking about oxygen when they fly high enough to exceed Froehling's reach. When that shot landed in court, Lutz must have questioned Thomas Tusser's maxim that Christmas comes but once a year. On Froehling's second match point, Lutz served an ace with his second ball. Both must have known then that the gods who govern these things had already written the result in the programme.

Lutz did not last long. Roy Emerson beat him in a match that contained three tie-breaks. Thus they temporarily upstaged Marty Riessen. Whatever else is happening, at any tournament anywhere, Riessen always seems to be playing a tie-break with somebody. At Wimbledon he played five of them in four matches. On the way this fine sportsman—a hustler who always gives maximum effort—beat Arthur Ashe, which was big news back in Illinois.

Before the tournament, Ashe spoke for everyone when he said: 'If Laver's in good shape, God help us all.' Only Ray Moore managed to take a set from Laver in his first three matches. Laver reached the last sixteen by bursting past the gloomy and intimidating Clark Graebner, whose game is all calculated violence. Graebner moves as if he had been manufactured rather than born. When he walks about between points, you feel that if there was a wall in front of him, he would go through it without even blinking. He is the sort of chap Jack found at the top of the beanstalk. But the waspish Laver reminded us that even a large man like Graebner has to leave a lot of the court uninhabited.

Laver then beat Tom Okker. This was not a great performance; but it contained enough of the stuff of greatness to stir apprehension in Laver's remaining rivals. Okker's backgammon buddy, Riessen, talks well about Laver: 'He doesn't stand out. Just to look at him walking around, you wouldn't think he was the world champion.

His stature isn't something that you expect—like a Gonzales or a Hoad. His personality seems shy, almost retiring, off the court. But it's as if he goes into a telephone booth or something, and changes. On court, he's aggressive. What impresses me is his quickness. This speed is why he handles almost everyone. Speed enables him to make the recovery when he's in trouble. The thing I learned from playing Laver is how consistent one can be with power. It's amazing how he can keep hitting with such accuracy. He combines everything. There are a lot of good competitors. But he's fantastic. Yet such a big change of personality—when a lot of players play the same as they act.'

When Laver played Okker that day, we noticed anew the lazily self-conscious walk, the blurred lightning of reflexes, footwork and control of the racket head. He swung hard and fast at almost everything. His co-ordination of eye and hand, his timing, his wrist action, were astonishing. Again he showed us the running forehands clouted from under the noses of front-row spectators, the startling whip of that cross-court backhand, the capacity to hit offensive shots when logic suggested defensive thinking. He was in a playfully good humour, too, as his hair tossed about amid the swirling breezes of the centre court. Okker was an admirable foil in this restlessly adventurous match. They continually stepped with dainty tread on the frontier between the brave and the reckless. Adversity eventually lent wings to Okker's assurance. But when it mattered most, he was a man trying to snatch sunbeams out of the air. Laver's efficiency level looked about 80 per cent: and he gave the impression he could draw the other 20 per cent out of the bank any time he needed it.

Tom Gorman beat him 9–7, 8–6, 6–3. The last player to beat Laver in straight sets at Wimbledon was Alex Olmedo in 1959.

One of many handsome economics graduates in big tennis, Gorman made a late start. His first tournament in Britain, and his first experience of loose-top courts, was at Guildford in 1969, when he was twenty-three. He was beaten by Stephen Warboys, aged fifteen. Shortly afterwards Istvan Gulyas and the clay courts of Paris taught him things he had never even suspected about tennis. Looking over my shoulder while watching another match, I saw Gorman turn his back on the court, take the stop netting in a simian-like grasp, and give the world a stare of glassy-eyed horror, as if to say: 'This is unbelievable. Open the cage!' During the 1970 Dewar Cup tournament at the Albert Hall, he again retreated to the stop netting after a crucial rally in a tight match, and asked the spectators: 'Did the Beatles really play here?'

One of America's most personable ambassadors, Gorman moves fast and plays the game that suits his nature—snappy and stylish, without being flashy. Before beating Laver, he discussed with Dennis Ralston ('probably one of the best students of other players' games') the way to set about it. Ralston had beaten Laver at Forest Hills ten months earlier, and now preached what he had practised. Gorman played it cool. He denied Laver the hot pace on which the man thrives ('He plays so well off other people's power that it gets discouraging'). He mixed his services well, volleyed like a dream, and had only four break points against him. He tested Laver's composure by volleying against the incoming volleyer, or by standing a yard or more inside the baseline to threaten Laver's second service. In the third set Gorman's temperament was impressive. Laver hit two typically flamboyant shots—a forehand down one line, a backhand down the other—and had break points in two games. For a few minutes, the balance of the match teetered. Gorman was impressed. But he was not intimidated. He held his curly head high and went back to work as though nothing had happened. A net cord gave him a decisive break to 4–2; without fuss, he confidently finished the job.

'I needed a taxi to get to the short volleys today,' said Laver. 'The trouble was, I didn't have a taxi.'

In the dressing room, Gorman's back was so stiff that he needed help taking off his socks. The weakness dates from a football match in 1964 ('I was trying to make a sensational catch, and fell in a hole'). That ailing back, abused by his endeavours against Laver, did not permit him to play his best tennis against Stan Smith. Gorman had a look of brave fragility. He was beaten in straight sets: then Smith stepped over the net and put a massive arm round a friend for whom he felt a lot of sympathy.

But the excitement did not wait upon Gorman and Laver. There comes a time in the course of every great tournament when the smouldering ashes of drama are sparked into flame. This does something startling to the pulse rate. It turns the small arena of a tennis court into a microcosm of life, with all its hopes and frustrations, all its agonies and ecstasies. It happened on the third day of that 1971 Wimbledon. Before a centre court crowd whose emotions were thrilled and bludgeoned in turn, Cliff Richey and Roger Taylor played for 2 hours 45 minutes before the referee rang down the curtain of twilight. In terms of Richey, the score stood at 6–2, 3–6, 6–4, 7–7.

Again Taylor carried the hope of a nation. Mike Coward, the best baritone to graduate from Adelaide to the Wimbledon press box ('After a few whiskies and dry, I can cover about three and a half octaves under extreme pressure'), watched him thoughtfully and observed: 'I like Taylor. He typifies the north of England. A gutsy, gritty player.'

This was a spectacular match with a sharp intensity of thrust and counter-thrust. Both men chased everything. Neither gave an inch. If they had known that the winner would be the only one to come out alive, they could not have tried harder. In addition to the strong meat it served as a main course, the match was flavoured with theatrical side dishes. When Richey was foot-faulted, he made as if to serve from a yard behind the baseline and then went through the motions again while standing in front of it. The cheeky implication of 'Where do you want me?' produced a slow handclap. Richey dropped his racket and joined in—then raised his hands as if conducting a choir. For a while after that, it seemed that the match was Richey against the world (a fixture he had often played before). In the fourth set Taylor had his chance: two break points for a 5–4 lead. But he lost the set with a double-fault. Whereupon Taylor appealed against the light and put on his sweater. While the appeal was being considered, the ball of fire called Richey practised services, bounced up and down for a while, and then went for a jog-trot around the court, with the startled crowd roaring him on as if he were an Olympic champion doing a lap of honour.

They played on until play was suspended at 7–all. In the darkness of the deserted stadium the mind's eye retained its moving pictures: Taylor swooping about the court like a human cannon-ball, and Richey running and jumping like a clockwork toy that had gone out of control. Next day, it quickly became apparent that whereas Richey's game was still at boiling point (it always is), Taylor's was not. Richey wrapped it up at 11–9 when a backhand service return induced Taylor to put a low volley into the net.

Richey against Adriano Panatta was American hustle against the stylish languor of Italy—the throbbing insistence of pop music drowning the soft strains of some Roman ballad played on a mandolin. Richey kept belting it out: the next man to fall was a long-haired musician called Jeff Borowiak. But Richey had now moved into Ken Rosewall's sphere of influence. Rosewall had been taken to five sets by Bob Carmichael, whose massive shoulders somehow seem to govern his every movement. Carmichael is a worried, self-critical perfectionist who continually pushes his talents to their limit in the hope that he can rearrange the boundaries. But he could not get past Rosewall.

The stage was set for the only great match of the tournament. Rosewall, who played at Wimbledon when Richey was five years old, conceded twelve years and a two sets' start and beat him 6-8, 5-7, 6-4, 9-7, 7-5 in 3 hours 58 minutes. Had this match been written as fiction, we would have thought it far-fetched. It began at 3.30. After ninety-four minutes Rosewall was two sets down and looked sad and tired—not in his limbs, but in his spirit. He had his back to the wall for so long that he seemed glued to it. Through all the frustration and fatigue, he fought on when everything in him—except some small, secret voice—must have told him he was done for. At 7.15 he had the first of five match points. At 7.28 he won: with a backhand down the line played so calmly that this might have been a practice match. Richey climbed wearily over the net to shake his hand. Two huge crowds roared ovations: the crowd inside, and that other crowd, watching the flickering digits of the electric scoreboard on the promenade. Those ovations rang and rang through the twilight of Wimbledon.

'I was happy for him, in an ironic and weird sort of way,' said Richey. He patted Rosewall on the head. He waved him off court first.

Richey was the first to break service in every set except the last. In the fourth he served for the match at 7-6. Rosewall responded with three glorious games. Richey was foot-faulted eleven times: 'That made me tentative. I hung back. My biggest mistake was not to attack enough at 7-6. I wanted to get in, and didn't.' Rosewall's volleying, previously unrecognizable, was now sweetly in tune. His racket was singing, his whole game was in harmony. But in the fifth set he had to survive seven break points (and was balked at four match points on 5–4) in a run of six successive deuce games. Every-one knew then that this was the match of the tournament.

That is a glimpse of the skeleton, the bare statistical design. But how to dress it with greatness of character? Here were the boxer and the fighter, the artist and the craftsman, the old matador and the young bull. The one was coolly surgical, the other hotly combative. Yet in the sharpness of contrast they were as one: quick little men with good ground strokes, a taste for lobs, and unyielding deter-mination. They hit drives like bullets and lobs that had a precise and delicate beauty. The patterns they wove covered the length and breadth of the court. They explored the angles with a subtle delight in the game's aesthetic possibilities. They used bluff and double-bluff. At times they drew each other to and fro like puppets. In these exchanges Rosewall was usually the puppet master. Yet his technique was often inconsistent. His volleys flew all over the place. His head sagged. The restless yet deliberate Richey was sounder. Yet we noticed how much he depended on his first service, how confidently Rosewall attacked his second, and how vulnerable Richey was to the arrow-thrust of a cross-court backhand. Richey's authority was precarious. All the time we felt the match trembling in the balance. Rosewall, desperately, was trying to fit together the wayward pieces of his game. Could he do it in time?

We know the answer now. But that afternoon all was taut un-certainty as one thrilling rally succeeded another. Richey reminded us that he will work until he drops—and then get up and work some more. Poker-faced and pale-eyed, he kept glancing up at his wife Mickey and his sister Nancy, to remind himself that there was kindness beyond the pain. But gradually, marvellously, we saw the magic settle on Rosewall. It says much for Richey's courage that, even then, we could not be sure of the result—until Rosewall, on his fifth match point, created an opening and carefully threaded his last needle of the day.

Technically this was not one of Rosewall's best performances ('I kept telling myself I could only get better'). But in all the essential qualities, which are to be found in a man's heart, it was one of his greatest. 'It's the closest match I've had here and I don't think I've won too many, anywhere, from two sets down. We both put in a few miles. It was probably as good a match as you can see.'

The last eight included a former customs immigration officer at

Sydney airport, Colin Dibley, who used to watch the stars go by and dream of going with them. He made his first overseas tour in 1970 and, on the strength of a £230 profit and the encouragement of Rosewall and Fred Stolle, gave up his job. Dibley is a big fellow with an erratic but explosive service that plays havoc with prevailing air currents. They say in the trade that a man is as good as his second service: and Dibley's can be good. He came back from two sets down to beat Dennis Ralston. In the last eight he played John Newcombe. Both hit hard. It was just as well that they were usually twenty-six yards apart. But for the intervening obstacles, their services would have endangered Channel shipping and the wild life of Norfolk.

Newcombe has supreme confidence in his strength, sense and skill. If he ever has doubts, he keeps them to himself. His drooping moustache suggests he has been to places most of us would rather avoid. He has the kind of face that emerges victoriously through smoke and dust and a sudden flutter of flags at the end of those battle films, while the credits roll and disembodied choirs surge into patriotic song. He kept puffing out his chest, showing his teeth and looking fierce. To pass the time between Dibley's double-faults, he wiped his brow and rearranged his muscles. It was all too much for Dibley. In his first full season on the circuit, here he was playing the Wimbledon champion on the centre court. He had the bemused air of some part-time footballer who suddenly finds himself marking George Best at Wembley, and cannot understand how it happened.

Newcombe barged Rosewall aside by the bruising margin of 6-1, 6-1, 6-3 in a semi-final. Rosewall did not play badly. But he was seldom allowed to play at all. Tennis is impossible when the other fellow does not give you time to get to the ball. Newcombe played as if his whole life had been dedicated to the single aim of winning this particular match as fast as possible. He grunted with effort as racket met ball with an impact that was instantly dismissive. The ball thudded into patches of the earth's surface that Rosewall had no hope of occupying in time. Poor Rosewall swayed in the draught as the shots sang past him. He had to play fine shots merely to stay in the rallies, never mind winning them. There was no question of sparring for an opening. Whenever the ball came within Rosewall's reach, he had to go for a winner. Newcombe showed us strength with finesse, power with polish. We could see the sense shining through. He said later: 'I played as well as I've ever played in a match of this importance.'

By this time the only other player around was Stan Smith, who had an easy run to the final and made the most of it. In six matches he lost one set—to Roy Emerson (the same Emerson who was Australian and French champion in 1963, the year Smith was turned down as a Davis Cup ball boy because he was considered awkward). Smith turned up at that 1971 Wimbledon as a private, first class, in the United States Army. But he looked more like a colonel. He had a military moustache, an erect bearing, and rose 6 ft 4 in. through the gases that surround the earth's crust. He was an awful lot of soldier.

Smith holds a racket as if it were a toothpick. He seems to hit his service from just in front of the gutter—the one on the roof of the stand. Lobbing him is like trying to toss buns over a lighthouse. When he gets off the ground you feel that the next time his feet touch anything solid, another lunar landing will be recorded. When he goes to the net, getting the ball past or over him is like trying to perforate a wall with a pea-shooter. This huge threat to the resilience of tennis balls plays with violently sound sense. Even when his big game is working well, he has the humility to work hard when it seems a good idea to do some scrambling. He moves well for his size (as with an elephant on its hind legs at a circus, the remarkable thing is not that it should be done well, but that it should be done at all). Smith has made himself a fine tennis player in the Newcombe mould, with a capacity to thrill if not enchant, to earn respect if not lyrical praise. He has the equable temperament, the qualities of character, that stamp him as a champion.

Newcombe needed all his skill and competitive experience to win 6–3, 5–7, 2–6, 6–4, 6–4. He began well. Smith could never be sure what would happen next, except that it would happen fast and he would not enjoy it. But Smith won the second set and, from 0–2 down in the third, took seven successive games. His tennis moved up a gear. Newcombe's looked vulnerable. 'At the beginning of the fourth I had a small feeling of being a loser,' Newcombe said later. 'I was a bit shaken up. I felt I had gone, mentally. Stan picked up his game extremely well and I started to drop my shots shorter. One gets a little tentative.'

Newcombe felt the chill of adversity upon him, but worked his way out of trouble and back into his best form like the great competitor he is. Both men punished anything loose, so both had to concentrate 100 per cent. The crux came in the fifth set when Newcombe broke service to 3–2 as Smith played a loose game that included two double-faults. Smith double-faulting is like someone using a sledgehammer to kill an ant—and missing. But he had to gamble with his second service. In the next game Newcombe was 30–40 down but saved himself with a service and a forehand volley. After that, the last few pieces of his vivid jigsaw were quickly put together.

The moustaches on these big and brawny men seemed utterly irrelevant as evidence of virility. I would choose neither to play for my pleasure, but either to play for my life. The final was an exemplary display of grass court tennis, which is to say that as a spectacle it was admirably boring. It would be unreasonable to expect charm and the subtlety of the chessboard from a men's final at Wimbledon. The prerequisites are strength, fitness, reflexes, a marriage of power and precision, and sufficient imagination to put forks in the lightning. Newcombe and Smith supplied all this. But one grass court specialist is enough for any match, and here we had two. So the spice of contrast was missing. At times it was so quiet you could hear a bird singing.

In the women's event Kerry Melville beat Rosemary Casals (who had won both their previous Wimbledon matches) and then reached the last eight for the first time by defeating Mary Ann Eisel. This match was an attractive advertisement for the women's game: both players gave the ball a healthy crack yet looked smartly feminine while they were doing it. Winnie Shaw reached the last eight unseeded for the second successive year. Wind made the ball wobble about in the oddest way during her touch-and-go win over Lesley Bowrey.

Much of Judy Dalton's 9–8, 6–3 win over Virginia Wade was contested before a crowd as sympathetically subdued as visitors in a sick room. In the first set both players were overwhelmed by nervous tension (as they had been when playing a Federation Cup match at Freiburg, in the Black Forest, the previous year). But once Mrs Dalton had won the tie-break, she came to terms with the enemy within. Miss Wade never did. Which meant that only once in five years had she justified her Wimbledon seeding. Her compatriot Ann Jones, in the book *A Game to Love*, came as close as anyone to diagnosing the cause: 'Wimbledon was a difficult place for me to play. Being English and having the support of the crowd and the television viewers should have spurred me on, but it merely added a crushing weight of responsibility. More so at Wimbledon than anywhere else, I could lose control of the ball and, with it, the situation.'

Billie Jean King beat Christine Janes 6–2, 7–5 on the centre court. Mrs Janes was a housewife and mother revisiting the playground of her youth for some exercise with an old but younger rival. The friends of the 1960s were still around her, still strong in their affection, but no longer expecting too much from a woman who seemed at last to have discarded the label of the eternal schoolgirl. They were applauding a memory, rather than nourishing a hope. Mrs King was still at her peak, whereas Mrs Janes had descended to the relaxing warmth of the valleys, where she could smell the urban flowers and look back on high endeavour without regret for the challenge that was yesterday. In the second set Mrs King's concentration faltered and she had a rash of errors. Mrs Janes responded with booming forehands. She had two set points. For a while the crowd dreamed and roared. A favoured friend had sung them a few lines from a well remembered song.

Julie Heldman matched her brains against Evonne Goolagong's instinctive talent and came off second best. Nancy Gunter (formerly Miss Richey) led Miss Goolagong in both sets but lost five successive games in the first and six successive games in the second. Miss Goolagong seemed to have a lot of time for her shots and a lot of court to hit them in. She made the game look so easy that we wondered why others found it so difficult. Already we were aware that she could become a great player if her will insisted on it.

Four generations of the Australian women's game were present that year: Thelma Long, their champion in 1952 and 1954; Lorraine Robinson, who reached a lot of big finals in 1958; Margaret Court; and Evonne Goolagong. So it was historically appropriate that, for the first time, Australia provided three of the last four—and both players in the final, which marked the twilight of one era and the dawn of another. The dramatic conventions were so neatly satisfied that the plot might have been written in advance.

Mrs Court beat Judy Dalton in a match that was all Australian steaks and sunshine. Big, robust and aggressive, they clouted the ball as though they hated it. Miss Goolagong beat Billie Jean King 6–4, 6–4. Considering the huge disparity in experience, it was remarkable that Miss Goolagong won five out of six deuce games. She came under considerable pressure but took only fifty-five minutes to win. She could not have looked more serene without falling asleep. That superb backhand earned her scorching winners on crucial points in each set. Another backhand won her the match. Whereupon she gathered her gear and her flask of glucose and water and tripped off court as if she had just finished an afternoon's shopping and had to hurry home to get the tea ready. The crowd were delighted. They had seen something new, and something special. Shortly afterwards, Miss Goolagong was so gaily relaxed that the peals of laughter made her first big press conference sound more like a party. But that is the way this bright and unaffected girl lives her life. She blew into tennis like a breeze fresh from the Murrumbidgee River.

Her story is like something out of schoolgirl fiction. She hails from the rolling wheat country of Barellan, New South Wales, from an area scattered with names that sound preposterous to Anglo-Saxon ears. Her father is a farm hand who shears sheep. Her ancestors were knocking about in Australia before Captain Cook (whose father was also a farm hand) even found the place. Vic Edwards recalls the days when two of his coaches asked him to look at her. He was impressed by her reflexes and her approach to the game ('Her strokes weren't too good'). In 1965 the Edwards family arranged with her parents that they would take over the responsibility for her education and training. So at the age of thirteen she joined the Edwards household in Sydney. The coach brought her along gradually, choosing every step on the climb with care before asking her to move up. He became her father-figure, her manager, her Svengali.

Miss Goolagong was just getting the feel of a tennis racket when Mrs Court became Australian champion for the first time, in 1960. Mrs Court gave women a new dignity and a new stature in Australian tennis, and came to dominate the world game. Now these country girls from New South Wales faced each other across the net in a Wimbledon final. Mrs Court was born at Albury, Miss Goolagong at Griffith. You can find the places on the map, between

Merriwagga and Yackandandah and a lot more etymological oddities. Which reminds me that in the early 1960s Mark Cox and Roger Taylor went to a place called Tallangatta, not far from Albury, to play an exhibition. The trip produced my favourite Taylor story. They were standing near the court when a local V.I.P. strolled up. The following exchange ensued:

V.I.P. to Cox: 'I hear you're going to Cambridge. Which college?'

Cox to V.I.P.: 'Downing.'

V.I.P. to Cox: 'Oh. I'm Jesus.'

Taylor (suddenly interested) to V.I.P.: 'I've always wanted to meet you.'

Back to Wimbledon, 1971. . . .

Miss Goolagong beat Mrs Court 6–4, 6–1 in sixty-two minutes. In terms of games lost, it was the most decisive result in the final since Althea Gibson beat Darlene Hard in 1957. In successive matches Miss Goolagong had beaten the top two seeds in straight sets. We learned later that Mrs Court was a month pregnant, which means that one day Daniel Lawrence Court may boast of playing a Wimbledon final before being born. It was not the first time a pregnant woman had played at Wimbledon (and not all of them had been married). In this case the mother-to-be was not weighed down by future responsibilities. She lost only one set on the way to the final, and was beaten on merit.

Mrs Court ('I never really got into it') looked so apprehensive about the possibility of losing that she lacked the assurance that was her only guarantee of victory—if guarantee there could be, with so much facile talent on the other side of the net. Her forehand had a hesitant ring about it. She did not take the offensive as much as she needed to. She was tentative. By contrast, Miss Goolagong played with all the confidence of a gifted youngster who had nothing to lose ('I was glad to get through to the final, never mind winning it'). She was inspired, imaginative: never more impressive than when applying the principle that attack is the best form of defence. Some of her loveliest strokes were conceived in the darkness of temporary adversity. It was much to Miss Goolagong's credit that, as against Mrs King, she won most of the deuce games against a far more experienced player: the score this time was eight out of ten.

The tennis was thrilling, with each player so resilient that time and again an apparent winner was turned into yet another shining link in a sweeping chain of shots. From 0–4 down in the first set Mrs Court won five games out of seven. She lost six in a row for the match. But the last four all went to deuce and in that sequence she had nine game points. The score lied. Because this was a consistently close match.

Miss Goolagong seemed to have put behind her the occasional lapses of concentration that had marked her tennis a year earlier. Except for one set against Lesley Hunt, she had shown no sign of 'going walkabout', as Vic Edwards puts it. But she had retained her brisk and buoyant enthusiasm, her serene enjoyment of the game. Our delight at the success of a player whose sunny nature is as refreshing as her tennis was tempered by sympathy for the champion she dethroned. Mrs Court and Miss Goolagong are the only Australian women to win Wimbledon. One generation grasped the torch for another.

After saving three match points, Mrs Court double-faulted. Up in the stands, her husband Barry stood, turned, and held out his hand to congratulate Vic Edwards—who, like his wife Eva, was weeping with joy. Minutes later, the country girl was receiving her trophy from Princess Alexandra.

The following evening, the lively strains of *Waltzing Matilda* rang through the plush sobriety of Grosvenor House as Miss Goolagong and John Newcombe opened the ball. That was a good moment for Australia after all the heat and dust of battle.

Back in New South Wales, Miss Goolagong was given civic receptions in Sydney and Narrandera, and was driven through the streets in open cars. And finally there was a victory ball in a small town called Barellan. . . . Evonne Goolagong had come home.

7

The United States Championships

Harold Zimman, a publisher who is also an officer of the United States LTA, told me once that the islands of New York had two problems—getting the food in and the garbage out. Ed Fernberger of Philadelphia, promoter and photographer, reckons the fastest way to beat a New York traffic jam is to buy the car off the man in front and sell yours to the man behind (he foresees a time when the United States will be entirely paved). But Manhattan does not have the feel of an island, and its traffic is by no means the worst in the world. The immediately striking thing is that walking about between skyscrapers is like taking a claustrophobic stroll through a maze of man-made gorges. The years have done nothing to amend my early conclusion that, in such an environment, the spirit must to some extent be contracted and perverted.

But the memory's selective processes are kind. To think of New York is to think primarily of players, though they do not appear in the draw for the United States tennis championships at Forest Hills. They have names like Wild Bill Davison, Buzzy Drootin, Roy Eldridge, Chuck Folds, Oliver Jackson, Budd Johnson, Dill Jones, Max Kaminsky, Gene Krupa, Joe Muranyi, Anita O'Day and Zutty Singleton. They make, or made, music.

The sounds of Manhattan are one of the fringe benefits of reporting Forest Hills. A familiar if thin slice of the city is Peter's Backyard or the Cattleman for food, Broadway for a show, perhaps an hour at Your Father's Mustache for fun (on Sundays, traditional jazz), and Jimmy Ryan's for winding down to more 'trad' while evening becomes night and night becomes morning. In the late 1960s we could also pop into the Metropole to see Krupa—a showpiece from the past, resplendent in scarlet jacket and ruffled shirt—sitting at his drum kit atop a platform behind the bar. He has gone now. In his place, restricted in footwork but waggling everything else with impressive energy, are go-go girls: straight in the face but otherwise smoothly convex. They look more at home than Krupa did, but Krupa will live longer in the memory.

Your Father's Mustache, in the heart of the seedy vitality called Greenwich Village, occupies the same address as Nick's, once famous for its jazz. For six days a week YFM features a banjo band with a trombone lead; Laurel and Hardy films; and straw-hatted waiters who jump about, and casually empty ashtrays by tipping them on the floor. There is rumbustious communal song from customers who drink beer, chew peanuts, and are actively discouraged from leaving the entertainment to the entertainers. The ambiance is that of many East End pubs in London. It is all rather brash and consciously amateurish, like an enormous, lusty family party. But go along with a few friends prepared to sing and shout and drink, and the place will slacken the nerves and do you good. It was at YFM that we discovered Lesley Bowrey had a better singing voice than Bill, that Margaret and Barry Court and Bob Howe had not forgotten the words to *Waltzing Matilda*, that Peter Curtis and Phillip Dent could occasionally be induced to have a beer, and that Bill Holmes (road manager for World Championship Tennis) knew some extraordinary songs.

But Sunday is the big night at YFM. The jazz is blasted out by such species as the Southampton Dixie, Racing & Clambake Society Jazz Band, or Balaban and Cats. With Reg Brace (*Yorkshire Post*), who knows what is what in the way of tennis and jazz, I had two memorable sessions there in 1971. We saw Buzzy Drootin—a more leathery version of Bud Collins—arrange his small frame behind the drums and achieve astonishing effects with the economy of effort prevalent among experts in any field. With the same professionalism a greying legend called Wild Bill Davison emerged from the past and blew an explosive lead without wasting a puff. Like Ricardo Gonzales, Davison has presence. A fidgety and meticulously dapper man with restless eyes and a lot of 'business', Davison commands attention even when he is doing nothing constructive. George Melly, the British jazz singer and art critic, arrived from London and went on the stand for a set. He enjoyed himself and delighted the customers with such primitive standards as *Careless Love, Doctor Jazz, St James Infirmary Blues* and *Nuts, Hot Nuts*. In the process he must have dispelled a few illusions about the inhibited reserve of the British.

More mellow is the traditional jazz brewed at Ryan's, which is on 54th Street at the back of the Hilton Hotel. The beer is cold, the temperature of the music variable. Roy Eldridge holds court in the genial, gravel-voiced manner of the late and great Louis 'Pops' Armstrong. In the small hours, when the casuals have mostly gone to bed, Eldridge and company play what you fancy: if one of them knows the number, the rest pick it up. Between sets, the band mingle at the bar: because Ryan's is a relaxed and relaxing 'trad' rendezvous (on Saturday nights, the stand can get congested with well-known customers sitting in). And at some stage Joe Muranyi, flexing his phalanges in readiness at the clarinet, reminds us of all our yesterdays by announcing gravely: 'Watch carefully, ladies and gentlemen, and you'll notice that my fingers never leave my hands.'

Muranyi played on Armstrong's last date. At three o'clock one morning in September, 1971—while rain rattled on the car and cascaded onto the night-gleaming streets of Manhattan, and the windscreen wipers swished softly—Muranyi sat at the wheel and talked about 'Pops' with quiet affection: 'I'm not the kind who cries. But it took me weeks to get over his death. He was the original nice man.'

Ryan's is my kind of place: the right kind of music, the right kind of professionals, and the right kind of beer. Reg Brace has more catholic tastes in jazz. We heard the lot. We even followed the JPJ quartet from the obscurity of the Half Note, down by the docks, to their next date—at Jimmy Weston's on 54th Street, a smart restaurant (jackets obligatory) that is popular with the sporting fraternity. The trouble with reporting in New York is that there is all this and plenty more to do in the evenings—and the evenings are long because, for British morning papers, the time lag guillotines the working day at about 6.30 p.m. At most tournaments, there is time for only one social outing each evening. In New York, we tend to fit in so many that it can be a hustle getting to bed before dawn. In 1968 I realized at the tennis one day that the night life had caught up with me. So I dutifully made a mental note: 'Bed by midnight.' At that moment the telephone rang. A friend, an Australian sports writer, was on his way back from London to Sydney:

'Hi Rex. Jim Webster here. I'm in New York for twenty-four hours. You going to show me the town?'

We saw the town, or at least a chunk of it. I passed so many tiredness peaks I risked altitude sickness.

But in New York, tennis reporters can sleep late. Then a bucking, clattering steam bath called a subway train—even the players are not pampered by door to door transport, as they are at several other major championships—takes us a few miles east of Manhattan. The respectably dingy suburbia of Forest Hills is the home of the West Side Tennis Club and the United States championships.

The club is apparently the hub of the entire New York transport system. Overhead are chugging, droning aircraft of all shapes and sizes. Helicopters sometimes pry round the premises. Beside the courts is the Long Island railroad: passing trains with clacking wheels and howling whistles. There is also a lot of road traffic about.

That is the din from outside the club.

Inside are the radios, the cries of wandering salesmen, the booming amplification of the umpire's calls from the main court, and strident reminders that the citizens of New York are not always the most restful of company. Court 23, by the clubhouse terrace, is an encyclopaedia of noise: to all the other assaults on the ears are added the chatter of diners and drinkers and the tinkle and crash of glasses, bottles, crockery and cutlery. Peter Curtis, playing Tom Gorman there one evening in 1967, observed that he would practise at Charing Cross Station before his next trip to Forest Hills. In 1971 Mark Cox, playing Owen Davidson on the adjacent court 22, had his concentration assailed first by a radio playing in a tented cafeteria, and then by a clanging avalanche of empty bottles. Cox, who tends to play with his nerves tightly wound, observed angrily: 'And people wonder why Forest Hills isn't like Wimbledon.'

The comment was acid. But it went straight to the point: or to one of them. If the New York Symphony Orchestra set their stall up in the road outside and played the *1812 Overture*, hardly anyone in the vicinity of courts 22 and 23 would notice the difference.

Nor are the irritants merely aural. The courts are so close together that even a modest crowd can make the promenades almost impassable. In addition, the dressing rooms are a long way from the main stadium and the referee's office. Add these factors together and it can be seen that slick scheduling is almost impossible.

All this would not matter so much if the courts were good, but they disgrace the stature of the championships. American grass courts tend to be poor. It seems that firmly rooted grass cannot be grown because of the climate. In the dripping humidity of Forest Hills the deficiencies are more obvious than anywhere else, because for two weeks in the year the courts attract a lot of attention and influence the distribution of a lot of money. There are not enough covers and those they have—or had in 1971—are inadequate and out of date (but full marks for the initiative shown in 1969, when a hovering helicopter was used as a spin drier). When it has been raining, a court can soon look like a farmyard after the cows have come home on a wet day. Divots fly about and are kicked or tossed aside—or trodden in by players, linesmen and ball boys. The ball skids, or stops and jumps. The bounce, if any, is so unpredictable that players in their senses do not allow the ball to touch the ground if they can avoid it. So they must forget many technical and tactical conventions, and improvise from stroke to stroke.

No other tournament offers such damning evidence of the extent to which the 'lawn' tennis tradition is inhibiting and damaging the development of the game. Grass court tennis is an inferior product, and at Forest Hills that inferiority is blatant. Great matches have been played there—but in spite of the courts, not because of them. Save for incidental absurdities, most matches are instantly forgettable. Of the seven major tournaments, the United States championships are by far the worst test of tennis.

The championships are an unsuccessful marriage between big-time tennis and an environment more suitable for the recreational exercise of a large amateur club. Until the late 1960s, few Europeans bothered to make the trip. But in recent years imaginative and determined efforts have been made to lend substance to the tournament's pretensions. The championships are now an energetic promotion with all the trappings of commercial sponsorship. The improved organization is earnest and thorough. Its workers are so affable, so painstaking, so eager to make the show a success, that they attract sympathy because they are lumbered with an unreasonably difficult task. In 1969 the committee imported Owen Williams from South Africa, as tournament director, and Captain Michael Williams from Britain, as referee. But the format in which these experienced professionals had to work, plus an extraordinary rainfall (in 24 hours there was 4.05 inches, which exceeded New York's usual total for the whole of September), ensured that the tournament still misfired.

The United States want their championships to be the best in the world—and good luck to them, because competition keeps everyone on his toes. But as long as the championships are played in the Forest Hills that existed in 1971, they will not come under starter's orders when it comes to challenging Wimbledon or Paris.

Many of the ills are probably incurable, which puts the United States LTA in a dilemma. Those commonplace courts could—and should—be replaced by a synthetic surface that would give the players a consistent bounce, a sure foothold, and a chance to play a game of skill rather than what can often be a game of luck. The superficially attractive court lay-out could be drastically rearranged on more effective lines. But these wholesale changes would be difficult and expensive. It might be better to shift the championships to the West Coast, where the courts and climate are better and visitors from overseas could see a more characteristic and engaging aspect of America.

The championships are the richest in the world (the 1971 prize money was £64,000) and the most diligently promoted. They have a strong and cosmopolitan entry. They are the last Big Four tournament and therefore, on distinguished occasions, the climax of a Grand Slam. The horseshoe-shaped main stadium (like the crater of a small volcano, with one side knocked out) is an impressively mighty arena. One custom that should be emulated elsewhere is that of taking players straight from the court to the interview room. This is good for the players because it gets the interviews done with, and good for the press because they often have to work fast.

In 1967 Christine Truman, who was about to become Mrs Janes, was questioned about the furniture she and her fiancé were installing in their new home (American reporters can be omnivorous in their curiosity). 'There was one thing I couldn't get married without,' she said, 'and that was a record player. Because I have to do everything to music.'

Whereupon the press paused, and speculated. . . .

We will not examine the championships closely, because we have already met most of the cast and studied similar plots. But let us flick over a few pages of the tournament's recent history and thus catch the flavour of the story. In 1967 Peaches Bartkowicz, three times American junior champion, caused a stir by beating Rosemary Casals and then losing an enchanting match with Ann Jones—whose spirits were revived by a cup of tea during the interval. As at Wimbledon, the champions were John Newcombe and Billie Jean King, the first American to win the women's title since Darlene Hard in 1961 (the runner-up on each occasion was Mrs Jones, who now played one of her best grass court matches, in spite of stretching a hamstring in the first set). Newcombe beat Clark Graebner, only the second American-born player to reach the men's final in twelve years.

In 1968, at Jimmy Ryan's one evening, we heard some of the great names of jazz history re-creating the magic of the past—and adding to it the facile expertise that only experience can buy. Next day we saw Ricardo Gonzales do the same thing. Some of the strength and staying power had gone. But wisdom had replaced it. He beat Tony Roche in straight sets. Tom Okker dismissed Gonzales and Ken Rosewall in successive matches to become the first Dutchman to reach the final. Gonzales was then forty, and the 30-game first set probably took a lot out of him. 'I didn't try to hit winners all the time,' said Okker, 'because that way you get short points. I tried to make low returns, so that he had to bend and work.'

Had the man no respect for his elders?

At the press conference Okker was gravely asked an involved question about his psychological reaction when Gonzales aced him three times in one game. He appeared to give the inquiry the deep consideration the manner of its asking indicated. Only his eyes smiled as he answered softly: 'Yes, I remember that. I thought: this guy's got a pretty good serve.'

There was some great tennis when Okker beat Rosewall. Okker ('It's the best I've ever played') excelled with his backhand passing shots. 'It wasn't that I played badly,' said Rosewall. 'He put something extra on the ball. His shots came very fast. Almost everything I gave him, he came back with one better.' Cliff Drysdale, who had never played Rod Laver before, beat him 4–6, 6–4, 3–6, 6–1, 6–1. The main reasons were Laver's service, which was vulnerable, Drysdale's ground strokes, which were good, and the court, which was relatively slow after rain. Laver had a lot of trouble guessing which way Drysdale's two-fisted backhand was going. Briefly, we were promised another surprise when Torben Ulrich served for the match against Newcombe. With his beard, his flowing hair, and his bandaged right knee, Ulrich looked like a battered Viking. He played to the measured tempo one expects from musicians.

That was an exciting tournament. Few were prepared to argue when Allison Danzig (*New York Times*), who had reported the event since 1922, said the quality of the players had never been higher and the number of fine matches never greater. The championships were dominated by the advent of open competition, and by the fact that the readmitted professionals were getting knocked about. Arthur Ashe, seeded fifth, and Virginia Wade, sixth, achieved a long-odds double. But Okker won the top prize of £5,800 because Ashe was competing only for expenses (down the years, the ILTF have had a lot of nonsense to answer for).

In successive matches Ashe beat Roy Emerson, Drysdale, Graebner and Okker. The final carried his winning sequence to twenty-six matches and gave him his first major title. He was also the first black man to secure an important championship (Althea Gibson, who had the same patron, preceded him); the first American man to gain a Big Four singles title since Chuck McKinley won Wimbledon in 1963 (the year Ashe began his trail-blazing by playing at Wimbledon and earning a place in the Davis Cup team); and the first American to win the men's singles at Forest Hills since Tony Trabert in 1955. It would be appropriate, but false, to suggest that the final was a great match. True, it lasted five sets and 2 hours 36 minutes. True, Ashe and Okker played well. But the tennis was at the mercy of an environment that insisted on the hot pace that is the enemy of variety. We shall not remember the match: merely the fact that Ashe won it.

After that startling success he became firmly established among the game's half-dozen best players, but he did not advance his stature as a winner of championships (he took the Australian title in 1970, but the opposition was not formidable). Ashe may have suffered because his game tends to be flashy, because he has the technique for fast courts and the temperament for slow ones, and because he is too gentle a man—too much the easy-going dreamer—to demand an unrelieved diet of success. His concentration on tennis may also have been affected by an accumulation of business interests and (because of his pigmentation, his influential reputation and his sociological concern) an inevitable involvement on the fringe of racial politics. In this direction he has done much good, both by speaking his mind with a usually discreet candour, and by dashing around Africa playing tennis. He also deserves much of the credit for opening the doors of the South African game to players with dusky skins: he could not get through the doors himself, but he helped to push them ajar for others.

Ashe's comportment—a disarmingly serene dignity—has buttressed his advocacy of the causes in which he believes. That serenity never wavered for an instant when a young lady, hunting for autographs at Bristol in 1971, approached the easily identifiable Ashe as he walked past in his tennis clothes, and said to him: 'I'm terribly sorry. I don't know who you are. But would you sign anyway?'

In his own profession Ashe is an engaging ideas man, though too imaginatively radical for some tastes. There is much support for his arguments that the rules were written for amateurs long ago and now need tightening up, and that there should be more flexibility in promoting and presenting a game that has become an increasingly commercial segment of the entertainment industry. His enthusiasm for coloured tennis clothes (which tend to look better on him than on those with lighter skins) has had a mixed reception. Even more controversial is his thinking on 'time out', as used in American football and basketball. He reckons it would add drama to a tennis match if, instead of having a brief interval when changing ends, players could ask for a break after any game—though each player would be restricted to a fixed amount of demanded 'time out' in each set.

Ashe is the kind of man who opens windows in the mind. His horizons are wide, and his sense of humour is never far from the surface. In Paris one evening, a gang of us clambered into a van leaving Roland Garros, and when I dumped my decaying brief-case on the floor, Ashe examined it thoughtfully.

'You had that a long time, Rex?'

'Right.'

'Means something special, does it? Something you want to hang on to—maybe a present?'

'Right again.'

'Because I'm telling you, man, that one day you're going to pick up that handle and there's going to be nothin' coming up with it.'

Back at Forest Hills, in 1968, we were reminded that Maria Bueno could still beat Margaret Court. But Virginia Wade was the star of the show. Perhaps it had to happen some time: because like Fred Perry (the last British player to win a United States singles championship) she has a nature that is in harmony with the bustling tempo of New York. Stephanie DeFina, now Mrs Johnson, a left-hander who writes up the page instead of across it, was the only player to take a set from Miss Wade. In successive matches Miss Wade bounded past Rosemary Casals, Judy Tegart, Ann Jones and Billie Jean King—a list that included three of the last four at Wimbledon. She was powerful but precise, bold yet disciplined. She had never played such consistently punishing tennis ('My game always was good: I just had lots of bad patches . . .'). She looked as though she felt like a champion. She played like a champion.

The final was rather an anticlimax because there never seemed much doubt that Miss Wade would win it ('I never had a chance to get into the match,' said Mrs King). At the end, Miss Wade appropriately shared a rostrum with Herman David, chairman of the All England Club, who had a lot to do with the introduction of open competition that year. Miss Wade won the first open event, at Bournemouth, and now she won the richest. She was the first British woman since Betty Nuthall, in 1930, to become United States champion.

Miss Wade is so strong and athletic and has such hard-eyed determination, such a tempestuous and striking court presence, that there is an aura of exceptional quality about her. It is genuine. But she was not a born tennis champion. She has the physique and the will. Up to a point, she has the flair and the powers of concentration. But her emotional resilience has often seemed limited. And her dedication to the game may be inhibited by a character that sees tennis as a part of life, not all of it. Unlike such players as Margaret Court, Billie Jean King and Ann Jones, she has seldom given the impression that her commitment is total. Nor has her intelligence always been matched by her common sense as a match player. She can be brilliant and she can be bad. She can beat anyone and she can lose to players who are, by her standards, mugs. This unpredictable streak is part of her attraction—that and the fact that she is a powerful and positive personality with a game to match. Casual observers often overrate her. Opponents do not. They just hope she has one of her off days. 'Against Virginia,' they say, 'you always give yourself a chance.'

If this seems a little severe, it is only because I assess her by the highest criteria. At Forest Hills in 1968, she was marvellous. That year, in addition to Bournemouth and Forest Hills, she was runner-up for the South African championship, reached the last four of the German championship, and was the prime force behind Britain's first Wightman Cup success since 1960. She was twenty-three, and climbing. Then she paused for a while. But in winning the 1971 Italian championship and the 1972 Australian title, she indicated that her game might still be advancing towards its most effective maturity. Winning or losing, she will never be dull company.

A stormy tide threw us together one day in May 1968. Many players and camp followers were stranded in Rome when the Federation Cup competition (to be followed by the game's first major open tournament) was due to begin in Paris. All flights and trains to Paris had been cancelled because riots, strikes and anarchy were gathering pace there. I decided that, if the pieces could be fitted together, the best idea was to fly to Brussels, hire a car, and drive to Paris. Miss Wade, the only British player left in Rome, was thinking on similar lines and agreed to join me. It seemed a rather dodgy scheme. But the LTA gave her *carte blanche*. We took what must have been the last two seats on a flight from Kuwait to Brussels. So many people flooded onto that aircraft in Rome that we decided they must be going out at the other end.

By the time we got to Brussels a deadline was pressing, so my first concern was to file a story (I was to break a personal record by telephoning stories from different capitals—Rome, Brussels and Paris—on successive days). Meantime Miss Wade, without being asked, was working quickly and well. She hired a car, collected two more tennis-playing passengers (the sisters Birgitta and Christina Lindström, whose first trip from Helsinki to Paris had come to a premature halt), and packed all our luggage into the Fiat.

I queued for an ample supply of Belgian and French currency—in case we should run into costly delays—and then shopped for provisions. On a board at the airport was a tattered, almost illegible map of north-western Europe. On the back of an envelope I jotted down the names of two or three places on what seemed a likely route. The trip was assuming the flavour of a rally-style initiative test. But we had all we needed, including a full tank: important because we were driving by night and there were rumours that French filling stations were closing down.

In fact there were all sorts of rumours, none of them comforting. Setting off into a disordered France with three young women, I just hoped nothing nasty happened. Particularly as I was feeling jaded, because I had been up half the night and had made a nerve-racking series of thirteen telephone calls—to airline companies, car hire firms and so on—when I should have been having breakfast. But Miss Wade was quietly shouldering more than her share of the chores. She did most of the driving, too.

We felt something like pioneers as we set off in the twilight from an airport chaotically crowded with people who wanted to get to Paris (and hoped buses might be forthcoming). Nothing went wrong, of course. Life spoils many of its best crises. Getting on for midnight, a speckled band of light called Montmartre appeared on the dark horizon. Miss Wade was doing another stint at the wheel, like a latter-day Boadicea. I turned to glance at the blonde Finns, who were gazing intently ahead with eyes that dreamed. Whatever happened to them on that first trip to Paris, they would not forget the manner of their coming.

'A splendid idea,' observed Miss Wade. 'I enjoyed it. I'm all for a little bit of fun.' Later that year she had some fun at Forest Hills too.

But in 1969 Ashe and Miss Wade were exposed as regents rather than monarchs. The true dynastic line was restored when Rod Laver and Margaret Court reclaimed their titles—and Laver completed his second Grand Slam. Vice-President Spiro Agnew turned up to keep an eye on the top people, and slick-suited G-men (hardware under their armpits) turned up to keep an eye on Spiro Agnew. One of them stood in the press box, and Barry Newcombe asked him if he liked tennis.

'Yup.' The man's eyes shifted. 'But if I clap, it will only be with one hand.'

It was in 1969, too, that Derek Penman, vice-chairman of the

British LTA, went back to his room in a roseate humour after a
farewell party and supper. A lady was asleep in his bed. Now there
are situations in which temptation may breach probity's most determined defences. But the intruder could not accurately be classified
as temptation. She was awoken with the suggestion that she should
return to her own room. And she tottered off, in her nightie. Later
our hero went to see the porter—'and she was down there having a
cup of tea!'

'Oh, yes,' said the porter. 'She often does this.'

Cryptic comments are seldom more cryptic than that. Was she
one of those ladies of the night who make it their duty to minister
to the needs of the deprived heterosexual? Perhaps, bored with
haggling, she was merely carrying her calling a little closer to its
desired conclusion. Or it may be that she was a victim of semantic
confusion about the activities of vice-chairmen—or just walked in
her sleep, or was vague about room numbers.

In New York, you never know. But some people, mostly the
impatient, find the place invigorating. On a tennis court, that often
applies to Miss Wade and to Mark Cox. It was at Forest Hills, in
1966, that Cox sprang from obscurity by beating Tony Roche. Now
he beat Tom Okker in the first match on the stadium court. Another
left-hander, Owen Davidson, served well to subdue Cliff Drysdale
in straight sets—but then lost to the 6 ft 4 in. Ove Bengtson, one of
the select breed of men who smoke pipes at breakfast without feeling
ill. Ilie Nastase, who had frustrated Britain's Davis Cup hopes by
beating Cox at Wimbledon a fortnight earlier, foxed Stan Smith in
blazing heat on the stadium court. Everybody noticed, because
Nastase was a rookie at Forest Hills and was not supposed to be able
to play on grass anyway.

Ricardo Gonzales and Torben Ulrich (combined ages eighty-one)
played five sets rich in character and dignity. Ulrich lost, but said
he was merely paying his respects to the master: 'The scoreboard
is just a painting on the wall.' But Tony Roche stopped Gonzales
and then reached the last four at the expense of that widely travelled
professional, Butch Buchholz. Compared with the time Buchholz
spent on the road, Marco Polo never left home. John Newcombe
won a 48-game set with Marty Riessen, who was playing tie-breaks
before they were invented.

By this time the apparently relentless heat and humidity had given way to rain—the kind that once made an old man called Noah (plus his folks and assorted livestock) thankful that the Boss had tipped him off about the weather and added some advice on boat-building and a reminder that he should pack plenty of grub.

The courts were swamped. The players lost their edge: mentally and physically. Their joints rusted. Stolle served an ace that jumped over Roger Taylor's head. Encouraged, he stretched Newcombe to 13–11 in the fifth set. Roche stretched Newcombe, too, and this time Newcombe's service finally let him down. Arthur Ashe sank Ken Rosewall in straight sets. Laver caught the tide after Dennis Ralston had led him by two sets to one. Then, moving better on the slippery deck, Laver won a tough argument with his old chum Roy Emerson and an easier one with the new generation, represented by Ashe.

Laver was now in sight of harbour. But his Grand Slam—and Mary Laver's baby—were both overdue. To give him a little more to worry about, the last man he had to play was Roche, who that year had beaten him more often than not. Indeed, back at Brisbane on a January day with the temperature over 100, Roche almost ruined that Grand Slam before it began. Their semi-final of the Australian championship lasted ninety games and more than four hours. The crux came with Roche serving at 3–4 and 15–30 in the fifth set. Laver played a shot Roche thought was out. The linesman disagreed. Two break points. Laver hit a backhand down the line, and Roche could not hold it.

Now here they were again, at the end of the road. The previous day, Laver had played for only four minutes, finishing off Ashe, but Roche had taken 169 minutes to beat Newcombe. So Laver was fresher. After ten games of the first set he also put on spikes because the court was greasy. Laver moved better than Roche and lobbed well enough to make it obvious. Roche took the first set 9–7 and had a break point in the first game of the second. But Laver's service settled that rally—and Roche won only five more games. This meant Laver had won thirty successive matches. He was also the first player to win two Grand Slams, the first to win an open Grand Slam, and the first to win more than 100,000 dollars from a year's tennis. His cheque for the singles was 16,000 dollars. 'Maybe all this money will slow him down a bit,' said Roche.

But Laver's expenses were going up. Because Mary Laver, too, delivered the goods.

In the women's championship Nell Truman led 5–4 and 6–5 in the third set before Julie Heldman weathered the storm. Miss Truman chases everything, attacks all the time, improvises some extraordinary shots, and plays to a pattern that never existed until she did. Another Briton to give us a line for the papers back home was Joyce Williams. A patriotic Scot married to an equally patriotic Welshman, she must have been flabbergasted when the umpire compounded one error with another by introducing her as '*Miss* Williams of *England*'.

Which reminds me that, in tennis at any rate, it sometimes seems that no one outside the island can grasp the fact that England, Scotland and Wales, though all part of Great Britain, are jealous of their separate identities. If any of our overseas friends want to use 'English', 'Scottish' or 'Welsh' in preference to the overall label 'British', let them be sure of their ground first—or they may get a frozen reception. Mrs Williams's friend and rival, Winnie Shaw (the youngest British player in six successive Wightman Cup ties from 1966 to 1971), is a neat, no-nonsense woman who inspires friendships that will long survive her playing days. She is not the kind to make a fuss on court, or anywhere else for that matter. But she is thoroughly Scottish, and during the 1969 Federation Cup series in Athens she found it necessary to help an umpire with his geography. It was so quietly done that the details of the exchange escaped our ears. We wondered what all the chat was about. Miss Shaw explained later: 'After we tossed, the umpire said "Who's serving?" and I said "I am". So he said "Miss Shaw of England will be serving from the north side". I said "Well, before you start, I'm not representing England". So he sort of said "Oh. . . ."' I explained that I was representing Great Britain and that Great Britain included England, Wales and Scotland for tennis purposes. He'd thought that England included the lot. I put him right on that one.'

Let me ram the point home with an analogy. Texas and California are both part of the United States. But that does not make Cliff Richey a Californian or Stan Smith a Texan. And when they play in the Davis Cup they represent neither Texas nor California, but the United States. For the record, Miss Shaw and Mrs Williams are

Scottish, Gerald Battrick is Welsh, none is English, but all are British.

Sorry to go on so. But really!

Now we have sorted that out, let us get back to the fact that at Forest Hills in 1969 Nancy Richey beat Mrs Williams and Miss Shaw in turn and then—as was usual in those days (it was one of those psychological things)—subdued Billie Jean King. Miss Richey next banged Rosemary Casals out of the way but was abruptly checked in the final by Margaret Court, who lost only twenty games in the six matches she played to become champion. The one thing to add about 1969 is that in the doubles Karen Krantzcke was stung on the lip by a bee, broke out in a rash, and had to retire. Which was a painful reminder that, even in the concrete jungle of New York, Nature can still hit back.

The 1970 championships must be interpreted from the results and the opinions of colleagues, because I did not make the trip. The odd thing was the piquant blend of tradition and innovation. On the one hand, the champions were players with long and remarkably consistent records: Ken Rosewall, who had been winning major championships since 1953, and Margaret Court, who gained her first big title in 1960. On the other hand, there was the introduction of a 'sudden death' tie-break system—the best of nine points when a set reached 6-all. The record eleven-day attendance of 122,996 (which included a record one-day crowd of 14,502) may to some extent have been related to the tie-break, which produced dramatic finishes much to the public's taste. Rosewall saved himself some sweat by winning three of the four tie-breaks he played.

Rosewall was the first man to win two United States singles championships fourteen years apart. At thirty-five he was the oldest winner since Bill Tilden (thirty-six) in 1929. Those of us who have been lucky enough to watch Rosewall playing will never forget the joy of it. Youngsters now in their cots and cradles will look at the record books one day and ask: 'Hey, were all these Rosewalls the same guy?' They will want to know, because Rosewall's most extraordinary legacy is the span of his excellence. To take the Big Four as samples, he won the Australian championship in 1953, 1955, 1971 and 1972; the French in 1953 and 1968; the United States in 1956 (the year he robbed Lew Hoad of the Grand Slam) and 1970; and was runner-up at Wimbledon in 1954, 1956 and 1970.

To do a little arithmetic with those dates is to realize that we should be grateful every time we see Rosewall—or for that matter, Rod Laver or Mrs Court—step out on court. Because we are in the presence of genuine greatness. A Laver *v.* Rosewall match does seem rather like another episode of Peyton Place. It is easy to take the little men for granted. But the kind of man who finds Laver *v.* Rosewall a bore is the kind of man who got fed up with listening to Paderewski.

Laver and Rosewall went to the top and stayed there because they worked hard and thoughtfully (and still do) to exploit the talent born in them. They turned professional at a time when that meant joining a small élite. Standards were severe, complete dedication essential. The habits acquired in those years have stayed with them. They are quiet men, painstaking and proud, satisfied with nothing less than their best form and always seeking ways of making it even better. They have accepted the personal discipline involved in the truth that, whatever a man's ability, there is no substitute for hard work—in physical and mental conditioning, practice and, when necessary, training. That discipline extends to their concentration, their court manners and their private lives.

Most of their rivals would rather play Laver, because his shots flirt more dangerously with the laws of probability. There is always a chance his game may misfire. By contrast, no one playing Rosewall can expect any unearned income. He seems to play to the principle that unforced errors are punishable by death ('When Rosewall misses a backhand return,' said Bud Collins once, 'he acts like his house burned down'). But he is positive in his precision, and anyone playing Rosewall can safely assume that the next shot he has to play will be the one he least fancies. Because Rosewall goes for the corners, moves his man about, never relaxes the pressure, and is adept at catching players on the wrong foot. 'He doesn't hit very hard,' says Tom Okker, 'but you still can't get to the ball. It's very frustrating.' All this: plus quick anticipation, footwork, and reflexes. Play a loose shot against Rosewall, and you can start concentrating on the next rally.

Underneath the hard, remorseless professionalism is the chap next door—sensitive to the good times and the bad, appreciating the one and tolerating the other, taking everything in his stride. Rosewall smiles a lot. He is a gentle man, with no fuss, no side: the modesty is genuine. Retiring rather than pushing, he has nothing to prove, no need to impress. He does that on court. Small wonder that Rosewall has an uncommon capacity for making friends and keeping them. Long after his career has ended, we shall remember the legend with the marvellous backhand—but even more, we shall remember the man behind it.

At Forest Hills in 1970, his hardest match was probably that against Nikola Pilic in the round of sixteen. Rosewall then beat Stan Smith and John Newcombe in straight sets, which was going some. The match with Newcombe, whose service was not at its best, was a repetition of the Wimbledon final. 'Rosewall played mind-boggling tennis,' wrote Richard Evans in *World Tennis*. 'There were moments when one felt one had never seen anyone, anywhere, play better.' For the second successive year, Tony Roche was runner-up. Which meant that Roche had reached six singles finals in Big Four tournaments, and had won only one of them (the French, in 1966). But he was only twenty-five. Still reconnoitring.

Rod Laver? Dennis Ralston beat him. Ralston had often finished second after giving Laver long, hard matches. This time, after winning two sets and losing two, Ralston found a new assurance that drove him through the crisis. He has seldom played better.

In the doubles, Pierre Barthes and Nikola Pilic became the first European winners since 1937. They played twelve tie-breaks and won eight of them. They beat Jaime Fillol and Patricio Cornejo by the bizarre margin of 6–7, 6–7, 7–6, 7–6, 7–5.

Margaret Court—who had won three of the four titles in 1962, 1965 and 1969—easily completed the Grand Slam, thus emulating Maureen Connolly's feat of 1953. For the first time Mrs Court arrived at Forest Hills three up with one to play: and Billie Jean King was unfit, recuperating from an operation on her right knee. In five matches Mrs Court lost only thirteen games. In the final, inevitably charged with the tension of every last stride to glory, she lost a set to Rosemary Casals. But towards the end the majesty of her game was overwhelming ('Each segment of her game was perfection,' wrote Mary Hardwick in *World Tennis*). Mrs Court shared both doubles titles, too. It must have been quite a day.

Mrs Court was present but pregnant in 1971. The men's field was weaker, too. Some of the leading World Championship Tennis professionals were missing and the tournament was played under a cloud imposed by the ILTF, who had announced that WCT would be barred altogether in 1972. In that case, said the sponsors, they were getting out, because the horse they had agreed to back no longer had four sound legs. Up in the bleachers one day, an American friend told me: 'There's a kind of spooky feeling about the tournament. It's like everybody's waiting for the axe to fall next year.' Though Rod Laver, Ken Rosewall and Tony Roche did not play, and John Newcombe was beaten in the first round, nine of the last sixteen men in that 1971 field were under contract to WCT—which meant their entries could not be accepted in 1972 (I write in March) unless the ILTF had a sudden attack of common sense.

There was indeed a spooky feeling about Forest Hills in 1971, as if a great era was drawing sadly to an end. The tournament was saved by two unseeded players: Jan Kodes, clay court champion of France and the world, and Chris Evert, sixteen years nine months old, who reached the last four at her first attempt. It helped, too, that Stan Smith and Billie Jean King became the first players since Tony Trabert and Doris Hart, in 1955, to win both singles titles for the United States. But in spite of all this, the championships had a dying fall. Because of rain and those inadequate covers, the tournament again dragged on into extra time. Before it finished, I deserted the streaming grey streets of New York and went to watch the Ryder Cup golf match in St Louis (where I insisted on an introduction to Mary Ann Eisel's dog—and it bit me. This would not have mattered but for the fact that it is a St Bernard, which is a lot of dog).

For the first time since seeding was introduced in 1927, the men's singles favourite, Newcombe, was beaten in round one. For the first time since 1926 two Europeans, Kodes and Tom Okker, reached the last four. Kodes was the first Czechoslovak to get that far since Jaroslav Drobny in 1948. He did it for three reasons. The first was confidence: Jack Kramer and Ted Schroeder had convinced him that he could play well on grass. The second was practice: he arrived six days early. The third was his realization that the important thing with his first volley was to get it in court, rather than going for an instant winner.

In the first round the boss of the clay courts, Kodes, beat the boss of the grass courts, Newcombe, and told the press conference what he thought about it. Kodes was quiet but forthright, even controversial. He said it was wrong that three of the Grand Slam tournaments should be on grass—and he had a point because, as we have seen, grass is only a minority surface. 'The game on grass is a joke,' said Kodes, warming to his theme. 'Sometimes the ball doesn't bounce. Anything can happen. Everybody says I'm lousy on grass. And sometimes I get a little mad, because in Europe we don't get the chance to play on grass—only Wimbledon and Forest Hills. But grass is still important and I wanted to find out if I could play on it. So I arrived last Thursday and I've practised three hours a day.'

Kodes lost the first two sets to that strange mixture of artist and artisan, the erratically facile Pierre Barthes—but came back to win. Whatever else was happening that day, Kodes always seemed to be playing Barthes. Having beaten two bigger and stronger men, Kodes put his head down and went for the tape. In successive matches he sorted out George Seewagen, Bob Lutz and Frank Froehling, all in straight sets (the bean-pole called Froehling was wearing a floppy sun hat that made him look like a skyscraper in low cumulus). In a match of pounding speed, Arthur Ashe led Kodes by two sets to one and was a break up in the fourth. But Kodes could not shake off the habit of winning—and in any case the rain was now spattering Ashe's glasses, which made it difficult for him to focus on the Czechoslovak's ground strokes.

It was not all Kodes, of course. Perhaps inspired by his example, another clay court specialist, Manuel Orantes, had a good run to the last eight, beating Ricardo Gonzales on the way. Reg Brace and I sat up in the bleachers one day watching a lovely match in which Tom Okker and Roger Taylor both played their best tennis. Okker's was a little better. Playing in a hat with a turned-up brim, he had the guise of an underweight Bud Flanagan. And Bob Carmichael was working again: he beat Ilie Nastase in straight sets. So much sweat was pouring off Carmichael that but for the burnished sky you would have thought he was standing in heavy rain.

Meantime Stan Smith was loping along in his unfussy way. He played well ('That was the best I ever served in a big match') to beat Okker in a five-set semi-final on a greasy surface. This earned Smith a crack at the souped-up little steamroller from Prague—and for Kodes, the party was over. Smith was too powerful, too consistent. His services, volleys and ground strokes manœuvred Kodes about the court and set him up for the kills. This was Smith's first major championship. He looked the part: and he will play it again.

Only four women's seeds reached the last eight. Laura DuPont beat Nancy Gunter. Joyce Williams, playing some of the best tennis of her life and showing an unflagging zest for work, dismissed Winnie Shaw and Julie Heldman and then pestered Rosemary Casals as far as 4–all in the third set (at which point Mrs Williams, serving at 30–40, was startled by a foot-fault call). But the player everyone was talking about was the 'Cinderella in Sneakers', 'Little Miss Cool', 'The Ice Dolly', 'Little Miss Sunshine'—baptismal name, Christine Marie Evert, a schoolgirl who at 5 ft 4 in. and 105 lb. did not look much of a threat to anybody.

She sprang from nowhere at the age of fifteen when she beat Françoise Durr and Margaret Court at Charlotte, North Carolina, in November 1970. The next year she won forty-six successive singles matches, including pulverizing wins over Miss Shaw and Virginia Wade under the pressure of Wightman Cup competition (Miss Evert was the youngest player ever to represent the United States). When she arrived at Forest Hills, she had already captured the public's imagination. Like Evonne Goolagong at Wimbledon, she caused excited speculation. All her matches were in the main stadium ('We had to put her there, or the crowd would have torn down the fences'). The tournament briefly threatened to be a box office flop, by 1970 standards. But Miss Evert, with the help of Kodes, turned it into a smash hit.

She won three consecutive matches after losing the first set: against Mary Ann Eisel (who had six match points), Miss Durr and Lesley Hunt. During those lost sets, she sapped her opponents' energy and concentration. Miss Evert was now earning comparison with the late Maureen Connolly. The day she was due to meet Billie Jean King in a semi-final, the subway trains out to Forest Hill were packed. The match attracted a record total of eleven television crews. Whenever Miss Evert changed ends, photographers clustered round her small, introspective figure like moths round a flame. Arrangements were made for her usual press conference to be shifted from the little room under the stand to a spacious marquee. But the fairy tale was over. Mrs King concentrated hard and played a match that was beautifully designed and executed. At last Miss

Evert showed signs of fallibility. By her previous standards she was tentative and erratic, even a little despondent.

So the leading lady was not on stage for the last scene. Mrs King beat Rosemary Casals in the first all-American final since 1958.

Miss Evert was brought up on clay courts at Fort Lauderdale, Florida, where her father is a coach. She sprays the length and width of the court with firm ground strokes hit to a good length. Her backhand is two-fisted. She uses the drop shot and occasionally the lob, and she is ruthlessly punishing with anything loose in midcourt. At the time of that Forest Hills début, her service, volley and smash were still commonplace. Temperamentally, this poker-faced young lady is cool and matter-of-fact, with superb concentration. Between rallies, she is no more demonstrative than a clockwork soldier. She has a remarkable capacity for 'switching off' between points—and she never plays more than one at a time. She plays tennis like a computer with a heart.

Miss Evert is pleasantly precocious, though she lacks the joyous, outgoing warmth of Evonne Goolagong. One of five children, she has a healthy family background to help her through the difficult years of teenage fame. She spoke from the heart when she told us: 'I'd rather be famous for being a girl than for being a tennis player.'

The splash she made with that forty-six-match winning sequence sent ripples around the world. I had a note from Bill Tucker, the London orthopaedic consultant, who is an expert on athletics injuries—which often spring from faults of technique. He said that when hitting her two-fisted backhand, Miss Evert's posture was 'perfect in every way'. He went on:

Dozens of people break down because they don't know about simple body mechanics. In executing perfect athletic actions the general posture at rest and in motion must carry out two fundamental mechanical laws. The first is that the load, force, and lever must be one above the other. The second is that activator muscles must be assisted by synergic muscles, and that both of these actions must work on a firm base, called the prime fixing level.

It is obvious that she hits the ball so that the load, force and lever are one above the other. The load is the ball. The force is obtained through all the muscles of both arms—which are firmly attached at the shoulder girdle lever to the rest of the body, which is held rigid throughout, right down to the foot. The lever is at the shoulder girdle level, where the arms should be firmly attached to the fixed trunk and the rest of the body.

The second law in action is also perfectly executed: that is to say the force obtained by the action of the arms is being assisted by synergic muscles of the back, hips and legs right down to the firm base, the ankle and the foot (prime fixing level), which is placed absolutely correctly with the weight on the outside. The patella is pointing forwards and the in-toeing is to permit this. At the same time all the muscles around the ankle and foot are braced.

Because she is doing her shot against a fixed right side from the low back down to the foot, she is getting tremendous power in her shot with consequent maximum recoil. She also has the head of her racket above the line of her wrists, as it should be.

Which just goes to show that most of us do not know half of what is going on. If a layman may dare to sum up, it amounts to this: to hit the ball properly is to achieve maximum effect without strain. But I always used to think synergism was the co-operation of human effort with divine grace in the salvation of the soul. Come to think of it, that may be what tennis is all about.

Index